D1639429

NOBEL
WISDOM

NOBEL
WISDOM

THE 1000 WISEST THINGS EVER SAID

Compiled by DAVID PRATT

BOOKS

First published in Great Britain in 2008 by
JR Books, 10 Greenland Street, London NW1 OND

A catalogue record for this book is available from the British Library.

ISBN 978-1-906217-42-6

1 3 5 7 9 10 8 6 4 2

Printed in the UK by Cromwell Press, Trowbridge Wiltshire BA14 0XB

CONTENTS

PREFACE

For more than a century, the Nobel Prize has been the hall-mark of genius. The lives and the work of the 768 men and women who have won the prize since the first prizes were awarded in 1901 show that this popular impression is not misplaced. What makes the Nobel laureates not merely interesting but inspiring is the fact that their intellectual brilliance is commonly accompanied by qualities of humanity and idealism. Not only are they extraordinary minds; they are extraordinary people, whose observations on a wide range of issues are of intrinsic interest.

The Nobel Foundation has, over the past century, carried out Alfred Nobel's wishes to honor "those who during the preceding year have conferred the greatest benefit on mankind." The benefits that this group of less than a thousand people has conferred on humanity are prodigious. Millions of lives have been saved or bettered by the work of Nobel laureates in medicine who gave us radium therapy, antibiotics, insulin, antidepressants, bone marrow and organ transplants, cardiac catheterization, the diphtheria serum, and the measles vaccine. Nobel Peace Prize winners played important roles in ending both World Wars, as well as the Suez Crisis of 1956, the Vietnam War, and the Cold War. Less historically visible are the tragedies and conflicts that have been prevented by the dedicated work of individual laureates and of Nobel Prize–winning organizations such as the Red Cross, Amnesty International, the United Nations Peacekeeping Forces, and Médecins Sans Frontières.

Nobel laureates pioneered many technical inventions, often persevering for years in the face of apathy or derision by colleagues and the public. Their inventions include X-rays, magnetic resonance imaging, transistors, semiconductors, integrated circuits, lasers, and the electron microscope. And the world would be spiritually and aesthetically poorer without the writers who gave us such works as *Lord of the Flies, Dr. Zhivago, Waiting for Godot, The Tin Drum, The Waste Land, The Forsyte Saga, The Old Man and the Sea, The Jungle Book, Man and Superman,* and *Of Mice and Men.*

In many of the quotations in this collection, Nobel laureates speak about their specialized work. Physicists comment with perception or irony on physics, poets on poetry. But laureates also address, often with great insight, issues outside their immediate specialization—in fact, they tend to be versatile in their interests. The conventional image of the Nobel Prize winner as an absent-minded genius, eccentric in habits and solitary in lifestyle, fits hardly any of them.

A number of laureates were publicly prominent in their time. They include three presidents of the United States and numerous presidents and prime ministers of other nations. When they speak of public events, they do so from a privileged position. "History will be kind to me," Winston Churchill averred, "for I intend to write it."[1]

Music may serve as an example of the versatility of many laureates. Among the physicists, for example, Max Planck and Werner Heisenberg were both concert-level pianists. Gerald Edelman played the violin in a symphony orchestra, Gerhard Herzberg was a noted bass-baritone, Albert Einstein's attachment to his violin is well known, and Richard Feynman would, at every opportunity, exercise his virtuosity on the bongo drums. Other Nobel laureates have excelled in sports. Niels Bohr was a soccer player, Dudley Herschbach a high school football star, Philip Noel-Baker ran in three Olympic Games, Max Perutz was a skier and mountaineer, and Henry Kendall was a scuba diver who lost his life on a *National Geographic* diving expedition. Ernest Hemingway once remarked, "My writing is nothing. My boxing is everything."[2]

With their high energy and restless minds, Nobel laureates are people whose tastes and interests are rarely limited to a single field. Thus we find the Russian physicist Pyotr Kapitsa remarking, "Ah, but it's impossible to live without poetry."[3] Or Einstein rushing to embrace the young violinist Yehudi Menuhin after a concert in Berlin in 1930 and saying, "Now I know there is a God in Heaven."[4]

Einstein is the best-known science laureate, and his many observations, both whimsical and profound, are frequently quoted in anthologies. Otherwise, the scientists tend to be neglected in such collections in favor of a few well-known Literature laureates. In this collection, close to half of the laureates represented earned the prize in one of the sciences. *Nobel Wisdom* includes quotations from 73 laureates who won the prize for Literature, 53 for Peace, 45 for Physics, 43 for Medicine, 24 for Chemistry, and 18 for Economics. As will be seen from the quotations from the science laureates, many of them are highly articulate individuals who think deeply about matters of general concern. Working as they do at the frontiers of knowledge, exploring the mysteries of the cosmic, the subatomic, and the organic worlds, they have much to tell us not only about science but about many of the significant issues of our time.

In these pages laureates from different fields share their views on such topics as belief and religion, good and evil, joy and grief, ethics and morals. Many thousands of documents were perused in the compilation of this collection: novels, plays, and poetry; biographies and autobiographies; scientific papers and monographs; newspaper reports and interviews; letters, journals, lectures, and Web pages.

Anyone who studies the lives of the laureates quickly recognizes that they do not escape the hardships and tragedies that are the lot of humankind. Indeed, they often seem to have suffered more than their share of difficulties. Several lost one or both parents in childhood, and a sizable minority grew up in poverty. The wars of the twentieth century took beloved sons from Theodore Roosevelt, Rudyard Kipling, William Henry Bragg, and Robert Aumann. A large number of the scientists became refugees from Nazi Germany, and many others became exiles from their homelands. Of the 259 laureates represented here, at least 30 endured the experience of prison, whether as prisoners of war like Konrad Lorenz and Jean-Paul Sartre, civilian internees like Albert Schweitzer or James Chadwick, prisoners of conscience like Bertrand Russell and Aung San Suu Kyi, or inmates of concentration camps like Roald Hoffmann and Elie Wiesel. Almost all of them, at one time or another, experienced discouragement or setbacks in their careers.

When Nobel laureates write of their work in literature, peace, economics, or science, they write of what they know firsthand. But very often, when they speak of prison and exile, communism and fascism, war and terrorism, success and failure, duty and courage, or dreams and nightmares, they likewise speak not from theory or speculation but with the voice of experience. At the beginning of the twenty-first century, we are the beneficiaries of a hundred years of insights and discoveries that Nobel laureates achieved with pain and effort. They constitute a source of wisdom that compels our attention.

ACKNOWLEDGMENTS

I gratefully acknowledge the permission of the Nobel Foundation to use its photographs of the laureates from the Nobel Museum. This is a virtual museum that contains more than thirty thousand documents, including biographies and autobiographies of Nobel laureates, their acceptance speeches, and their Nobel lectures. It has been an invaluable resource.

I would like to acknowledge a particular debt to three authors whose work I have found especially valuable: István Hargittai (five books in his Candid Science series; *The Road to Stockholm*, 2002; and *Our Lives: Encounters of a Scientist*, 2004); Louise S. Sherby (*The Who's Who of Nobel Prize Winners, 1901-2000*, 4th ed., 2002); and Tyler Wasson (*Nobel Prize Winners*, 1983, and supplements). For interested readers, these works can be recommended as a rich source of information about a truly remarkable company of men and women.

I wish to thank Michael Pratt, M.D., and Timothy Pratt, Ph.D., for their help with the biographies of scientists.

The final shape of the book owes much to the gifted help of Hugh Brewster. It has been a pleasure to work with Jacqueline Johnson and Mike O'Connor of Walker & Company. Most important, Beverley Slopen of the Slopen Agency had faith in the project from the beginning and has been an unfailing source of encouragement. To all of these people I express my warmest thanks.

NOBEL WISDOM

Achievement

The supreme achievement of a Nobel Prize is almost invariably the reward for supreme effort. Whether in science, medicine, economics, literature, or peace, Nobel laureates are, almost without exception, men and women who have persisted in their endeavors regardless of setbacks, discouragement, and failures. We owe the development of penicillin, Prozac, Viagra, the diphtheria serum, vitamin therapy, organ transplants, the measles and mumps vaccines, and innumerable other medical advances to Nobel laureates whose persistence drove them to conduct repeated experiments in the face of failure and skepticism. Writers such as Hemingway, Faulkner, Steinbeck, Beckett, and Naipaul refused to be discouraged by early rejection and apathy. Pasternak and Solzhenitsyn are well known for the official persecution they endured, but many other Nobel writers suffered without being defeated by neglect, censure, exile, and imprisonment. And if the world is a slightly safer place today than it was a half century ago, this is partly due to the tenacity and dedication of the men and women who have been honored with the Nobel Peace Prize.

Such commitment springs in large part from passion for their vocations. Most Nobel laureates find their mission in life early and never abandon it. Arbitrary retirement age rarely stops them or even slows them down. An exception was Frederick

Sanger, who won the Nobel Prize for Chemistry in 1958 and again in 1980. He worked at his bench in the Laboratory of Molecular Biology at Cambridge up to the eve of his retirement at age sixty-five, at which point he closed the door of his laboratory and left science completely in favor of gardening.

But the traditional image of the workaholic genius matches few Nobel laureates. While some have worked exclusively in a single specialized area, others have excelled in more than one field. Many laureates served with distinction as soldiers or with wartime resistance organizations. Others nurtured private excellence in sports or music. And the biographies of most of them reveal these men and women as individuals marked by personal charm and integrity.

Something of the character of Nobel Prize winners is manifested by their reactions on winning the award. Despite the fanfare, the pomp and circumstance of the award ceremonies, and the expectation of the media that new Nobels will have informed opinions on everything within and outside their subject, modesty rather than arrogance characterizes the response of the prize winners. Laureates from the University of California at Berkeley and Stanford University claim that the main benefit of the prize is the lifetime right to one of the "Reserved for NL" parking spaces. An incident involving Glenn Seaborg is illustrative. At a U.S. Senate hearing in 1970, an elderly senator from Louisiana asked Seaborg sarcastically, "What do you know about plutonium?" With admirable restraint, Seaborg gave a "vague but reassuring answer." He was the discoverer of plutonium.

ACHIEVEMENT

1. The difficult is what takes a little time; the impossible is what takes a little longer.
   Fridtjof Nansen PEACE, 1922

2. Ever tried. Ever failed. No matter. Try Again. Fail again. Fail better.
   Samuel Beckett LITERATURE, 1969

3. All of us failed to match our dreams of perfection. So I rate us on the basis of our splendid failure to do the impossible.
   William Faulkner LITERATURE, 1949

4. A man can be destroyed but not defeated.
   Ernest Hemingway LITERATURE, 1954

5. I don't like people who have never fallen or stumbled. Their virtue is lifeless and it isn't of much value. Life hasn't revealed its beauty to them.
   Boris Pasternak LITERATURE, 1958

6. Have you not succeeded? Continue! Have you succeeded? Continue!
   Fridtjof Nansen PEACE, 1922

7. I don't believe I have special talents. I have persistence . . . After the first failure, second failure, third failure, I kept trying.
   Carlo Rubbia PHYSICS, 1984

8. I think and think for months and years, ninety-nine times, the conclusion is false. The hundredth time I am right.
   Albert Einstein PHYSICS, 1921

9. Just take a risk. Go for it. I think if you crash and burn trying, it's still going to be better than if you never tried at all.

Roderick MacKinnon CHEMISTRY, 2003

10. Saints, it has been said, are the sinners who go on trying. So free men and women are the oppressed who go on trying and who in the process make themselves fit to bear the responsibilities and uphold the disciplines which will maintain a free society.

Aung San Suu Kyi PEACE, 1991

11. I have, despite all disillusionment, never, never allowed myself to feel like giving up. This is my message today; it is not worthy of a human being to give up.

Alva Myrdal PEACE, 1982

12. The greatest joy of life is to accomplish. It is the getting, not the having. It is the giving, not the keeping. I am a firm believer in the theory that you can do or be anything that you wish in this world, within reason, if you are prepared to make the sacrifices, think and work hard enough and long enough.

Frederick Banting MEDICINE, 1923

13. Never give in, never give in, never, never, never, never—in nothing, great or small, large or petty—never give in except to convictions of honor and good sense. Never yield to force; never yield to the apparently overwhelming might of the enemy.

Winston Churchill LITERATURE, 1953

WORK

14. Work is the only good thing.
    John Steinbeck LITERATURE, 1962

15. Work is the only thing that gives substance to life.
    Albert Einstein PHYSICS, 1921

16. Without a vocation, man's existence would be meaningless.
    Anwar al-Sadat PEACE, 1978

17. Happiness depends on one being exactly fitted to the nature of one's work.
    Alexis Carrel MEDICINE, 1912

18. Those whose work and pleasure are one . . . are . . . Fortune's favoured children.
    Winston Churchill LITERATURE, 1953

19. When I ask myself, "Who are the happiest people on the planet?" my answer is, "Those who can't wait to wake up in the morning to get back to what they were doing the day before."
    James Cronin PHYSICS, 1980

20. The scientist has in common with the artist only this: that he can find no better retreat from the world than his work and no stronger link with the world than his work.
    Max Delbrück MEDICINE, 1969

21. Far and away the best prize that life offers is the chance to work hard at work worth doing.
    Theodore Roosevelt PEACE, 1906

22. All the people who do well work very hard. Nobody who has a record of achievement has been lazy about it.
    Sidney Altman CHEMISTRY, 1989

23. Nothing is going to happen unless you work with your life's blood.
    Riccardo Giacconi PHYSICS, 2002

24. I am a very lucky person, and the harder I work, the luckier I seem to be.
    Alan MacDiarmid CHEMISTRY, 2000

25. All my life I've been surrounded by people who are smarter than I am, but I found I could always keep up by working hard.
    Glenn Seaborg CHEMISTRY, 1951

26. Work is of two kinds: first, altering the position of matter at or near the earth's surface relative to other matter; second, telling other people to do so. The former is unpleasant and badly paid. The latter is pleasant and well paid.
    Bertrand Russell LITERATURE, 1950

27. Loveless work, boring work, work valued only because others haven't got even that much, however loveless and boring—this is one of the harshest human miseries.
    Wislawa Szymborska LITERATURE, 1996

28. A situation where people can grow old without having a job that rewards them individually while adding to the collective well-being is morally unacceptable.
    Franco Modigliani ECONOMICS, 1985

29. After all, it is hard to master both life and work equally well. So if you are bound to fake one of them, it had better be life.

Joseph Brodsky LITERATURE, 1987

30. The intellect of man is forced to choose Perfection of the life, or of the work.

William Butler Yeats LITERATURE, 1923

31. The human worker will go the way of the horse.

Wassily Leontief ECONOMICS, 1973

THE NOBEL PRIZE

32. I had never, ever thought of winning the Nobel Prize. That is really true. I had grown up never expecting to get my name in the newspapers without doing something wicked.

Eugene Wigner PHYSICS, 1963

33. In any case, let's eat breakfast.

Isaac Bashevis Singer LITERATURE, 1978

To his wife, on hearing he had won the Nobel Prize

34. Almost instantly the phone rang again. He had heard me just as he'd hung up. "Congratulations, Dr. Mullis. I am pleased to be able to announce to you that you have been awarded the Nobel Prize." "I'll take it!" I said.

Kary Mullis CHEMISTRY, 1993

35. I didn't do this work; the young people in the lab did it. I just made the coffee and sharpened the pencils.

Peter Agre CHEMISTRY, 2003

36. I was delighted too when I heard about the Nobel Prize, thinking as you did that my bongo playing was at last recognized.

Richard Feynman PHYSICS, 1965

37. What am I supposed to be, a pompous fool because I got a medal?

Jody Williams PEACE, 1997

38. Local geriatrics were going, "What's a Nobel? Is that a bagel?"

Derek Walcott LITERATURE, 1992

39. In my whole life since my kids became teen-agers, this is the first time they've come home and said, "Dad, my friends think this is so cool."

Peter Agre CHEMISTRY, 2003

40. Your Majesties, Your Royal Highnesses, Ladies and Gentlemen . . . I know of no other place where Princes assemble to pay their respect to molecules . . . Because of you, our wives hesitate for just an instant before summoning us to do the dishes.

John Polanyi CHEMISTRY, 1986

41. As a child, I wanted to be a physicist. I begged my mother to let me go to Tokyo to study physics. I promised I would win the Nobel Prize for Physics. So, 50 years later, I returned to my village and said to my mother, "See, I have kept my promise. I won the Nobel Prize." "No," said my mother, who has a very fine sense of humor, "You promised it would be in physics!"

Kenzaburo Oe LITERATURE, 1994

42. It is as good as going to one's funeral without having to die first.

Emily Balch PEACE, 1946

On reading her Nobel nominations

43. It is really very, very nice for a week. It would corrupt you utterly if it lasted much longer.

Milton Friedman ECONOMICS, 1976

Of the Nobel celebrations in Stockholm

44. The Prize is also wonderful for the individual. I've jokingly said it's like being given a lifetime depot injection of Prozac.

Alfred Gilman MEDICINE, 1994

45. People keep e-mailing me to ask, "What is the meaning of life?" And they want me to e-mail them back quickly with an answer!

David Baltimore MEDICINE, 1975

46. Oh, no, I was afraid of that! I better go and hide.

Torsten Wiesel MEDICINE, 1981

47. This is the end of me. This is fatal. I cannot live up to it.

Sinclair Lewis LITERATURE, 1930

48. The Nobel is a ticket to one's own funeral. No one has ever done anything after he got it.

T. S. Eliot LITERATURE, 1948

49. If you're not careful, the Nobel Prize is a career-ender. If I allowed myself to slip into it, I'd spend all my time going around cutting ribbons.

Daniel McFadden ECONOMICS, 2000

50. If I could explain it in three minutes, it wouldn't be worth the Nobel Prize.
   Richard Feynman PHYSICS, 1965

51. If I knew what leads one to the Nobel Prize, I wouldn't tell you, but go get another one.
   Robert Laughlin PHYSICS, 1998

52. You too can win Nobel Prizes. Study diligently. Respect DNA. Don't smoke. Don't drink. Avoid women and politics. That's my formula.
   George Beadle MEDICINE, 1958

53. You people think it's hard to win a Nobel Prize, but it's easy. Trivial. Just put protons and antiprotons in a box, and shake them up, and then collect your prize.
   Carlo Rubbia PHYSICS, 1984
To colleagues at Harvard University

54. A deal is a deal. It's hard to be unpleasant after winning a prize like that.
   Robert Lucas ECONOMICS, 1995
The clause in the divorce settlement of Lucas and his wife read, "Wife shall receive 50 percent of any Nobel Prize" if won within seven years of their divorce on October 31, 1988. Lucas's prize was announced on October 10, 1995, so he had to split the $600,000.

55. Some have extolled the use of frozen sperm from judiciously chosen donors. Some have even praised the sperm of Nobel Prize winners. Only if one does not know Nobel laureates would one want to reproduce them like that.
   François Jacob MEDICINE, 1965

56. I feel that this award was not made to me as a man, but to my work—a life's work in the agony and sweat of the human spirit, not for glory and least of all for profit, but to create out of the materials of the human spirit something which did not exist before.

William Faulkner LITERATURE, 1949

57. Why, that's a hundred miles away. That's a long way to go just to eat.

William Faulkner LITERATURE, 1949

Explaining why he declined President Kennedy's invitation to dinner with forty-nine Nobel laureates

Beliefs

Alfred Nobel's will directed that the prizes be awarded to persons "who during the preceding year have conferred the greatest benefit on mankind." This humanitarian ethos has been maintained by the Nobel selection committees. While Nobel laureates represent all shades of political, religious, and social belief, idealism and humanitarianism are general characteristics.

Few laureates could be described as extremist in their beliefs. Only a minuscule number have at any time been doctrinaire communists or fascists. A minority are passionate in their religious belief, a similar minority in their atheism. Insofar as Nobel laureates share a set of beliefs, these would be belief in their work, in the welfare of humanity, in freedom, and in the search for truth.

BELIEFS

58. There are two objectionable types of believers: those who believe the incredible, and those who believe that "belief" must be discarded and replaced by "the scientific method."
     Max Born PHYSICS, 1954

59. Someone who believes everything he is told simply can't be a scientist, but someone who believes nothing will wind up in jail or prematurely buried.
     Luis Alvarez PHYSICS, 1968

60. I am astonished at the ease with which uninformed persons come to a settled, a passionate opinion when they have no grounds for judgment.
     William Golding LITERATURE, 1983

61. Human beings . . . are far too prone to generalize from one instance. The technical word for this, interestingly enough, is superstition.
     Francis Crick MEDICINE, 1902

62. I certainly do not believe in this superstition. But you know, they say it does bring luck even if you don't believe in it!
     Niels Bohr PHYSICS, 1922
In answer to a visitor's question about the horseshoe above the door of his country cottage

63. I feel no need for any other faith than my faith in human beings.
     Pearl S. Buck LITERATURE, 1938

64. I believe in God—in spite of God! I believe in Mankind—in spite of Mankind! I believe in the Future—in spite of the Past!

Elie Wiesel PEACE, 1986

MEANING AND SIGNIFICANCE

65. What man seeks, to the point of anguish, in his gods, in his art, in his science, is meaning. He cannot bear the void. He pours meaning on events like salt on his food.

François Jacob MEDICINE, 1965

66. If, after all, men cannot always make history have a meaning, they can always act so that their own lives have one.

Albert Camus LITERATURE, 1957

67. I believe that I am not responsible for the meaningfulness or meaninglessness of life, but that I am responsible for what I do with the life I've got.

Hermann Hesse LITERATURE, 1946

68. The meaning of life consists in the fact that it makes no sense to say that life has no meaning.

Niels Bohr PHYSICS, 1922

69. Not everything that counts can be counted, and not everything that can be counted counts.

Albert Einstein PHYSICS, 1921

70. I have one life and one chance to make it count for something . . . My faith demands that I do whatever I can, wherever I am, whenever I can, for as long as I can with whatever I have to try to make a difference.

Jimmy Carter PEACE, 2002

71. The ancient covenant is in pieces; man knows at last that he is alone in the universe's unfeeling immensity, out of which he emerged only by chance. His destiny is nowhere spelled out, nor is his duty. The kingdom above or the darkness below: it is for him to choose.
    Jacques Monod MEDICINE, 1965

72. In roadside ditches, in washed-out trenches, among the ruins of burned houses, he learned the value of a can of soup, an hour of quiet, the meaning of true friendship, of life itself.
    Alexandr Solzhenitsyn LITERATURE, 1970

TRUTH AND FALSEHOOD

73. The truth isn't always beauty, but the hunger for it is.
    Nadine Gordimer LITERATURE, 1991

74. With the beginning of life, comes the thirst for truth, whereas the ability to lie is gradually acquired in the process of trying to stay alive.
    Gao Xingjian LITERATURE, 2000

75. Believe those who seek the truth, doubt those who find it.
    André Gide LITERATURE, 1947

76. Discussion is impossible with someone who claims not to seek the truth, but already to possess it.
    Romain Rolland LITERATURE, 1915

77. Science has nothing to do with any dogma. Science ceases to exist when there is a dogma.
    Jean-Marie Lehn CHEMISTRY, 1987

78. It is the certainty that they possess the truth that makes men cruel.
      Anatole France LITERATURE, 1921

79. I believe that ideas such as absolute certitude, absolute exactness, final truth, etc. are figments of the imagination which should not be admissible in any field of science . . . This loosening of thinking seems to me to be the greatest blessing which modern science has given to us. For the belief in a single truth and in being the possessor thereof is the root cause of all evil in the world.
      Max Born PHYSICS, 1954

80. Men occasionally stumble over the truth, but most of them pick themselves up and hurry off as if nothing had happened.
      Winston Churchill LITERATURE, 1953

81. The opposite of a correct statement is a false statement. The opposite of a profound truth may well be another profound truth.
      Niels Bohr PHYSICS, 1922

82. No deep truth has ever been shouted.
      Juan Ramón Jiménez LITERATURE, 1956

83. A man may say, "From now on I'm going to speak the truth." But the truth hears him and runs away and hides before he's even done speaking.
      Saul Bellow LITERATURE, 1976

84. Humankind cannot bear very much reality.
      T. S. Eliot LITERATURE, 1948

85. Nothing factual that I write or say will be as truthful as my fiction.

  Nadine Gordimer LITERATURE, 1991

86. In a room where people unanimously maintain a conspiracy of silence, one word of truth sounds like a pistol shot.

  Czeslaw Milosz LITERATURE, 1980

87. A person obsessed with ultimate truth is a person asking to be relieved of money.

  Robert Laughlin PHYSICS, 1998

88. You can resolve to live your life with integrity. Let your credo be this: Let the lie come into the world, let it even triumph. But not through me.

  Alexandr Solzhenitsyn LITERATURE, 1970

89. Lying is not only saying what isn't true. It is also, in fact especially, saying more than is true, and, in the case of the human heart, saying more than one feels.

  Albert Camus LITERATURE, 1957

90. The only lies for which we are truly punished are those we tell ourselves.

  V. S. Naipaul LITERATURE, 2001

91. In all my fifty years of public service I have never seen a document that was more crowded with infamous falsehoods and distortions—infamous falsehoods and distortions on a scale so huge that I never imagined until today that any government on this planet was capable of uttering them.

  Cordell Hull PEACE, 1945

To the Japanese ambassador, who brought a note to Secretary of State Hull immediately after Pearl Harbor, December 7, 1941

92. Men will clutch at illusions when they have nothing else to hold to.
Czeslaw Milosz LITERATURE, 1980

93. As I was standing in the drawing-room at Trinity, a clergyman came in. And I said to him: "I'm Lord Rutherford." And he said to me, "I'm the Archbishop of York." And I don't suppose either of us believed the other.
Ernest Rutherford CHEMISTRY, 1908

IDEAS

94. I'm enough of an academic to believe that ideas are even more powerful than nuclear weapons.
John Polanyi CHEMISTRY, 1986

95. For an idea that does not first seem insane, there is no hope.
Albert Einstein PHYSICS, 1921

96. As a rule, the man who first thinks of a new idea is so much ahead of his time that everyone thinks him silly, so that he remains obscure and is soon forgotten. Then, gradually, the world becomes ready for his idea, and the man who proclaims it at the fortunate moment gets all the credit.
Bertrand Russell LITERATURE, 1950

97. How do you get good ideas? You have a lot of ideas and throw out the bad ones.
Linus Pauling CHEMISTRY, 1954; PEACE, 1962

98. Ideas are like rabbits. You get a couple, learn how to handle them, and pretty soon you have a dozen.
John Steinbeck LITERATURE, 1962

99. The only way I can tell that a new idea is really important
is the feeling of terror that seizes me.

James Franck PHYSICS, 1925

100. I distrust scientists who complain about others stealing
their ideas—I have always had to force new ideas down
people's throats.

Max Perutz CHEMISTRY, 1962

101. There's a saying among scientists, that you don't know
you've got a really good idea until at least three Nobel
laureates have told you it's wrong.

Paul Lauterbur MEDICINE, 2003

102. No one has ever had an idea in a dress suit.

Frederick Banting MEDICINE, 1923

IDEALS

103. You must begin with an ideal and end with an ideal.

Frederick Banting MEDICINE, 1923

104. Idealism increases in direct proportion to one's distance
from the problem.

John Galsworthy LITERATURE, 1932

105. Much that passes as idealism is disguised hatred or
disguised love of power.

Bertrand Russell LITERATURE, 1950

106. We are not asked to subscribe to any utopia or to believe
in a perfect world. We are asked to equip ourselves with
courage, hope, readiness for hard work and to cherish
large and generous ideals.

Emily Balch PEACE, 1946

107. They call us romantics, weak, stupid, sentimental idealists, perhaps because we have some faith in the good which exists even in our opponents and because we believe that kindness achieves more than cruelty.
Fridtjof Nansen PEACE, 1922

108. The ideals that have lighted my way and time after time have given me new courage to face life cheerfully, have been Kindness, Beauty, and Truth.
Albert Einstein PHYSICS, 1921

IDEOLOGY

109. One of the important distinctions between *ideology* and *science* is that science recognizes the limitations on what one knows.
Joseph Stiglitz ECONOMICS, 2001

110. Ideology—that is what gives evildoing its long-sought justification and gives the evildoer the necessary steadfastness and determination.
Alexandr Solzhenitsyn LITERATURE, 1970

111. I don't know whose crime is worse, the establishment intellectual or the intellectual who trots out ideological dogma.
Wole Soyinka LITERATURE, 1986

112. Bid farewell to ideologies and instead return to the truth of being human.
Gao Xingjian LITERATURE, 2000

113. Now that the cruel utopias that bloodied our century have vanished, the time has come at last to begin a radical, more human reform of liberal capitalist society.
Octavio Paz LITERATURE, 1990

114. After the collapse of socialism, capitalism remained without a rival. This unusual situation unleashed its greedy and—above all—its suicidal power. The belief is now that everything—and everyone—is fair game.
Günter Grass LITERATURE, 1999

115. Every reasonable human being should be a moderate Socialist.
Thomas Mann LITERATURE, 1929

116. Any anti-Communist is a dog.
Jean-Paul Sartre LITERATURE, 1964

117. By "radical," I understand one who goes too far; by "conservative," one who does not go far enough; by "reactionary," one who won't go at all.
Woodrow Wilson PEACE, 1919

118. It is time to fight the fashionable notion that self-fulfilment, the development of one's personality and fulfilment of one's wishes at no matter what cost to one's family, friends, colleagues, and community, should be man's or woman's ultimate aim.
Max Perutz CHEMISTRY, 1962

RELIGION

119. Man is man because he can recognize supernatural realities, not because he can invent them.
T. S. Eliot LITERATURE, 1948

120. Man is born broken. He lives by mending. The grace of God is glue.
Eugene O'Neill LITERATURE, 1936

121. I think only an idiot can be an atheist.
Christian Anfinsen CHEMISTRY, 1972

122. I was merely an electrician and the only things I had were my belief in God, and my belief in what I was doing.
Lech Walesa PEACE, 1983

123. We have to recognize that we are spiritual beings with souls existing in a spiritual world as well as material beings with bodies and brains existing in a material world.
John Eccles MEDICINE, 1963

124. We know too much, and are convinced of too little. Our literature is a substitute for religion, and so is our religion.
T. S. Eliot LITERATURE, 1948

125. Science without religion is lame, religion without science is blind.
Albert Einstein PHYSICS, 1921

126. Religion is very different from science . . . When you play the piano, when you climb a mountain, does this contradict your scientific endeavors? . . . In science we have certain ways of thinking about the world, and in religion we have different ways of thinking about the world. Those two things coexist side by side without conflict.
Robert Aumann ECONOMICS, 2005

127. Wherever we may look, far and wide, we nowhere find a contradiction between religion and natural science. Quite the contrary, precisely on the decisive points we find complete agreement.
Otto Hahn CHEMISTRY, 1944

128. I do not believe that anyone should ever say that science agrees with religion. What I would say, which I think is

a far more powerful statement, and one which allows people to be religious, is to say, the modern observations of science do not disagree with religion.

Arno Penzias PHYSICS, 1978

129. I consider the power to believe to be one of the great divine gifts to man through which he is allowed in some inexplicable manner to come near to the mysteries of the Universe without understanding them.

Ernst Chain MEDICINE, 1945

130. The most beautiful emotion we can experience is the mystical. It is the power of all true art and science.

Albert Einstein PHYSICS, 1921

131. I feel that my faith and my scientific work have mutually reinforced each other . . . The wondrous experience of understanding, perhaps understanding for the first time, something about the natural world is a deep religious experience.

Walter Kohn CHEMISTRY, 1998

132. Being an ordinary scientist and an ordinary Christian seems perfectly natural to me.

William Phillips PHYSICS, 1997

133. Whether or not God is dead, it is impossible to keep silent about him who was there for so long.

Elias Canetti LITERATURE, 1981

134. One of the great achievements of science has been, if not to make it impossible for intelligent people to be religious, then at least to make it possible for them not to be religious.

Steven Weinberg PHYSICS, 1979

135. I think in many respects religion is a dream—a beautiful dream often. Often a nightmare. But it's a dream from which I think it's about time we awoke.

Steven Weinberg PHYSICS, 1979

136. I can believe in God's wisdom but I cannot see his mercy.

Isaac Bashevis Singer LITERATURE, 1978

137. The Churches and the Faith have really done too much harm! . . . While there's a breath left in me I shall cry "No!" to the Churches.

André Gide LITERATURE, 1947

On his deathbed

138. Christianity might be a good thing if anyone ever tried it.

George Bernard Shaw LITERATURE, 1925

139. We should live our lives as though Christ were coming this afternoon.

Jimmy Carter PEACE, 2002

Talk to Bible class

140. Turn your face to God and he becomes light but turn your face away from him and he becomes darkness.

William Golding LITERATURE, 1983

141. Whenever I'm in trouble, I pray. And because I'm in trouble all of the time, I pray almost constantly.

Isaac Bashevis Singer LITERATURE, 1978

142. It is a fact—and I saw it with my own eyes—that man in his downfall has nothing to lean on, nothing to solace him, except faith. The NKVD brought many back to the religious fold . . . Lukishki nights taught us that faith takes better care of man, when things go badly with

24

him, than man does of his faith when things are well
with him.

Menachem Begin PEACE, 1978

143. I have lived, and continue to live, in the belief that God is
always with me. I know this from experience. In August of
1973, while exiled in Japan, I was kidnapped from my hotel
room in Tokyo by intelligence agents of the then military
government of South Korea. The news of the incident
startled the world. The agents took me to their boat at
anchor along the seashore. They tied me up, blinded me,
and stuffed my mouth. Just when they were about to throw
me overboard, Jesus Christ appeared before me with such
clarity. I clung to him and begged him to save me. At that
very moment, an airplane came down from the sky to
rescue me from the moment of death.

Kim Dae-jung PEACE, 2000

144. For four and a half months in 1918 I was in prison for
pacifist propaganda . . . I was much cheered on my arrival
by the warder at the gate, who had to take particulars about
me. He asked my religion, and I replied "agnostic." He
asked how to spell it, and remarked with a sigh: "Well,
there are many religions, but I suppose they all worship the
same God." This remark kept me cheerful for about a week.

Bertrand Russell LITERATURE, 1950

MATERIALISM

145. Man does not live by GNP alone.

Paul Samuelson ECONOMICS, 1970

146. Most people seek after what they do not possess and are
thus enslaved by the very things they want to acquire . . .

Only when he has ceased to need things can a man truly
be his own master and so really exist.
Anwar al-Sadat PEACE, 1978

147. The craving for possessions and money, from the humble
hire-purchase level, to the smash and grab tactics of the
tirelessly acquisitive rich, from the alderman to the union
leader and cabinet minister, and finally the dictator of a
superpower, has become an epidemic disease.
Patrick White LITERATURE, 1973

148. You have riches and freedom here but I feel no sense of
faith or direction. You have so many computers, why don't
you use them in the search for love?
Lech Walesa PEACE, 1983
In Paris, on his first visit to the West

149. In the past people's mentality was formed within a large
space which still exists, called the cathedral. Today human
mentality is formed within another large space called the
shopping centre. And the illusion there is constant.
José Saramago LITERATURE, 1998

150. What is more insidious than any censorship, is the
steady influence which operates silently in any mass
society organized for profit, for the depression of
standards of art and culture.
T. S. Eliot LITERATURE, 1948

151. Americans suffer from this notion that somehow they can
possess their souls by means of possessing commodities.
Don't they recognize that they'll end up a nation and an
empire who has the capacity to conquer the world, but has
completely lost its soul?
Eugene O'Neill LITERATURE, 1936

152. I don't know how to own things . . . I cling like a miser to the freedom that disappears as soon as there is an excess of things.
   Albert Camus LITERATURE, 1957

153. All of the other shallow things will not matter. I won't have any money to leave behind. I won't have the fine and luxurious things of life to leave behind. But I just want to leave a committed life behind.
   Martin Luther King PEACE, 1964

154. Free-market societies produce unjust and very stupid societies. I don't believe that the production and consumption of things can be the meaning of human life.
   Octavio Paz LITERATURE, 1990

155. To defend oneself, one must also be ready to die; there is little such readiness in a society raised in the cult of material well-being.
   Alexandr Solzhenitsyn LITERATURE, 1970

156. I rather like materialism. The poor need it.
   V. S. Naipaul LITERATURE, 2001
   In answer to a question from the audience in India

Time, Life, and Death
◇◈◇◈◇

Nobel Prize laureates often appear not only to achieve more in their lifetimes than other mortals but also to live longer lives. Although no Nobel Prize winner has, up to this point, lived to a hundred years—Hans Bethe, so far the longest lived, died in 2005 at the age of ninety-eight—many do exceed the average life expectancy. The statistics, however, are biased by the fact that in order to become a laureate one must have lived long enough for one's accomplishments to be recognized. The prize is not awarded posthumously, although in the past it was awarded to Erik Karlfeldt and Dag Hammarskjöld, both of whom died after nomination, but before public announcement of the prize. It is awarded if the recipient dies after the announcement but prior to the award ceremony, as in the case of William Vickrey in 1996 who died three days after his prize for Economics was announced.

The youngest Nobel laureate was William Lawrence Bragg, who in 1915 at the age of twenty-five shared the Physics Prize with his father, William Henry Bragg. The youngest laureates to win the prize in Chemistry, Medicine, and Peace were in their thirties, whereas the youngest laureate for Literature was forty-two and for Economics fifty-one. The earliest-born Nobel Prize winner was Theodor Mommsen, who won the Literature Prize in 1902; he was born in 1817, and in 1903 became the first laureate to die. The laureate who died youngest was Martin Luther King, who was assassinated at the age of thirty-nine, four years after winning the prize.

TIME

157. We are not the father of time. We are the children of time.
      Ilya Prigogine CHEMISTRY, 1977

158. Now he has departed from this strange world a little ahead of me. That signifies nothing. For us believing physicists, the distinction between past, present, and future is only an illusion, however persistent.
      Albert Einstein PHYSICS, 1921
      Letter to the family of his friend Michelangelo Besso, March 21, 1955, written a month before Einstein's own death

159. The only reason for time is so that everything doesn't happen at once.
      Albert Einstein PHYSICS, 1921

160. It is an experimental fact that time runs slower in the vicinity of babies, especially at night. Who of us cannot remember learning the true measure of eternity by spending the first night alone with an alert baby? And who would deny the iron certainty of Heisenberg's famous Uncertainty Principle, which states that two new parents cannot possibly get a good night's sleep simultaneously?
      Robert Laughlin PHYSICS, 1998

LIFE AND LIFESPAN

161. Life—the way it really is—is a battle not between Bad and Good but between Bad and Worse.
     Joseph Brodsky LITERATURE, 1987

162. Life is perhaps best regarded as a bad dream between two awakenings.
     Eugene O'Neill LITERATURE, 1936

163. No one who lives in the sunlight makes a failure of his life.
     Albert Camus LITERATURE, 1957

164. To oppression, plundering and abandonment, we respond with life. Neither flood nor plagues, famines nor cataclysms, nor even the eternal wars of century upon century, have been able to subdue the persistent advantage of life over death.
     Gabriel García Márquez LITERATURE, 1982

165. Life continues to be a mystery too great to understand. I only know that I cling to it. I fear its cessation—death. I dread its diminution—pain. I seek its enlargement—joy.
     Albert Schweitzer PEACE, 1952

166. In every human being's life there is one period when he manifests himself most fully, feels most profoundly himself, and acts with the deepest effect on himself and on others. And whatever happens to that person from that time on, no matter how outwardly significant, it is all a letdown. We remember, get drunk on, play over and over in many different keys, sing over and over to ourselves that snatch of a song that sounded just once within us.
     Alexandr Solzhenitsyn LITERATURE, 1970

167. Unless you stake your life, life will not be won.
Werner Heisenberg PHYSICS, 1932

168. I wish to preach, not the doctrine of ignoble ease, but the doctrine of the strenuous life.
Theodore Roosevelt PEACE, 1906

169. *We shall not cease from exploration*
And the end of all our exploring
Will be to arrive where we started
And know the place for the first time.
T. S. Eliot LITERATURE, 1948

170. For every year one works beyond age 55, one loses 2 years of life span on average . . . If you . . . have to keep on working very hard until the age of 65 or older before your retirement, then you probably will die within 18 months of retirement.
Leo Esaki PHYSICS, 1973

Based on retirement statistics at Boeing and Lockheed. Leo Esaki himself, however, was still working at the age of eighty.

171. I think there is a limit to how long one can live even if you eradicate disease. Mice have a natural lifespan of 2 ½ years. And humans, 120 years.
Linda Buck MEDICINE, 2004

172. The average man does not know what to do with his life, yet wants another one which will last forever.
Anatole France LITERATURE, 1921

YOUTH AND AGE

173. Birth was the death of him.
Samuel Beckett LITERATURE, 1969

174. Youth longs not for that which was, but rather for that which could be.

Willy Brandt PEACE, 1971

175. Students of Stockholm, Nature will begin to harden your arteries and your attitudes soon enough, without your help. You are not obligated to speed the process along.

Arno Penzias PHYSICS, 1978

176. The most aggravating thing about the younger generation is that I no longer belong to it.

Albert Einstein PHYSICS, 1921

177. Eighteen is a good time for suffering. One has all the necessary strength, and no defenses.

William Golding LITERATURE, 1983

178. Twenty to twenty-five! These are the years! Don't be content with things as they are . . . You will make all kinds of mistakes; but as long as you are generous and true, and also fierce, you cannot hurt the world or even seriously distress her.

Winston Churchill LITERATURE, 1953

179. The most precious, creative and innovative period in your life is the 10-year period around the age of 32. Plan your career path to use this precious 10-year period wisely and effectively to produce your greatest achievement in your life.

Leo Esaki PHYSICS, 1973

180. Most of the progress in understanding how the universe works is made by people under 40, which is just as well, or we'd end up like the Kremlin run by people over 80.

Sheldon Glashow PHYSICS, 1979

181. The young girls in the flower of their youth still laugh and chatter on the seashore, but he who watches them gradually loses his right to love them, just as those he has loved lose the power to be loved.
Albert Camus LITERATURE, 1957

182. Every man over forty is a scoundrel.
George Bernard Shaw LITERATURE, 1925

183. The years between fifty and seventy are the hardest. You are always being asked to do things, and yet you are not decrepit enough to turn them down.
T. S. Eliot LITERATURE, 1948

184. It's better to be seventy years young than forty years old.
Jimmy Carter PEACE, 2002

185. The excitement of learning separates youth from old age. As long as you're learning, you're not old.
Rosalyn Yalow MEDICINE, 1977

186. Perhaps one has to be very old before one learns to be amused rather than shocked.
Pearl S. Buck LITERATURE, 1938

187. When I cease to be indignant, I will have begun my old age.
André Gide LITERATURE, 1947

188. We breathe, we change! We lose our hair, our teeth! Our bloom! Our ideals!
Samuel Beckett LITERATURE, 1969

189. I don't believe one grows older. I think that what happens early on in life is that at a certain age one stands still and stagnates.
T. S. Eliot LITERATURE, 1948

190. I think we may take it, gentlemen, that the evening light is much the same for all men. When the shadows lengthen one contrasts what one had intended to do in the beginning with what one has accomplished.
Rudyard Kipling LITERATURE, 1907

191. I used to think getting old was about vanity—but actually it's about losing people you love. Getting wrinkles is trivial.
Eugene O'Neill LITERATURE, 1936

192. The secret of a good old age is simply an honorable pact with solitude.
Gabriel García Márquez LITERATURE, 1982

193. Old age is wonderful . . . A pity it ends so badly.
François Mauriac LITERATURE, 1952

194. I don't see why not, you look healthy enough to me.
George Bernard Shaw LITERATURE, 1925
On his ninetieth birthday, 1946, to a young reporter who said, "I hope to interview you again on your 100th birthday." This quip is also attributed to Winston Churchill.

DEATH AND MORTALITY

195. There's nothing in biology yet found that indicates the inevitability of death.
Richard Feynman PHYSICS, 1965

196. On our arrival in Cambridge, we had a rather frightening reception. On all the big hoardings was written in large letters: "The Man Born to be Hanged"! but soon we found out that it did not refer to me, and that it was quite harmless: the title of a cinema film, made from a crime novel.
Max Born PHYSICS, 1954

197. I curse death. I can't help it. And if I should go blind in the process, I can't help it, I repulse death with all my strength. If I accepted it, I would be a murderer.
     Elias Canetti LITERATURE, 1981

198. *Never to have lived is best, ancient writers say;*
     Never to have drawn the breath of life, never to have looked
     into the eye of day;
     The second best's a gay goodnight and quickly turn away.
     William Butler Yeats LITERATURE, 1923

199. To lose the touch of flowers and women's hands is the supreme separation.
     Albert Camus LITERATURE, 1957

200. The newspapers, at one time, said that I was dead, but after carefully examining the evidence I came to the conclusion that the statement was false.
     Bertrand Russell LITERATURE, 1950

201. Death is only an incident, and not the most important which happens to us in this state of being . . . Look forward, feel free, rejoice in life, cherish the children, guard my memory. God bless you. Good bye. W.
     Winston Churchill LITERATURE, 1953
     Letter to his wife before his departure for France in 1915, to be delivered only after his death

202. Californians, alone among humans, seem to be blissfully unaware of their own personal mortality.
     Sheldon Glashow PHYSICS, 1979

203. We should all like to go out in full summer, with beauty stepping towards us across a lawn.
     John Galsworthy LITERATURE, 1932

204. Jerónimo, my grandfather, swineherd and story-teller,
feeling death about to arrive and take him, went and said
goodbye to the trees in the yard, one by one, embracing
them and crying because he knew he wouldn't see them
again.
    José Saramago LITERATURE, 1998

205. That's exactly what is going to happen to me.
    Martin Luther King PEACE, 1964
Dr. and Mrs. King were sitting together when they learned that
President John F. Kennedy had been assassinated, November 22,
1963

206. All our knowledge merely helps us to die a more painful
death than the animals that know nothing. A day will
come when science will turn upon its error and no longer
hesitate to shorten our woes. A day will come when it will
dare and act with certainty; when life, grown wiser, will
depart silently at its hour, knowing that it has reached
its term.
    Maurice Maeterlinck LITERATURE, 1911

207. It isn't decent for Society to make a man do this thing
himself.
    Percy Bridgman PHYSICS, 1946
Suicide note; Bridgman was suffering from rapidly advancing bone
cancer

208. Man cannot boast of his intelligence until he knows how
to contrive a serene death. We cultivate the exact opposite
of euthanasia, we know only dysthanasia.
    Charles Richet MEDICINE, 1913

209. The termination of life is becoming more and more a
voluntary matter. People can be put on life sustaining

machines. They can be kept going more or less indefinitely . . . The questions about life termination are going to affect everybody. And I put that as the top most ethical issue, how we confront that.

Joshua Lederberg MEDICINE, 1958

EPITAPHS AND EULOGIES

210. *My son was killed while laughing at some jest. I would I knew*
What it was, and it might serve me in a time when jests are few.

Rudyard Kipling LITERATURE, 1907

211. *If any question why we died,*
Tell them, because our fathers lied.

Rudyard Kipling LITERATURE, 1907

212. *From little towns in a far land we came,*
To save our honor and a world aflame,
By little towns in a far land we sleep,
And trust that world we won for you to keep!

Rudyard Kipling LITERATURE, 1907

213. Never in the whole field of human conflict has so much been owed by so many to so few.

Winston Churchill LITERATURE, 1953

Of the Royal Air Force pilots in the Battle of Britain

214. "Not in vain" may be the pride of those who survived and the epitaph of those who fell.

Winston Churchill LITERATURE, 1953

215. So long as English is spoken, and history studied, men will marvel at the greatness of Sir Winston.

John Cockcroft PHYSICS, 1951

Tribute to Churchill at Churchill College, Cambridge, January 24, 1965

216. Standing here today, I wish to salute loved ones—and foes. I wish to salute all the fallen of all the countries in all the wars; the members of their families who bear the enduring burden of bereavement; the disabled whose scars will never heal.

Yitzhak Rabin PEACE, 1994

217. My life's work has been accomplished. I did all that I could.

Mikhail Gorbachev PEACE, 1990

218. Here lies someone who tried to screw his fellow man as little as possible.

Camilo José Cela LITERATURE, 1989

Epitaph Cela chose for himself

219. He lies here, somewhere.

Werner Heisenberg PHYSICS, 1932

Epitaph on his gravestone, composed by Heisenberg, author of the Heisenberg Uncertainty Principle

220. When I go from hence, let this be my parting word, that what I have seen is unsurpassable.

Rabindranath Tagore LITERATURE, 1913

HISTORY AND THE PAST

221. Man does not live in a state of nature but in history.

Boris Pasternak LITERATURE, 1958

222. The past is never dead. It's not even past.
William Faulkner LITERATURE, 1949

223. No one is free from the history he has inherited.
Willy Brandt PEACE, 1971

224. It is difficult at times to repress the thought that history
is about as instructive as an abattoir.
Seamus Heaney LITERATURE, 1995

225. He who puts out his hand to stop the wheel of history will
have his fingers crushed.
Lech Walesa PEACE, 1983

226. History is neither made nor written without love or hate.
Theodor Mommsen LITERATURE, 1902

227. History will be kind to me, for I intend to write it.
Winston Churchill LITERATURE, 1953

THE FUTURE

228. The vision of the future should shape the agenda for the
present.
Shimon Peres PEACE, 1994

229. A nation which never looks ahead is in for rude
awakenings.
John Galsworthy LITERATURE, 1932

230. The best way to predict the future is to ask a Nobel
laureate what is impossible to do.
Paul Lauterbur MEDICINE, 2003

231. In the near future the developments in biology will make problems like no one has ever seen before.
     Richard Feynman PHYSICS, 1965

232. In the year 2020 you will be able to go into the drug store, have your DNA sequence read in an hour or so, and given back to you on a compact disk so you can analyze it.
     Walter Gilbert CHEMISTRY, 1980

233. If the history of technology tells us anything, it is that the future lies in the world of the very small.
     Eric Cornell PHYSICS, 2001

234. Already the clash of empires is in process of becoming secondary to the clash of civilizations . . . Perhaps in ten years, perhaps in fifty, the dominance of Western civilization itself will be called into question.
     Albert Camus LITERATURE, 1957

235. You have only to wish it and you can have a world without hunger, disease, cancer and toil—anything you wish, wish anything and it can be done. Or else we can exterminate ourselves . . . at present we are on the road to extermination.
     Albert Szent-Györgyi MEDICINE, 1937

236. At every crossroads on the path that leads to the future, tradition has placed 10,000 men to guard the past.
     Maurice Maeterlinck LITERATURE, 1911

237. Currently, the central region of the sun, in which hydrogen is converted into helium is moving outward toward the solar surface as more and more hydrogen is consumed. When this helium core grows sufficiently large—in about 6 billion years—the sun will expand into

a red giant and move away from its present position on the main sequence. At that time the earth's surface will be hot enough to melt lead, the oceans will boil, and life on earth will end.

Max Delbrück MEDICINE, 1969

238. Building for the future is a very difficult thing to do; we cannot hope to complete the work in one generation; all the more reason to begin at once.

René Cassin PEACE, 1968

Human Qualities

The humane character of Nobel laureates is identified most clearly in the public mind with such Peace laureates as Albert Schweitzer, Mother Teresa, and Desmond Tutu. The Peace Prize has also been awarded more than twenty times to humanitarian organizations such as the Red Cross, Médecins sans Frontières, and the International Campaign to Ban Landmines.

Altruism is a quality that may be observed in the lives of many Nobel laureates. The Swedish writer Selma Lägerlof saved the future laureate Nelly Sachs from the Holocaust in 1940 by sponsoring her emigration to Sweden. Pyotr Kapitsa saved the life of his fellow physicist Lev Landau by intervening with the Soviet authorities to release him from prison. In the 1930s, the laboratory of Niels Bohr in Copenhagen became a haven for Jewish scientists fleeing Nazi Germany, and Bohr was a leading participant in the operation that successfully sent almost all the Danish Jews to Sweden just ahead of the roundup planned by the Nazis. Ernest Rutherford's Cavendish Laboratory in Cambridge was another refuge for German scientists, while the efforts of many other laureates in Britain and the United States were instrumental in saving numerous refugees. Many Nobel laureates gave away all or part of their prize money. As a child, Günter Blobel, in flight with his family from the Russians, saw the magnificent Frauenkirche in

Dresden, which a few days later was destroyed by Allied bombing. When he won the Nobel Prize for Medicine in 1999, he donated the entire prize money for the restoration of the church and for the construction of a new synagogue in Dresden.

Courage is a subject on which many Nobel laureates can speak with authority. A substantial number served with distinction in the armed forces of their countries. During World War II, many current and future laureates worked in the Resistance in France, Poland, Hungary, and Italy. In fact, almost all the laureates living in France at that time were members of the Resistance, including the Irishman Samuel Beckett and the Pole Georges Charpak.

Imprisonment has been another challenging experience for many winners of the Nobel Prize. They found themselves in prison camps in wartime, as prisoners of war, enemy aliens, persecuted minorities, or resistance fighters. But in addition a number of Peace laureates suffered imprisonment for their work and beliefs, including Menachem Begin, Nelson Mandela, Martin Luther King, Shirin Ebadi, Anwar al-Sadat, Andrei Sakharov, Lech Walesa, and Wangari Maathai. Some Literature Prize winners were also prisoners of conscience, including Bertrand Russell, Alexandr Solzhenitsyn, Joseph Brodsky, and Wole Soyinka.

GOOD AND EVIL

239. Evil is not the norm. Injustice is not the norm. Poverty is not the norm. War is not the norm . . . The norm is goodness. The norm is compassion. The norm is gentleness.
Desmond Tutu PEACE, 1984

240. There is no simple choice between the children of light and the children of darkness. Good and evil are not symmetrically distributed along political lines.
Saul Bellow LITERATURE, 1976

241. It was only when I lay there on rotting prison straw that I sensed within myself the first stirring of the good. Gradually it was disclosed to me that the line separating good and evil passes, not through states, not between classes, not between political parties either, but right through every human heart and through all human hearts.
Alexandr Solzhenitsyn LITERATURE, 1970

242. Evil takes root when one man starts to think that he is better than another.
Joseph Brodsky LITERATURE, 1987

243. All things truly wicked start from an innocence.
Ernest Hemingway LITERATURE, 1954

244. I, and few others, know what must be done, if not to reduce evil, at least not to add to it. Perhaps we cannot prevent this world from being a world in which children are tortured. But we can reduce the number of tortured children.
Albert Camus LITERATURE, 1957

245. A man does not have to be an angel in order to be a saint.
Albert Schweitzer PEACE, 1952

246. If this is a world of vice and woe, I'll take the vice and you
can have the woe.
Winston Churchill LITERATURE, 1953

CHARACTER AND SELF-CONCEPT

247. If you cannot be gold, be silver.
Juan Ramón Jiménez LITERATURE, 1956

248. Try not to become a man of success, but rather try to
become a man of value.
Albert Einstein PHYSICS, 1921

249. I can no longer bear to be human and I will no longer try.
Samuel Beckett LITERATURE, 1969

250. Man is nothing else but what he makes of himself. Such is
the first principle of existentialism.
Jean-Paul Sartre LITERATURE, 1964

251. A human being is never what he is but the self he seeks.
Octavio Paz LITERATURE, 1990

252. Great suffering builds up a human being and puts him
within reach of self-knowledge.
Anwar al-Sadat PEACE, 1978

253. He did not remember when he had attained humility,
but he knew he had attained it, and he knew it was not
disgraceful, and it carried no loss to pride.
Ernest Hemingway LITERATURE, 1954

254. I have been called indispensable and a miracle worker.
I know, because I remember every word I say.
Henry Kissinger PEACE, 1973

255. The main advantage of being famous is that when you
bore people at dinner parties they think it is their fault.
Henry Kissinger PEACE, 1973

256. At all costs try to avoid granting yourself the status of the
victim . . . No matter how abominable your condition
may be, try not to blame anything or anybody.
Joseph Brodsky LITERATURE, 1987

257. The tendency to see oneself perpetually as a victim will lead
to the evasion of responsibility and the condoning of evil.
Albert Lutuli PEACE, 1960

COURAGE AND HEROISM

258. Courage is rightly esteemed the first of human qualities,
because . . . it is the quality which guarantees all others.
Winston Churchill LITERATURE, 1953

259. We do not know how to retreat, we know how to advance.
Yasser Arafat PEACE, 1994

260. When you are in the last ditch, there is nothing left but
to sing.
Samuel Beckett LITERATURE, 1969

261. Grace under pressure.
Ernest Hemingway LITERATURE, 1954
When asked what he meant by *guts* in an interview with Dorothy
Parker

262. If people bring so much courage to this world the world
has to kill them to break them, so of course it kills them.
The world breaks everyone and afterward many are strong

46

at the broken places. But those that will not break it kills.
It kills the very good and the very gentle and very brave
impartially. If you are none of these you can be sure that
it will kill you too but there will be no special hurry.
Ernest Hemingway LITERATURE, 1954

263. A hero is someone who does what he can.
Romain Rolland LITERATURE, 1915

264. How can we justify our dreams? How can we confirm our
beliefs? How can we prove to ourselves that what we have
been taught as children is true? How can we alleviate our
doubts? How can we, in our own often naturally dormant
lives, be inspired to action, sometimes even at the sacrifice
of our own immediate well-being? We derive those
inspirations from our heroes.
Jimmy Carter PEACE, 2002

265. One day the South will recognize its real heroes . . . They
will be the young high school and college students, the
young ministers of the gospel and a host of their elders,
courageously and nonviolently sitting in at lunch counters
and willingly going to jail for conscience' sake.
Martin Luther King PEACE, 1964

266. The coward makes himself cowardly. The hero makes
himself heroic.
Jean-Paul Sartre LITERATURE, 1964

267. There are no heroes of action: only heroes of renunciation
and suffering. But few of them are known, and even these
not to the crowd, but to the few.
Albert Schweitzer PEACE, 1952

268. What the future has in store for me I do not know. It
might be ridicule, imprisonment, concentration camp,

47

flogging, banishment and even death. I only pray to the
Almighty to strengthen my resolve so that none of these
grim possibilities may deter me from striving, for the sake
of the good name of our beloved country, the Union of
South Africa, to make it a true democracy and a true union
in form and spirit of all the communities in the land.

Albert Lutuli PEACE, 1960

Statement in November 1952 when dismissed from his position
as chief of his Zulu tribe for refusing to resign from the African
National Congress

269. It's strange and it's also wonderful to live in a country
where there are still heroes.

Nadine Gordimer LITERATURE, 1991

Speaking of South Africa

270. During my lifetime I have dedicated my life to this
struggle of the African people. I have fought against white
domination, and I have fought against black domination.
I have cherished the ideal of a democratic and free society
in which all people live together in harmony and with
equal opportunities. It is an ideal which I hope to live for,
and to see realized. But, my lord, if it needs be, it is an
ideal for which I am prepared to die.

Nelson Mandela PEACE, 1993

Speech at his trial in Johannesburg, April 20, 1964

271. The politician wants men to know how to die
courageously; the poet wants men to live courageously.

Salvatore Quasimodo LITERATURE, 1959

272. Don't be downhearted in the thick of the battle. It is the
place where all good men would wish to be.

Lester Pearson PEACE, 1957

273. I would say to the House, as I said to those who have
joined this government, that I have nothing to offer but
blood, toil, tears and sweat.
Winston Churchill LITERATURE, 1953

274. Let us therefore brace ourselves to our duties, and so bear
ourselves that, if the British Empire and its Commonwealth
last for a thousand years, men will still say, "This was their
finest hour."
Winston Churchill LITERATURE, 1953

275. Friends, I shall ask you to be as quiet as possible. I don't
know whether you fully understand that I have just been
shot; but it takes more than that to kill a Bull Moose. But
fortunately I had my manuscript, so you see I was going to
make a long speech, and there is a bullet—there is where
the bullet went through—and it probably saved me from it
going into my heart. The bullet is in me now, so that I
cannot make a very long speech, but I will try my best.
Theodore Roosevelt PEACE, 1906
On October 14, 1912, Roosevelt was shot in the chest by a deranged
immigrant just before entering a hall in Milwaukee to give a campaign
speech

276. If we wanted to regain freedom, we were forced to strike.
We told the Soviets that you can enter with your tanks if
you wish. Then, we will put flowers in the guns of those
tanks and your soldiers will sooner or later be forced to
open the tanks and get out and get some air. When they
are out, our girls will kiss them to death. However, we are
not going to work for you anymore.
Lech Walesa PEACE, 1983

277. For more than forty years I have selected my collaborators
on the basis of their intelligence and their character and

not on the basis of their grandmothers, and I am not
willing for the rest of my life to change this method.
Fritz Haber CHEMISTRY, 1918
Letter of resignation as director of the Kaiser Wilhelm Institute,
1933, after being instructed to dismiss the Jews in his department

278. Losing an arm is more an inconvenience than a catastrophe.
Eric Cornell PHYSICS, 2001
Cornell lost an arm and shoulder to necrotizing fasciitis in 2004

DUTY AND RESPONSIBILITY

279. Freedom is choosing your responsibility. It's not having
no responsibilities; it's choosing the ones you want.
Toni Morrison LITERATURE, 1993

280. Only a life lived for others is a life worthwhile.
Albert Einstein PHYSICS, 1921

281. The real definition of loneliness . . . is to live without
responsibility.
Nadine Gordimer LITERATURE, 1991

282. I slept and dreamt that life was joy. I awoke and saw that
life was service. I acted and behold, service was joy.
Rabindranath Tagore LITERATURE, 1913

283. A sense of duty is useful in work but offensive in personal
relations.
Bertrand Russell LITERATURE, 1950

284. When a stupid man is doing something he is ashamed of,
he always declares that it is his duty.
George Bernard Shaw LITERATURE, 1925

COMPASSION

285. If you want others to be happy, practice compassion. If you want to be happy, practice compassion.
The Fourteenth Dalai Lama PEACE, 1989

286. The highest forms of understanding we can achieve are laughter and human compassion.
Richard Feynman PHYSICS, 1965

287. You and I belong, good friends, to a group that gets up early. We get up early because we don't sleep much. And we don't sleep much because the world doesn't let us sleep. And in turn, we try our best not to let the world sleep. That when people suffer anywhere, either we shout or we whisper, but at least we try to wake it up.
Elie Wiesel PEACE, 1986

288. Three passions, simple but overwhelmingly strong, have governed my life: the longing for love, the search for knowledge, and unbearable pity for the suffering of mankind.
Bertrand Russell LITERATURE, 1950

289. What matters today is not the difference between those who believe and those who do not believe, but the difference between those who care and those who don't.
Georges Pire PEACE, 1958

290. Only the tortured can understand those who have endured torture.
Yasser Arafat PEACE, 1994

291. How can you expect a man who is warm to understand one who is cold?
Alexandr Solzhenitsyn LITERATURE, 1970

FORGIVENESS

292. Without forgiveness there is no future.
Desmond Tutu PEACE, 1984

293. In every language, every culture, the most difficult words
you have to say are: "I'm sorry. Forgive me."
Desmond Tutu PEACE, 1984

294. True reconciliation does not consist in merely forgetting
the past.
Nelson Mandela PEACE, 1993

295. We have gone on our knees before God Almighty to pray
for his forgiveness.
F. W. de Klerk PEACE, 1993

CONFORMITY AND ECCENTRICITY

296. I have always thought respectable people scoundrels, and
I look anxiously at my face every morning for signs of my
becoming a scoundrel.
Bertrand Russell LITERATURE, 1950

297. Great spirits have always found violent opposition from
mediocre minds. The mediocre mind is incapable of
understanding the man who refuses to bow blindly to
conventional prejudices and chooses instead to express
his opinions courageously and honestly.
Albert Einstein PHYSICS, 1921
On Bertrand Russell, whose appointment to a post at City College,
New York, was revoked on grounds that he was "morally unfit"

298. It is always from a minority acting in ways different from what the majority would prescribe that the majority in the end learns to do better.

Friedrich von Hayek ECONOMICS, 1974

299. Don't yell at me. But if you must yell, at least don't do it in unison.

Boris Pasternak LITERATURE, 1958

To hecklers during his address to the Plenum of the Soviet Writers Union, 1957

300. A man of great common sense and good taste—meaning thereby a man without originality or moral courage.

George Bernard Shaw LITERATURE, 1925

301. Do not fear to be eccentric in opinion, for every opinion now accepted was once eccentric.

Bertrand Russell LITERATURE, 1950

302. When I was young, I found out that the big toe always ends up making a hole in a sock. So I stopped wearing socks.

Albert Einstein PHYSICS, 1921

STUPIDITY

303. If fifty million people say a foolish thing, it is still a foolish thing.

Anatole France LITERATURE, 1921

304. Two things are infinite, the universe and human stupidity, and I am not yet completely sure about the universe.

Albert Einstein PHYSICS, 1921

305. Nothing in the world is more dangerous than sincere ignorance and conscientious stupidity.
       Martin Luther King PEACE, 1964

306. The melancholy thing about the world is that it is full of stupid and common people; and the world is run for the benefit of the stupid and the common.
       V. S. Naipaul LITERATURE, 2001

307. The trouble with the world is that the stupid are cocksure and the intelligent are full of doubt.
       Bertrand Russell LITERATURE, 1950

308. It is precisely the stupidest people who are most sincere in their mistaken beliefs.
       Norman Angell PEACE, 1933

309. Ignorant people in preppy clothes are more dangerous to America than oil embargoes.
       V. S. Naipaul LITERATURE, 2001
       After teaching at Wellesley College for a year

310. Do not feel envious of the happiness of those who live in a fool's paradise, for only a fool will think that it is happiness.
       Bertrand Russell LITERATURE, 1950

311. To succeed in science, you have to avoid dumb people.
       James Watson MEDICINE, 1962

312. As history has repeatedly proven, it is not with the brass hats but with the brass heads that the danger to our country lies.
       George C. Marshall PEACE, 1953

Emotions

Much has been written about the emotions by authors who have been awarded the Nobel Prize for Literature. But reflection on this topic is not the exclusive domain of professional writers.

Nobel laureates who write of human experiences tend to do so with authority, often informed by extreme experiences in their own lives. This is readily apparent in the Holocaust writings of Elie Wiesel and Imre Kertész. Other examples include Kenzaburo Oe and Pearl S. Buck, both of whom brought up brain-damaged children. Heinrich Böll, René-Samuel Cassin, Camilo José Cela, Renato Dulbecco, Ernest Hemingway, and François Jacob were all gravely wounded in battle; in the case of Jacob, forcing him to give up his long-cherished ambition to become a surgeon.

Laureates are no more immune to tragedy than are the rest of humanity. Richard Feynman's beloved wife died of TB at the age of twenty-two. Ilya Mechnikov's wife also died of TB after only five years of marriage, causing him such anguish that he attempted suicide. Other laureates, including Albert Camus, Kenzaburo Oe, Donald Cram, Roald Hoffmann, Harry Martinson, and Gabriela Mistral, lost, by death or abandonment, one or both parents when young. Theodore Roosevelt's mother and his first wife died of different causes on the same day. The life of Max Planck, the father of quantum physics, was particularly tragic. His wife died after twenty-two years of marriage, he lost two daughters in childbirth, his elder son was killed in World War I, and the younger was executed after the 1944 bomb plot against Hitler.

But despite such traumas, when they write about emotions, the mood of most Nobel laureates is one of affirmation rather than of despair. Few could be described as hardened pessimists. In experiencing the joys and tragedies of life, and emerging with more insight and compassion, Nobel laureates are often models of sanity and fortitude in the face of the human predicament.

JOY AND HAPPINESS

313. What sky! What light! Ah in spite of all it is a blessed thing to be alive in such weather, and out of hospital.
Samuel Beckett LITERATURE, 1969

314. You must embrace joy as a moral obligation.
André Gide LITERATURE, 1947

315. The man who for the first time picks a small flower so that he can have it near him while he works has taken a step toward joy in life.
Hermann Hesse LITERATURE, 1946

316. Pleasure may be achieved without paying the price of strenuous effort, but joy cannot.
Konrad Lorenz MEDICINE, 1973

317. An unshared happiness is not happiness.
Boris Pasternak LITERATURE, 1958

318. An act of goodness is of itself an act of happiness. No reward coming after the event can compare with the sweet reward that went with it.
Maurice Maeterlinck LITERATURE, 1911

319. To be without some of the things you want is an
     indispensable part of happiness.
     Bertrand Russell LITERATURE, 1950

320. There is no better way to clothe one's grief than to
     celebrate another's joy.
     Sheldon Glashow PHYSICS, 1979

321. Happiness in intelligent people is the rarest thing I know.
     Ernest Hemingway LITERATURE, 1954

322. Junk mail is the mail that gives me the greatest pleasure
     in the world, because I know immediately what to do
     with it.
     Roald Hoffmann CHEMISTRY, 1981

323. A colleague who met me strolling rather aimlessly in the
     beautiful streets of Copenhagen said to me in a friendly
     manner, "You look very unhappy"; whereupon I
     answered fiercely, "How can one look happy when he
     is thinking about the anomalous Zeeman effect?"
     Wolfgang Pauli PHYSICS, 1945

AFFIRMATION AND GRATITUDE

324. For all that has been—Thanks! To all that shall be—Yes!
     Dag Hammarskjöld PEACE, 1961

325. To say Yes to life is at one and the same time to say Yes to
     oneself.
     Dag Hammarskjöld PEACE, 1961

326. Thank you, God. I'm not sure why. But thank you.
     Juan Ramón Jiménez LITERATURE, 1956

327. Gratitude is a word that I cherish. Gratitude is what
defines the humanity of the human being.
Elie Wiesel PEACE, 1986

328. To state quite simply what we learn in a time of pestilence:
that there are more things to admire in men than to despise.
Albert Camus LITERATURE, 1957

BEAUTY

329. Man should consider himself fortunate to have been a
contemporary of the rose.
Juan Ramón Jiménez LITERATURE, 1956

330. In the presence of the most beautiful things we always
experience not only pleasure but also grief or fear.
Hermann Hesse LITERATURE, 1946

331. One either serves the whole of man or does not serve him
at all. And if man needs bread and justice, and if what has
to be done must be done to serve this need, he also needs
pure beauty which is the bread of his heart.
Albert Camus LITERATURE, 1957

332. It is more important to have beauty in one's equations
than to have them fit experiment.
Paul Dirac PHYSICS, 1933

PAIN AND GRIEF

333. Between grief and nothing I will take grief.
William Faulkner LITERATURE, 1949

334. Unearned suffering is redemptive.
     Martin Luther King PEACE, 1964

335. One can find so many pains when the rain is falling.
     John Steinbeck LITERATURE, 1962

336. This is a crushing blow, to be left out of this sperm bank.
     I felt badly enough when I only made it into President
     Nixon's second enemies list.
        George Wald MEDICINE, 1967
     The short-lived "Repository for Germinal Choice" was founded in
     the 1970s. It was reported that three Nobel laureates contributed,
     but no Nobel babies resulted.

337. There is a general place in your brain, I think, reserved
     for "melancholy of relationships past." It grows and
     prospers as life progresses, forcing you finally, against
     your better judgment, to listen to country music.
        Kary Mullis CHEMISTRY, 1993

338. I am one of the millions everywhere in the world who will
     never recover from the death of John Fitzgerald Kennedy
     and the way it came about.
        Pearl S. Buck LITERATURE, 1938

INDIFFERENCE

339. I have always preferred the folly of the passions to the
     wisdom of indifference.
        Anatole France LITERATURE, 1921

340. If you are neutral in situations of injustice, you have
     chosen the side of the oppressor. If an elephant has its foot

on the tail of a mouse and you say that you are neutral, the mouse will not appreciate your neutrality.

Desmond Tutu PEACE, 1984

341. Better an unjust God than an indifferent one.

Elie Wiesel PEACE, 1986

342. The opposite of love is not hate, it's indifference. The opposite of art is not ugliness, it's indifference. The opposite of faith is not heresy, it's indifference. And the opposite of life is not death, it's indifference.

Elie Wiesel PEACE, 1986

343. The world did know and remained silent. And that is why I swore never to be silent when and wherever human beings endure suffering and humiliation. We must always take sides. Neutrality helps the oppressor, never the victim. Silence encourages the tormentor, never the tormented. Sometimes we must interfere. When human lives are endangered, when human dignity is in jeopardy, national borders and sensitivities become irrelevant. Wherever men and women are persecuted because of their race, religion, or political views, that place must—at that moment—become the center of the universe.

Elie Wiesel PEACE, 1986

HOPE AND DESPAIR

344. I have always thought that if the man who places hope in the human condition is a fool, then he who gives up hope in the face of circumstances is a coward.

Albert Camus LITERATURE, 1957

345. It is hope that gives life a meaning. And hope is based on the prospect of being able one day to turn the actual world into a possible one that looks better. When the French writer Tristan Bernard was arrested with his wife by the Gestapo, he told her: "The time of fear is over. Now comes the time of hope."
François Jacob MEDICINE, 1965

346. Remember: you must never, under any circumstances, despair. To hope and to act, these are our duties in misfortune.
Boris Pasternak LITERATURE, 1958

347. Never flinch, never weary, never despair.
Winston Churchill LITERATURE, 1953

348. In the depth of winter, I finally learned that within me there lay an invincible summer.
Albert Camus LITERATURE, 1957

349. Without confidence in a cause, there is no action. Ignorance may be enlightened, superstition wiped out; intolerance may become tolerant, and hate be changed into love; ideas may be quickened, intelligence widened, and men's hearts may be ennobled; but from pessimism which can see nothing but gloomy visions nothing is to be expected.
Klas Arnoldson PEACE, 1908

350. No horse named Morbid ever won a race.
Ernest Hemingway LITERATURE, 1954

351. To deride the hope of progress is the ultimate fatuity, the last word in poverty of spirit and meanness of mind.
Peter Medawar MEDICINE, 1960

352. Defeatism about the past is a grievous error; defeatism about the future is a crime.
Philip Noel-Baker PEACE, 1959

353. Because I remember, I despair. Because I remember, I have the duty to reject despair. I remember the killers, I remember the victims, even as I struggle to invent a thousand and one reasons to hope.
Elie Wiesel PEACE, 1986

354. You have pessimists and optimists, and of the two the pessimists are the better informed.
Imre Kertész LITERATURE, 2002

355. If you keep saying things are going to be bad, you have a good chance of being a prophet.
Isaac Bashevis Singer LITERATURE, 1978

FEAR

356. As we let our own light shine, we unconsciously give other people permission to do the same. As we are liberated from our own fear, our presence automatically liberates others.
Nelson Mandela PEACE, 1993

357. It is not power that corrupts but fear. Fear of losing power corrupts those who wield it and fear of the scourge of power corrupts those who are subject to it.
Aung San Suu Kyi PEACE, 1991

358. Emotional memories involving fear are permanently engrained in the brain. They can be suppressed but never erased.
Francis Crick MEDICINE, 1962

359. The worst of all fears is the fear of living.
     Theodore Roosevelt PEACE, 1906

360. To fear love is to fear life, and those who fear life are
     already three parts dead.
     Bertrand Russell LITERATURE, 1950

361. The 17th century was the century of mathematics, the 18th
     that of the physical sciences, and the 19th that of biology.
     Our 20th century is the century of fear.
     Albert Camus LITERATURE, 1957

Human Relations

The popular myth that brilliant people are socially retarded is refuted by the lives of Nobel laureates. A remarkable proportion of them, particularly the scientists, married once and stayed married. Saul Bellow was married five times, and Ernest Hemingway and Bertrand Russell four times, but these are exceptions. Erwin Schrödinger, after fleeing Nazi Germany, achieved the feat of sharing his house in a staid Dublin suburb with his wife and his mistress, while carrying on affairs with his university students and fathering children with two other Irish women. One laureate, Abdus Salam, a Muslim, had two wives, which presented unusual problems of protocol at the Nobel ceremonies in Stockholm, where by tradition the wife of the Physics laureate goes in to dinner on the arm of the king of Sweden.

In their autobiographies, laureates frequently pay tribute to their families. Although a number of laureates emerged from very modest backgrounds, the great majority were children of professional or academic parents. The physicist Maria Goeppert-Mayer, for example, was the seventh straight generation of university professors. Eight laureates had a parent who also won the Nobel Prize. Fortunately for the world, most laureates pass on their genes. Theodor Mommsen holds the record with sixteen children. Pearl S. Buck adopted nine children and founded Welcome

House, which arranged for the adoption of thousands of children fathered by American servicemen in Asia. Robert Aumann has eighteen grandchildren.

Nobel Prize winners are rarely solitary geniuses. Although the lone scientist was not unusual when the Nobel Prize was instituted in 1901, science no longer advances by means of the reclusive researcher working in a cramped laboratory. Theorists may work alone, but given the scale and complexity of experimental science today, it almost invariably requires collaboration. Many science laureates credit their success primarily to their collaboration with a brilliant senior scientist in the early years of their career. In the last twenty years, the science prizes have usually been awarded to pairs or trios of researchers. Unshared prizes, however, are still the norm for literature; few works of literature are the product of joint authorship.

Four married couples have won Nobel prizes. Marie and Pierre Curie, who shared the Physics Prize in 1903, epitomized married collaboration, which ended only when Pierre was tragically run over by a wagon on a Paris street. Many women have played significant roles in scientific discoveries, but women are underrepresented in the Nobel awards. Up to 2006, the Nobel Prize has been won by 735 men and 33 women. Two women have won the prize for Physics, three for Chemistry, seven for Medicine, ten for Literature, and twelve for Peace.

LOVE AND AFFECTION

362. Love is an illness, but it is not mortal.
Selma Lagerlöf LITERATURE, 1909

363. Love that stammers, that stutters, is apt to be the love that loves best.
Gabriela Mistral LITERATURE, 1945

364. Like all the great creations of humanity, love is twofold: it is the supreme happiness and supreme misfortune.
Octavio Paz LITERATURE, 1990

365. Love is not a desire for beauty; it is a yearning for completion.
Octavio Paz LITERATURE, 1990

366. One makes mistakes; that is life. But it is never a mistake to have loved.
Romain Rolland LITERATURE, 1915

367. Of all forms of caution, caution in love is perhaps the most fatal to true happiness.
Bertrand Russell LITERATURE, 1950

368. We cannot all do great things, but we can do small things with great love.
Mother Teresa PEACE, 1979

369. The spectacle of the Christians loving all men was the most astounding Rome had ever seen.
Jane Addams PEACE, 1931

370. Love is the only force capable of pulling down barriers which may stand between matter and spirit, visible and invisible, individual and God.

Anwar al-Sadat PEACE, 1978

371. How strange is the lot of us mortals! Each of us is here for a brief sojourn; for what purpose we know not, though sometimes sense it. But we know from daily life that we exist for other people first of all for whose smiles and well-being our own happiness depends.

Albert Einstein PHYSICS, 1921

372. There can be no deep disappointment where there is not deep love.

Martin Luther King PEACE, 1964

373. No one will ever know how many novels, poems, analyses, confessions, sufferings and joys have been piled up on this continent called Love, without it ever having turned out to be totally investigated.

Heinrich Böll LITERATURE, 1972

374. A loveless world is a dead world, and always there comes an hour when one is weary of prisons, of one's work, and of devotion to duty, and all one craves for is a loved face, the warmth and wonder of a loving heart.

Albert Camus LITERATURE, 1957

375. What goes by the name of love is banishment, with now and then a postcard from the homeland.

Samuel Beckett LITERATURE, 1969

376. If two people love each other there can be no happy end to it.

Ernest Hemingway LITERATURE, 1954

377. Love reciprocated is always rejuvenating.

T. S. Eliot LITERATURE, 1948

Replying to a toast by the sculptor Jacob Epstein on his seventieth birthday in 1958, the year after his marriage at sixty-eight to Valerie Fletcher, age thirty

378. In the security bred of many harmless marriages, it had been forgotten that love is no hothouse flower, but a wild plant, born of a wet night, born of an hour of sunshine; sprung from wild seed, blown along the road by a wild wind. A wild plant that, when it blooms by chance within the hedge of our gardens, we call a flower; and when it blooms outside we call a weed, but, flower or weed, whose scent and color are always wild!

John Galsworthy LITERATURE, 1932

379. You don't love because: you love despite; not for the virtues, but despite the faults.

William Faulkner LITERATURE, 1949

380. How unbearable, for women, is the tenderness which a man can give them without love.

Albert Camus LITERATURE, 1957

381. The fickleness of the women I love is only equalled by the infernal constancy of the women who love me.

George Bernard Shaw LITERATURE, 1925

MARRIAGE

382. Married love, enduring through a thousand vicissitudes, seems to me the most beautiful of miracles, even if the most common.

François Mauriac LITERATURE, 1952

383. I believe marriage to be the best and most important relation that can exist between two human beings.
Bertrand Russell LITERATURE, 1950

384. If the world of the twentieth century cannot succeed in this one thing, married love, then it has committed suicide.
Sinclair Lewis LITERATURE, 1930

385. You should look around carefully at the members of the opposite sex, and pick one out that you'd like to be with all your life. Get married young, and stay married.
Linus Pauling CHEMISTRY, 1954; PEACE, 1962

386. Incidentally, you're my fiancée now.
George Hitchings MEDICINE, 1988
Proposal to Joyce Shaver Hitchings, M.D., while she was driving him to an event

387. You can be married in the church if you want to, but not to me.
John Bardeen PHYSICS, 1956; PHYSICS, 1972
To his fiancée

388. I remember after I got that marriage license I went across from the license bureau to a bar for a drink. The bartender said, "What will you have, sir?" And I said, "A glass of hemlock."
Ernest Hemingway LITERATURE, 1954

389. It's only an improbable accident when a woman and a man who are both of them big enough not to be jealous of each other's bigness do meet—and then, probably, when they do meet, one of them will already be married to some little pretentious squirt and they can't marry!
Sinclair Lewis LITERATURE, 1930

390. The American girl makes a servant of her husband and
then finds him contemptible for being a servant.
John Steinbeck LITERATURE, 1962

391. An unhappy marriage! No ill treatment—only that
indefinable malaise, that terrible blight which killed all
sweetness under Heaven; and so from day to day, from
night to night, from week to week, from year to year, till
death should end it!
John Galsworthy LITERATURE, 1932

392. Had she taken a bullfighter I would have understood, but
an ordinary chemist!
Wolfgang Pauli PHYSICS, 1945
On his ex-wife's remarriage

SEX

393. Nobody will ever win the Battle of the Sexes. There's just
too much fraternizing with the enemy.
Henry Kissinger PEACE, 1973

394. Why two sexes rather than three? What a source of new
plots three sexes would provide for novelists, of new
variations for psychologists, of new complications for
lawyers.
François Jacob MEDICINE, 1965

395. How is it that, in the human body, reproduction is the
only function to be performed by an organ of which an
individual carries only one half so that he has to spend an
enormous amount of time and energy to find another half?
François Jacob MEDICINE, 1965

396. I've never turned over a fig leaf yet that didn't have a price tag on the other side.
    Saul Bellow LITERATURE, 1976

397. I learned that the sexual revolution is a very bloody affair, like most revolutions.
    Saul Bellow LITERATURE, 1976
    When asked his views on marriage in 1997

398. To fully experience the joys of adultery, one must be a person of piety.
    Anatole France LITERATURE, 1921

399. Of all the sexual aberrations, chastity is the strangest.
    Anatole France LITERATURE, 1921

WOMEN AND MEN

400. In societies where men are truly confident of their own worth, women are not merely tolerated but valued.
    Aung San Suu Kyi PEACE, 1991

401. The basic discovery about any people is the discovery of the relationship between its men and its women.
    Pearl S. Buck LITERATURE, 1938

402. Men and women can face anything, can endure anything, if they are sure of each other's loyalty and liking. They can endure nothing if they are not sure of each other.
    Pearl S. Buck LITERATURE, 1938

403. I have never seen in any country—and I have seen most of the countries of the world—such an unsatisfactory

relationship between men and women as there is in
America.

Pearl S. Buck LITERATURE, 1938

404. Of privileges women have had plenty, and yet most of
them have been denied the one great blessing of man's
life—the necessity to go out in the world and earn their
bread directly.

Pearl S. Buck LITERATURE, 1938

405. You can have it all!

Rosalyn Yalow MEDICINE, 1977

406. The humiliation inflicted on women is the result of a
diseased gene that is passed to every generation of men,
not only by society as a whole but also by their mothers. It
is mothers who raise boys who become men. It is up to
mothers not to pass on that diseased cultural gene.

Shirin Ebadi PEACE, 2003

407. Instead of telling girls to cover their hair, we should teach
them to use their heads.

Shirin Ebadi PEACE, 2003

408. What begins as the neglect of the interests of women ends
in causing adversity for the health and survival of all.

Amartya Sen ECONOMICS, 1998

409. Women are ultimately the key to development, they are
the key to eradication of poverty. Once you empower
them, you empower a nation.

Desmond Tutu PEACE, 1984

CHILDREN AND FAMILIES

410. Every child comes with the message that God is not yet discouraged of man.
Rabindranath Tagore LITERATURE, 1913

411. To be childlike is one of the most important, indispensable, and, in the best sense, human characteristics of man.
Konrad Lorenz MEDICINE, 1973

412. To have the heart of a child is not a disgrace. It is an honor.
Ernest Hemingway LITERATURE, 1954

413. People, especially young people, need compliments and admiration. We must give them a sense of their importance and dignity, and we must encourage them to use and develop all their talents. If ever I have children, I'll certainly do so. I'll tell them outright that they're important and that they're beautiful.
Mairead Corrigan PEACE, 1976

414. I have lived in a world of children and of child humor, child fantasy, and child passions for four decades. If only I can grow old, foolishly old in this same world—if it is my fate to grow old—I shall be most fortunate.
Carleton Gajdusek MEDICINE, 1976

415. I've written maybe thirty books, I don't remember exactly; but I have five children, and that is my real blessing.
Knut Hamsun LITERATURE, 1920

416. To be the father of a nation is a great honor, but to be the father of a family is a greater joy.
Nelson Mandela PEACE, 1993

417. Unless the child learns how to love a parent profoundly, I believe that he will never learn how to love anyone else profoundly, and not knowing how to love means the loss of the meaning of life and its fulfillment.

Pearl S. Buck LITERATURE, 1938

418. All kids are scientists. They're born scientists. They ask all these terrible questions that nobody can answer because they're scientists. So, what do you do? You beat that curiosity out of them and they stop asking questions. It's very hard to survive that.

Leon Lederman PHYSICS, 1988

419. Everywhere, everywhere, children are the scorned people of the earth.

Toni Morrison LITERATURE, 1993

420. Two parents can't raise a child any more than one. You need a whole community—everybody—to raise a child.

Toni Morrison LITERATURE, 1993

421. The fundamental defect of fathers is that they want their children to be a credit to them.

Bertrand Russell LITERATURE, 1950

422. You don't choose your family. They are God's gift to you, as you are to them.

Desmond Tutu PEACE, 1984

423. Families, I hate you! Shut-in homes, closed doors, jealous possessions of happiness.

André Gide LITERATURE, 1947

424. Family solidarity is after all the only good thing.

Marie Curie PHYSICS, 1903; CHEMISTRY, 1911

FRIENDSHIP

425. When the ways of friends converge, the whole world looks like home for an hour.
    Hermann Hesse LITERATURE, 1946

426. *Think where man's glory most begins and ends,*
    And say my glory was I had such friends.
    William Butler Yeats LITERATURE, 1923

427. When the whole world's against you, the thousandth man will stand your friend.
    Rudyard Kipling LITERATURE, 1907

428. I said earlier that love is tragic; I add here that friendship is a response to tragedy.
    Octavio Paz LITERATURE, 1990

429. If you sacrifice a friend in a difficult hour, you never make another friend again.
    Shimon Peres PEACE, 1994

430. Choose your friends carefully. Your enemies will choose you.
    Yasser Arafat PEACE, 1994

SOLITUDE AND LONELINESS

431. Today, there is no greater joy than to live alone and unknown.
    Albert Camus LITERATURE, 1957

432. Solitude is the grandest prize that anybody could receive.
    Camilo José Cela LITERATURE, 1989

433. I live in that solitude which is painful in youth, but delicious in the years of maturity.
Albert Einstein PHYSICS, 1921

434. My whole life presents a unity. Everything I have done, even my writing, grows out of a fascinated interest in human beings, in the wonders of their minds and hearts, their sensitivities, their needs, and the essential loneliness of their position in the universe.
Pearl S. Buck LITERATURE, 1938

435. We are alone, absolutely alone on this chance planet: and, amid all the forms of life that surround us, not one, excepting the dog, has made an alliance with us.
Maurice Maeterlinck LITERATURE, 1911

436. Life is for each man a solitary cell whose walls are mirrors.
Eugene O'Neill LITERATURE, 1936

437. Nearly all the great creators were almost recluses. Either one has many ideas and few friends, or many friends and few ideas.
Santiago Ramón y Cajal MEDICINE, 1906

438. In the West there is loneliness, which I call the leprosy of the West. In many ways it is worse than our poor in Calcutta.
Mother Teresa PEACE, 1979

439. Pray that your loneliness may spur you into finding something to live for great enough to die for.
Dag Hammarskjöld PEACE, 1961

Mind, Knowledge, and Learning
◇∞◇∞◇

The work that leads to the Nobel Prize is conducted primarily in the minds of men and women, minds focused and disciplined, well trained and well educated. Analysis of mind, however, as opposed to its exercise, is the domain of philosophers, and there is no Nobel Prize for philosophy. Nonetheless, many laureates have made astute observations on the subjects of the human mind and human learning.

Educational institutions play a major role in the lives of laureates. Among the universities, England's Cambridge University is the undisputed leader. It claims over sixty laureates, and if it were a country, it would stand sixth in the number of Nobel Prize winners it has produced. Harvard comes next with over forty laureates. City College of New York is singled out for praise on account of its free tuition, which enabled nine future laureates to attend. However, some universities also have Nobel skeletons in their closets. Cambridge University dismissed Bertrand Russell from his fellowship in 1918 for his pacifism, and in the same year, Emily Balch was fired by Wellesley College for the same reason. Brooklyn Polytechnic obliged Gertrude Elion to abandon her doctoral studies because she could not afford to give up her part-time job, and she became one of only a handful of science laureates never to earn a doctorate.

Schools can be difficult places for precocious youngsters, and a number of Nobel laureates have been highly critical of educational practice. Others have taken steps to remedy the deficiencies of schools. Marie Curie, Bertrand Russell, and Rabindranath Tagore all founded schools. Several science laureates have been dedicated and popular university teachers. The physicist Carl Wieman and the chemist Harold Kroto committed their Nobel Prize money to projects to improve the teaching and understanding of science. Three weeks before his death, Richard Feynman, although seriously ill, accepted an invitation to participate in a panel on education at his local high school.

THINKING AND THOUGHT

440. Never try to discourage thinking, for you are sure to succeed.
> *Bertrand Russell* LITERATURE, 1950

441. Never express yourself more clearly than you are able to think.
> *Niels Bohr* PHYSICS, 1922

442. No, no. You are not thinking, you are only being logical.
> *Niels Bohr* PHYSICS, 1922

443. I don't mind if you think slowly, doctor, but I do mind if you publish faster than you think.
> *Wolfgang Pauli* PHYSICS, 1945

444. One must think like a man of action, act like a man of thought.
> *Henri Bergson* LITERATURE, 1927

445. Many people would rather die than think. In fact they do.
Bertrand Russell LITERATURE, 1950

446. If we fail to teach our children the skills they need to think clearly, they will march behind whatever guru wears the shiniest cloak.
Paul Boyer CHEMISTRY, 1997

447. Some subjects are so serious that one can only joke about them.
Niels Bohr PHYSICS, 1922

INTELLECT AND REASON

448. Man is a rational animal—so at least I have been told. Throughout a long life, I have looked diligently for evidence in favor of this statement, but so far I have not had the good fortune to come across it.
Bertrand Russell LITERATURE, 1950

449. I've seen more common sense expressed around the table in a farm house than I have around the table in the United Nations committee room.
Lester Pearson PEACE, 1957

450. Common sense is the collection of prejudices acquired by age eighteen.
Albert Einstein PHYSICS, 1921

451. There's zero change in human intelligence in a million years and it won't change in the next million.
Carleton Gajdusek MEDICINE, 1976

452. It is an exceptional, almost pathological constitution one has if one follows thoughts logically through, regardless of

consequences. Such people make martyrs, apostles, or scientists, and mostly end up on the stake or in a chair, electric or academic.
Albert Szent-Györgyi MEDICINE, 1937

453. I emphasize the distinction between the ideas of the necessity and of the sufficiency of reason as a defense against that mad and self-destructive form of anti-rationalism which seems to declare that because reason is not sufficient, it is not necessary.
Peter Medawar MEDICINE, 1960

454. I know as well as anyone that the intellectual is a dangerous animal ever ready to betray.
Albert Camus LITERATURE, 1957

455. When an old and distinguished person speaks to you, listen to him carefully and with respect—but do not believe him. Never put your trust in anything but your own intellect.
Linus Pauling CHEMISTRY, 1954; PEACE, 1962

456. I think that it is much more likely that the reports of flying saucers are the results of the known irrational characteristics of terrestrial intelligence than of the unknown rational efforts of extra-terrestrial intelligence.
Richard Feynman PHYSICS, 1965

INSANITY

457. We all are born mad. Some remain so.
Samuel Beckett LITERATURE, 1969

458. Insanity: doing the same thing over and over again and expecting different results.
Albert Einstein PHYSICS, 1921

459. If I had any nerves, I'd have a nervous breakdown.
Eugene O'Neill LITERATURE, 1936

460. One of the symptoms of an approaching nervous breakdown is the belief that one's work is terribly important.
Bertrand Russell LITERATURE, 1950

461. Nobody would be so demented as to imagine for a moment that when you go to a shrink you get anything resembling good mental health.
Kary Mullis CHEMISTRY, 1993

462. You *never* understand everything. When one understands everything, one has gone crazy.
Philip Anderson PHYSICS, 1977

463. On one occasion a man came to ask me to recommend some of my books, as he was interested in philosophy. I did so, but he returned next day saying that he had been reading one of them, and had found only one statement he could understand, and that one seemed to him false. I asked him what it was, and he said it was the statement that Julius Caesar is dead. When I asked him why he did not agree, he drew himself up and said: "Because I am Julius Caesar."
Bertrand Russell LITERATURE, 1950

GENIUS AND TALENT

464. Without passion there is no genius.
Theodor Mommsen LITERATURE, 1902

465. The popular mind imagines the scientist as a lonely genius. In reality, few of us are geniuses, and even fewer are lonely.
J. Michael Bishop MEDICINE, 1989

466. Talent fulfilled brings the deepest content that an individual can know.

Pearl S. Buck LITERATURE, 1938

467. How quickly the visions of genius become the canned goods of the intellectuals!

Saul Bellow LITERATURE, 1976

468. Everyone thinks that having a talent is a matter of luck; no one thinks that luck could be a matter of talent.

Jacinto Benavente LITERATURE, 1922

KNOWLEDGE AND IMAGINATION

469. The larger the circle of light becomes, the greater the perimeter of darkness around it.

Albert Einstein PHYSICS, 1921

470. I can live with doubt and uncertainty and not knowing. I think it's much more interesting to live not knowing than to have answers which might be wrong.

Richard Feynman PHYSICS, 1965

471. I am enough of an artist to draw freely upon my imagination. Imagination is more important than knowledge. Knowledge is limited. Imagination encircles the world.

Albert Einstein PHYSICS, 1921

472. If no one has been annoyed for some time by what he sees to be your irresponsibility, you should consider whether you are holding your imagination too much in check.

Edmund Phelps ECONOMICS, 2006

MEMORY AND OBLIVION

473. Everybody needs his memories. They keep the wolf of insignificance from the door.
Saul Bellow LITERATURE, 1976

474. An individual, a society without memory, is a sick individual, a sick society.
Heinrich Böll LITERATURE, 1972

475. I personally have never believed in the therapeutic effect of "letting grass grow over the past."
Willy Brandt PEACE, 1971

476. I seek in my writing to hold back time so that the present is not forgotten.
Günter Grass LITERATURE, 1999

477. Forgetting is a virtue, memory, a vice.
Juan Ramón Jiménez LITERATURE, 1956

478. In old age we no longer live our lives, we merely keep on our feet with the aid of memories.
Knut Hamsun LITERATURE, 1920

479. When we lose one we love, our bitterest tears are called forth by the memory of hours when we did not love enough.
Maurice Maeterlinck LITERATURE, 1911

480. The best we can expect from people is to be forgotten.
François Mauriac LITERATURE, 1952

481. Love is so short, and forgetting so long.
Pablo Neruda LITERATURE, 1971

482. Everyone, deep down within, carries a small cemetery of those he has loved.
     Romain Rolland LITERATURE, 1915

483. I have tried to keep memory alive . . . I have tried to fight those who would forget. Because if we forget, we are guilty, we are accomplices.
     Elie Wiesel PEACE, 1986

484. If anything can, it is memory that will save humanity. For me, hope without memory is like memory without hope. Just as man cannot live without dreams, he cannot live without hope. If dreams reflect the past, hope summons the future.
     Elie Wiesel PEACE, 1986

485. If the failure of memory irks me, it also intrigues and pleases me. For the process of forgetting can also be a great and subtle pleasure.
     Eugene Wigner PHYSICS, 1963

DREAMS AND NIGHTMARES

486. I have had dreams and I've had nightmares. It is because of my dreams that I have overcome my nightmares.
     Linus Pauling CHEMISTRY, 1954; PEACE, 1962

487. In bed my real love has always been the sleep that rescued me by allowing me to dream.
     Luigi Pirandello LITERATURE, 1934

488. All the things one has forgotten scream for help in dreams.
     Elias Canetti LITERATURE, 1981

489. Sleep is when all the unsorted stuff comes flying out as from a dustbin upset in a high wind.
William Golding LITERATURE, 1983

490. Find your own dream. Keep this dream and take good care of it and then sometime you will accomplish something.
Koichi Tanaka CHEMISTRY, 2002

491. You see things; and you say, "Why?" But I dream things that never were; and I say, "Why not?"
George Bernard Shaw LITERATURE, 1925

492. There were many ways of breaking a heart. Stories were full of hearts broken by love, but what really broke a heart was taking away its dream—whatever that dream might be.
Pearl S. Buck LITERATURE, 1938

493. From my earliest youth, I have known that while one is obliged to plan with care the stages of one's journey, one is entitled to dream, and keep dreaming, of its destination. A man may feel as old as his years, yet as young as his dreams.
Shimon Peres PEACE, 1994

494. I have a dream that one day on the red hills of Georgia the sons of former slaves and the sons of former slave owners will be able to sit down together at a table of brotherhood. I have a dream that one day even the state of Mississippi, a desert state, sweltering with the heat of injustice and oppression, will be transformed into an oasis of freedom and justice. I have a dream that my four little children will one day live in a nation where they will not be judged by the color of their skin but by the content of their character.
Martin Luther King PEACE, 1964

PHILOSOPHY

495. The balm that heals the wound of time is called religion; the knowledge that we must live for a lifetime with our wound is called philosophy.
Octavio Paz LITERATURE, 1990

496. Scientists are explorers, philosophers are tourists.
Richard Feynman PHYSICS, 1965

497. The point of philosophy is to start with something so simple as not to seem worth stating, and to end with something so paradoxical that no one will believe it.
Bertrand Russell LITERATURE, 1950

498. Roughly, you'd say science is what we know and philosophy is what we don't know.
Bertrand Russell LITERATURE, 1950

499. I have made a great discovery, a very great discovery: all that philosophers have ever written is pure drivel.
Niels Bohr PHYSICS, 1922

500. That's metaphysics, my dear fellow. It's forbidden me by my doctor, my stomach won't take it.
Boris Pasternak LITERATURE, 1958

501. There is only one truly serious philosophical problem, and that is suicide. Judging whether life is or is not worth living amounts to answering the fundamental question of philosophy.
Albert Camus LITERATURE, 1957

ETHICS AND MORALS

502. If someone here told me to write a book on morality, it would have a hundred pages and ninety-nine would be blank. On the last page I should write: "I recognize only one duty, and that is to love."
       Albert Camus LITERATURE, 1957

503. The most important human endeavor is the striving for morality in our actions. Our inner balance and even our very existence depend on it. Only morality in our actions can give beauty and dignity to life. To make this a living force and bring it to clear consciousness is perhaps the foremost task of education.
       Albert Einstein PHYSICS, 1921

504. Morality must have its roots in conscience, not in dogma.
       Franco Modigliani ECONOMICS, 1985

505. *The last temptation is the greatest treason:*
      To do the right deed for the wrong reason.
       T. S. Eliot LITERATURE, 1948

506. Personally, I would not judge ethical issues based on absolute rights and wrongs. Whenever you see the word ethics, I see the word politics, which to me means personal, fixed, vested interests.
       Sydney Brenner MEDICINE, 2002

CRITICS AND CRITICISM

507. I have derived continued benefit from criticism at all
     periods of my life, and I do not remember any time when
     I was ever short of it.
     Winston Churchill LITERATURE, 1953

508. To announce that there must be no criticism of the
     President, or that we are to stand by the President, right
     or wrong, is not only unpatriotic and servile, but is
     morally treasonable to the American public.
     Theodore Roosevelt PEACE, 1906

509. Our American professors like their literature clear and
     cold and pure and very dead.
     Sinclair Lewis LITERATURE, 1930

510. Unless a reviewer has the courage to give you unqualified
     praise, I say ignore the bastard.
     John Steinbeck LITERATURE, 1962
     John Kenneth Galbraith describes a chance meeting with Steinbeck
     in an airport in 1958, when both were reading a hostile review of
     Galbraith's *The Affluent Society*

WISDOM

511. Wisdom is not in reason, but in love.
     André Gide LITERATURE, 1947

512. Where is the Life we have lost in living? Where is the
     wisdom we have lost in knowledge? Where is the
     knowledge we have lost in information?
     T. S. Eliot LITERATURE, 1948

513. Wisdom lies neither in fixity nor in change, but in the dialectic between the two.
Octavio Paz LITERATURE, 1990

514. You can tell whether a man is clever by his answers. You can tell whether a man is wise by his questions.
Naguib Mahfouz LITERATURE, 1988

515. Nine-tenths of wisdom consists in being wise in time.
Theodore Roosevelt PEACE, 1906

516. Think like a wise man but express yourself like the common people.
William Butler Yeats LITERATURE, 1923

517. The fool is silent because he has nothing to say. But the wise man is silent because he has too much to say.
Elie Wiesel PEACE, 1986

518. A wise man gets wiser by suffering. A person without any wisdom may suffer for a hundred years and die a fool.
Isaac Bashevis Singer LITERATURE, 1978

FANATICISM

519. Just as the clouds cannot stop the light, so religious extremism cannot stop modernization.
Shirin Ebadi PEACE, 2003

520. From the saintly and single-minded idealist to the fanatic is often but a step.
Friedrich von Hayek ECONOMICS, 1974

521. Fanaticism remains the greatest carrier of the spores of fear, and the rhetoric of religion, with the hysteria it so

readily generates, is fast becoming the readiest killing device of contemporary times.

Wole Soyinka LITERATURE, 1986

522. A few fanatics are not a fundamental problem. No, the problem arises if political fanatics bury themselves within a morally legitimate political movement.

David Trimble PEACE, 1998

523. A fanatic is one who can't change his mind and won't change the subject.

Winston Churchill LITERATURE, 1953

SCHOOLS AND TEACHERS

524. Education is the most backward of all large industries.

Arthur Lewis ECONOMICS, 1979

525. There is, on the whole, nothing on earth intended for innocent people so horrible as a school.

George Bernard Shaw LITERATURE, 1925

526. It is, in fact, nothing short of a miracle that the modern methods of instruction have not yet entirely strangled the holy curiosity of enquiry; for the delicate little plant, aside from stimulation, stands mainly in need of freedom; without this it goes to wrack and ruin without fail.

Albert Einstein PHYSICS, 1921

527. I sometimes think it would be better to drown children than to lock them up in present-day schools.

Marie Curie PHYSICS, 1903; CHEMISTRY, 1911

528. It was fortunate for me that I never in my life had what is called an education.
     Rabindranath Tagore LITERATURE, 1913

529. Nearly 12 years of school . . . form not only the least agreeable, but the only barren and unhappy period of my life . . . a time of discomfort, restriction and purposeless monotony . . . I would far rather have been apprenticed as a bricklayer's mate, or run errands as a messenger boy, or helped my father to dress the front windows of a grocer's shop. It would have been real; it would have been natural; it would have taught me more; and I should have done it much better.
     Winston Churchill LITERATURE, 1953

530. The desire to teach is visceral: it requires no defense, it permits no explanation, it is a cultural obligation, it is a vocation. Scholarship and research without the vocation to teach are sterile.
     J. Michael Bishop MEDICINE, 1989

531. Anytime you try to teach the subject without teachers who love the subject, it is doomed to failure and is a foolish thing to do.
     Richard Feynman PHYSICS, 1965
     At a local high school, three months before his death

532. Teaching is not entertainment, but it is unlikely to be successful unless it is entertaining.
     Herbert Simon ECONOMICS, 1978

533. The message I would give to young people is: Don't be the best in your class. If you're the best in your class you're in the wrong class.
     James Watson MEDICINE, 1962

534. Being a professor in an American university is the best job in Western civilization.
Leon Lederman PHYSICS, 1988

535. The typical university catalogue would never stop Diogenes in his search for an honest man.
George Stigler ECONOMICS, 1982

536. The last really notable advance in college teaching in recent times was the invention of the printing press.
George Stigler ECONOMICS, 1982

537. I've always thought of universities in a grand way, as seats of learning and inquiry. Well, it's bogus. You get bogus students taking bogus courses in bogus writing.
V. S. Naipaul LITERATURE, 2001

538. I hate university towns and university people, who are the same everywhere, with pregnant wives, sprawling children, many books and hideous pictures on the walls . . . Oxford is very pretty, but I don't like to be dead.
T. S. Eliot LITERATURE, 1948

539. Not one of you sitting round this table could run a fish-and-chip shop.
Howard Florey MEDICINE, 1945
To the governing body of Queen's College, Oxford, of which he was provost

540. My old Cambridge friend, T. R. Glover, used to tell me that there were three ways of being unpopular in Cambridge. One was to be known outside Cambridge. Another was to know something about a subject other than that which you had taken in your degree

examination. And the third was to be able to write
simple English which anybody could understand.
Edward Appleton PHYSICS, 1947

541. This is the first time we have elected an art historian
to a fellowship, and I very much hope it will also be
the last.
J. J. Thomson PHYSICS, 1906
As master of Trinity College, Cambridge, introducing the art historian
and subsequently unmasked traitor Anthony Blunt

542. The rivalry between Yale and Harvard is quite as keen
as that between Cambridge and Oxford and shows itself
in more unconventional ways. I saw at the house of one
of the professors [at Yale] a dog who had been trained
to pretend to be sick whenever he heard the name
Harvard.
J. J. Thomson PHYSICS, 1906

543. Bryn Mawr had done what a four-year dose of liberal
education was designed to do: unfit her for eighty percent
of the useful work of the world.
Toni Morrison LITERATURE, 1993

544. When we spliced the profit gene into academic culture,
we created a new organism—the recombinant university.
We reprogrammed the incentives that guide science.
The rule in academe used to be "publish or perish."
Now bioscientists have an alternative—"patent and
profit."
Paul Berg CHEMISTRY, 1980

545. There are no politics that are as dirty as academic politics.
Milton Friedman ECONOMICS, 1976

546. The disputes are so bitter because the stakes are so small.
Henry Kissinger PEACE, 1973

On university politics

547. A professor whose hands do not shake by the end of the academic year has not performed his duties properly.
Allvar Gullstrand MEDICINE, 1911

Arts and Culture

Although most of the quotations in this section are from Literature laureates, this group has no monopoly on interest in the arts. Several science laureates were talented musicians, some of them performing at the symphony level. The writer Gao Xingjian exhibits his paintings internationally; Harold Kroto chose chemistry as a career over graphic arts; the chemist Roald Hoffmann is a widely published poet.

It is difficult to find a Nobel Prize winner in any field who was not also a gifted writer. Their Nobel lectures are eloquent. Most laureates also write their autobiographies for the Nobel archive; these documents can be found in the Nobel Museum (http://nobelprize.org). It is the rare prize winner who has not published at least a handful of books, and the average output of Literature laureates is about three dozen volumes. Winston Churchill published forty books, Pearl S. Buck published over eighty, and Bertrand Russell's bibliography runs to over four thousand items.

THE ARTS AND ARTISTS

548. Art is contemplation of the world in a state of grace.
     Hermann Hesse LITERATURE, 1946

549. That life is worth living is the essential message and
     assurance of all art.
     Hermann Hesse LITERATURE, 1946

550. Art is always a good hiding-place, not for dynamite, but
     for intellectual explosives and social time bombs.
     Heinrich Böll LITERATURE, 1972

551. Art is a recoilless weapon.
     Joseph Brodsky LITERATURE, 1987

552. A guilty conscience needs to confess. A work of art is a
     confession.
     Albert Camus LITERATURE, 1957

553. There is not a single true work of art that has not in the
     end added to the inner freedom of each person who has
     known and loved it.
     Albert Camus LITERATURE, 1957

554. Art is unthinkable without risk and self-sacrifice.
     Boris Pasternak LITERATURE, 1958

555. To admire an artist, you should not know him personally.
     Jacinto Benavente LITERATURE, 1922

556. Art that submits to orthodoxy, to even the soundest
     doctrines, is lost.
     André Gide LITERATURE, 1947

557. It is the artist's job to create sunshine when there is none.
   Romain Rolland LITERATURE, 1915

LANGUAGE AND LITERATURE

558. Literature is the union of suffering with the instinct for form.
   Thomas Mann LITERATURE, 1929

559. As a form of moral insurance, at least, literature is much more dependable than a system of beliefs or a philosophical doctrine.
   Joseph Brodsky LITERATURE, 1987

560. Literature is a science one has to learn and there are 10,000 years standing behind every short story that gets written.
   Gabriel García Márquez LITERATURE, 1982

561. Literature is hazardously and irreversibly my life, my death and my suffering, my vocation and my servitude, my constant yearning and my well merited consolation.
   Camilo José Cela LITERATURE, 1989

562. Even if one day people stop or are forced to stop writing and publishing, if books are no longer available, there will still be storytellers giving us mouth-to-ear artificial respiration, spinning old stories in new ways: loud and soft, heckling and halting, now close to laughter, now on the brink of tears.
   Günter Grass LITERATURE, 1999

563. A novel is never anything but a philosophy expressed in images.
   Albert Camus LITERATURE, 1957

564. There is something similar about all stories, but I still don't know what it is.
Elias Canetti LITERATURE, 1981

565. Words are all we have.
Samuel Beckett LITERATURE, 1969

566. Short words are best and old words when short are best of all.
Winston Churchill LITERATURE, 1953

WRITERS AND WRITING

567. When I was a little boy, they called me a liar, but now that I am grown up, they call me a writer.
Isaac Bashevis Singer LITERATURE, 1978

568. To the question always asked, "Why do you write?" the response of the poet will always be the briefest "In order to live better."
Saint-John Perse LITERATURE, 1960

569. I believe that man will not merely endure: he will prevail. He is immortal, not because he alone among creatures has an inexhaustible voice, but because he has a soul, a spirit capable of compassion and sacrifice and endurance. The poet's, the writer's, duty is to write about these things. It is his privilege to help man endure by lifting his heart, by reminding him of the courage and honor and hope and pride and compassion and pity and sacrifice which have been the glory of his past.
William Faulkner LITERATURE, 1949

570. All good books are alike in that they are truer than if they had really happened and after you are finished reading one

you will feel that all that happened to you and afterwards it
all belongs to you: the good and the bad, the ecstasy, the
remorse and sorrow, the people and the places and how
the weather was. If you can get so that you can give that to
people, then you are a writer.

Ernest Hemingway LITERATURE, 1954

571. If you write novels merely to entertain—then burn
them! . . . Just consider how many writers there have been
who—down the ages—have written novels to entertain!
And who remembers them now?

Miguel Ángel Asturias LITERATURE, 1967

572. Pushed out of sight in any writer, no matter how austere
a front he presents to others, is the desire for someone to
read what he has written.

William Golding LITERATURE, 1983

573. Getting published isn't the important thing. You write in
order to be able to breathe.

Samuel Beckett LITERATURE, 1969

574. A man's writing is himself. A kind man writes kindly. A
mean man writes meanly. A sick man writes sickly. And
a wise man writes wisely.

John Steinbeck LITERATURE, 1962

575. Sometimes when I was starting a new story and I could not
get it going . . . I would stand and look out over the roofs
of Paris and think, "Do not worry. You have always
written before and you will write now. All you have to do
is write one true sentence. Write the truest sentence that
you know."

Ernest Hemingway LITERATURE, 1954

576. If the urge to write should ever leave me, I want that day to be my last.

Naguib Mahfouz LITERATURE, 1988

577. I couldn't have done it otherwise, gone on, I mean. I could not have gone on through the awful wretchedness of life without having left a stain upon the silence.

Samuel Beckett LITERATURE, 1969

578. The writer's only responsibility is to his art. He will be completely ruthless if he is a good one. He has a dream. It anguishes him so much he must get rid of it. He has no peace until then. Everything goes by the board: honor, pride, decency, security, happiness, all, to get the book written. If a writer has to rob his mother, he will not hesitate; the "Ode on a Grecian Urn" is worth any number of old ladies.

William Faulkner LITERATURE, 1949

579. The most essential gift for a good writer is a built-in shock-proof shit detector. This is the writer's radar and all great writers have had it.

Ernest Hemingway LITERATURE, 1954

580. Writing, at its best, is a lonely life . . . He does his work alone and if he is a good enough writer he must face eternity, or the lack of it, each day.

Ernest Hemingway LITERATURE, 1954

581. The profession of book writing makes horse racing seem like a solid, stable business.

John Steinbeck LITERATURE, 1962

582. When the writer becomes the center of his attention he becomes a nudnik. And a nudnik who believes he's profound is even worse than just a plain nudnik.

Isaac Bashevis Singer LITERATURE, 1978

583. Those who write clearly have readers; those who write obscurely have commentators.
     Albert Camus LITERATURE, 1957

584. For me, to be a writer is to acknowledge the secret wounds that we carry inside us, the wounds so secret that we ourselves are barely aware of them, and to patiently explore them, know them, illuminate them, to own these pains and wounds, and to make them a conscious part of our spirits and our writing.
     Orhan Pamuk LITERATURE, 2006

585. My own experience has been that the tools I need for my trade are paper, tobacco, food, and a little whisky.
     William Faulkner LITERATURE, 1949

586. When audiences come to see us authors lecture, it is largely in the hope that we'll be funnier to look at than to read.
     Sinclair Lewis LITERATURE, 1930

587. When it comes to reading galley proofs, I always feel reminded of an awful sight once seen in a prisoner-of-war camp: a man slowly and deliberately eating his own vomit.
     Konrad Lorenz MEDICINE, 1973

588. If Moses had been paid newspaper rates for the Ten Commandments, he might have written the Two Thousand Commandments.
     Isaac Bashevis Singer LITERATURE, 1978

589. I have always believed in fierce, devoted apprenticeship . . . Originality is the obsession of ambitious talent. Contemptible from early on and insufferable in the young.
     Derek Walcott LITERATURE, 1992

590. There are two moments worthwhile in writing. The one
    when you start and the other when you throw it in the
    waste-paper basket.
    Samuel Beckett LITERATURE, 1969

POETS AND POETRY

591. Poetry must be human. If it is not human, it is not
    poetry.
    Vicente Aleixandre LITERATURE, 1977

592. Literature is a state of culture, poetry is a state of grace.
    Juan Ramón Jiménez LITERATURE, 1956

593. I don't think poetry comes from an education . . . I think
    that it comes from God.
    Joseph Brodsky LITERATURE, 1987
    At his trial in Moscow in 1964

594. The fate of poetry is to fall in love with the world in spite
    of History.
    Derek Walcott LITERATURE, 1992

595. Poetry . . . is the only insurance available against the
    vulgarity of the human heart.
    Joseph Brodsky LITERATURE, 1987

596. Ah, but it's impossible to live without poetry.
    Pyotr Kapitsa PHYSICS, 1978

597. Literature that does not rise to the level of poetry—
    whether it takes the form of verse or prose—bears no
    relation to literature at all.
    Naguib Mahfouz LITERATURE, 1988

598. The only thing politics and poetry have in common is the letter "p" and the letter "o."
    Joseph Brodsky LITERATURE, 1987

599. We make out of the quarrel with others, rhetoric, but of the quarrel with ourselves, poetry.
    William Butler Yeats LITERATURE, 1923

600. Love is a metaphysical affair whose goal is either accomplishing or liberating one's soul . . . That is and always has been the core of lyric poetry.
    Joseph Brodsky LITERATURE, 1987

601. Genuine poetry can communicate before it is understood.
    T. S. Eliot LITERATURE, 1948

602. The relationship between eroticism and poetry is such that it can be said, without affectation, that the former is a poetry of the body and the latter an eroticism of language.
    Octavio Paz LITERATURE, 1990

603. Between poetry and literature there is the same distance, as, for example, between love and appetite, sensuality and sexuality, word and wordiness.
    Juan Ramón Jiménez LITERATURE, 1956

604. The experience of a poem is the experience both of a moment and of a lifetime.
    T. S. Eliot LITERATURE, 1948

605. In the house of poetry nothing endures that is not written with blood to be heard with blood.
    Pablo Neruda LITERATURE, 1971

606. The closest thing to poetry is a loaf of bread or a ceramic dish or a piece of wood lovingly carved, even if by clumsy hands.
Pablo Neruda LITERATURE, 1971

607. Contemporary poetry should be such that the listener or reader can say, "That is how I should talk if I could talk poetry."
T. S. Eliot LITERATURE, 1948

608. Immature poets imitate; mature poets steal.
T. S. Eliot LITERATURE, 1948

609. No poetry is free for the man who wants to do a good job.
T. S. Eliot LITERATURE, 1948

610. The instinct to rhyme is one we're born with . . . The delight of the two sounds joining means there's some sense in something . . . Everything is a couplet: two eyes, husband and wife, man and woman . . . As you travel towards the rhyme, it's a form of prayer. It's a form of prayer that says, I'm heading toward something that appears to be wisdom, saying, I hope for an order, there is order, I'm obedient to that order . . . The sort of anarchy and atheism or agnosticism that's contained in free verse is inferior to rhyme, because it's inferior as agnosticism is to the idea of God.
Derek Walcott LITERATURE, 1992

611. The feature of my schooling that in retrospect I value most is one that modern American educational theory rejects: the practice of memorizing poetry.
Salvador Luria MEDICINE, 1969

612. I do not go in search of poetry. I wait for poetry to visit me.
Eugenio Montale LITERATURE, 1975

613. I think inspiration is a refuge for poets. All poets are
generally very lazy. They're loafers!
Camilo José Cela LITERATURE, 1989

614. I was born in Sardinia. My family consisted of wise as well
as violent people, and primitive artists. The family was
respected and of good standing, and had a private library.
But when I started writing at thirteen, they objected. As
the philosopher says: If your son is writing poems, send
him to the mountain paths; the next time you may punish
him; but the third time, leave him alone, because then he
is a poet.
Grazia Deledda LITERATURE, 1926

615. As things are, and as fundamentally they must always be,
poetry is not a career, but a mug's game. No honest poet
can ever feel quite sure of the permanent value of what he
has written: He may have wasted his time and messed up
his life for nothing.
T. S. Eliot LITERATURE, 1948

616. To read a poem is to hear it with our eyes: to hear it is to
see it with our ears.
T. S. Eliot LITERATURE, 1948

617. If a society without social justice is not a good society,
a society without poetry is a society without dreams . . .
If society abolishes poetry it commits spiritual suicide.
Octavio Paz LITERATURE, 1990

618. The only job in which one cannot lie is poetry. You can't
lie in poetry. If you are a liar you'll always be discovered.
Perhaps now, perhaps in five years, in ten years, but
you are going to be discovered eventually if you are lying.
Giorgos Seferis LITERATURE, 1963

619. Bureaucrats and bus passengers respond with a touch of incredulity and alarm when they find out that they're dealing with a poet.
Wislawa Szymborska LITERATURE, 1996

620. Been writing much poetry lately, Mr. Keats?
J. J. Thomson PHYSICS, 1906
To William Butler Yeats, guest of honor at dinner

BOOKS

621. There is no friend as loyal as a book.
Ernest Hemingway LITERATURE, 1954

622. A man can never have too many books, too much red wine, or too much ammunition.
Rudyard Kipling LITERATURE, 1907

623. I'm old-fashioned and think that reading books is the most glorious pastime that humankind has yet devised.
Wislawa Szymborska LITERATURE, 1996

624. There are worse crimes than burning books. One of them is not reading them.
Joseph Brodsky LITERATURE, 1987

625. Never lend books, for no one ever returns them; the only books I have in my library are books that other folk have lent me.
Anatole France LITERATURE, 1921

626. I do not know any reading more easy, more fascinating, more delightful than a catalog.
Anatole France LITERATURE, 1921

627. All these people who call themselves publishers—they are no better than people who sell books off a barrow.
V. S. Naipaul LITERATURE, 2001

628. Almost all publishers belong to the ruling technocracies and therefore worship the dubious social sciences, scorn the classics, and mistrust poetry, considering it a fruitless activity or an archaic pastime.
Octavio Paz LITERATURE, 1990

629. Best-sellers are not works of literature, they are merchandise.
Octavio Paz LITERATURE, 1990

THE MEDIA

630. As long as I don't read the newspapers, I feel fine.
Otto Hahn CHEMISTRY, 1944

631. Turn off the television. Don't read the newspaper. It's all full of what went wrong yesterday.
Betty Williams PEACE, 1976

632. No poem can be the true image of our world. The true, the appalling image of our world is the newspaper.
Elias Canetti LITERATURE, 1981

633. Newspapers are unable, seemingly, to discriminate between a bicycle accident and the collapse of civilisation.
George Bernard Shaw LITERATURE, 1925

634. As journalists have occasionally said, What is there that will happen next that you can't even imagine?
Paul Lauterbur MEDICINE, 2003

635. Probably the most important thing my parents did to encourage me was to NOT get a television. We lived way out in the woods and once a week we would drive into town (nearly an hour away) to buy groceries. On those trips my parents always took us to the public library.
Carl Wieman PHYSICS, 2001

636. Television has proved that millions of people passionately love lust and violence.
Saul Bellow LITERATURE, 1976

637. Television has made dictatorship impossible, but democracy unbearable.
Shimon Peres PEACE, 1994

Places

Nobel prizes are geographically concentrated in North America and western Europe. Less than 5 percent of all prize winners were born south of the equator, almost all of them in Australia or New Zealand. About 40 percent of laureates have been citizens of the United States. Germany comes second, closely followed by Britain, then France. The tiny Caribbean island of St. Lucia, population 150,000, has produced two laureates, Arthur Lewis in Economics and Derek Walcott in Literature.

The most significant event affecting the distribution of prizes by nationality was the accession of the Nazis to power in Germany. Dismissed from German universities, many Jewish scientists, including several who had won or would later win the Nobel Prize, left Axis-dominated Europe, mainly for Britain and the United States. Before Hitler took charge, Germany was the acknowledged world leader in the sciences. Up to 1932, Germany won 40 percent of the prizes in Chemistry and Physics, with the United States taking 9 percent. Since 1932, these figures have been reversed; Germany has won 9 percent, while American scientists have won 45 percent. Poland was similarly affected by the politics of the twentieth century, losing ten of its fifteen laureates to emigration.

Exile has consequently been the experience of many Nobel

laureates, while many others have left their native land in the pursuit of their calling. This gives a particular poignancy to their observations on their countries of birth and adoption.

AMERICA AND AMERICANS

638. I'm the happiest combination you can think of. I'm a
    Russian poet, an English essayist, and an American citizen!
    Joseph Brodsky LITERATURE, 1987

639. I am proud to have become an American. Here is the last
    refuge of freedom. It is only the United States that can
    save the world.
    Albert Einstein PHYSICS, 1921

640. What America means to the rest of the world is the hope
    for people everywhere that they shall be able to walk with
    their heads erect.
    Henry Kissinger PEACE, 1973

641. I had never come across so many good people ready to
    help their neighbor.
    Czeslaw Milosz LITERATURE, 1980
    Referring to the United States

642. The most fascinating and exotic people in the world—the
    Average Citizens of the United States, with their friendliness
    to strangers and their rough teasing, their passion for
    material advancement and their shy idealism, their interest
    in all the world and their boastful provincialism.
    Sinclair Lewis LITERATURE, 1930

643. The Americans will always do the right thing after trying
    all other alternatives.
    Winston Churchill LITERATURE, 1953

644. History had created something new in the USA, namely crookedness with self-respect or duplicity with honor.
Saul Bellow LITERATURE, 1976

645. Intellectually I know that America is no better than any other country; emotionally I know she is better than every other country.
Sinclair Lewis LITERATURE, 1930

646. You've got to have a society which is concerned with justice. It's quite clear that American society for the past decade has been concerned with greed, not justice.
James Watson MEDICINE, 1962

647. The poor in America are unorganized and largely mute . . . They are the least revolutionary proletariat in the world.
Gunnar Myrdal ECONOMICS, 1974

648. We are determined that before the sun sets on this terrible struggle, our flag will be recognized throughout the world as a symbol of freedom on the one hand and of overwhelming power on the other.
George C. Marshall PEACE, 1953

649. For the moment we are the strongest power in the world. It is very important that we do not become the most hated.
Ernest Hemingway LITERATURE, 1954

650. If America's soul becomes totally poisoned, part of the autopsy must read Vietnam.
Martin Luther King PEACE, 1964

651. The United States leads the world economically and militarily, but it no longer does so morally . . . You have to prove your high moral standing by deeds, not words.
Lech Walesa PEACE, 1983

652. I put it to you that the United States is without doubt the greatest show on the road. Brutal, indifferent, scornful and ruthless it may be but it is also very clever. As a salesman it is out on its own and its most saleable commodity is self love.

Harold Pinter LITERATURE, 2005

653. My feeling about the United States is this. To live alongside this great country is like living with your wife. At times it is difficult to live with her. At all times it is impossible to live without her.

Lester Pearson PEACE, 1957

As Prime Minister of Canada to General Charles de Gaulle

654. The municipal authorities here consist of thieves so skilled in their profession that European corruption pales into insignificance in comparison.

Henryk Sienkiewicz LITERATURE, 1905

655. It is easy to earn much money in America but difficult to spend it in pleasant ways.

Wolfgang Pauli PHYSICS, 1945

656. Potatoes.

Paul Dirac PHYSICS, 1933

Answer to an American reporter's question, "What do you like best in America?"

657. There are too many famous people in America.

Eugene Wigner PHYSICS, 1963

658. I have always thought that in the United States a liberal is a conservative with a heart and a conservative is a liberal without one.

Franco Modigliani ECONOMICS, 1985

BRITAIN AND THE BRITISH

659. Unconquerable England that did not submit to the war,
but submitted the war to its habits and traditions.
Adapted it to its proprieties. What a debt to her we had
contracted when, alone, she stood fast against the
monster!

François Jacob MEDICINE, 1965

660. No sum of money can adequately and appropriately
express our gratefulness to the British people. What this
country of our adoption gave us was not just a new home
and livelihood . . . We also found a new and better way
of life coming from an atmosphere of political oppression
and persecution . . . We found a spirit of friendliness,
humanity, tolerance and fairness. It is this way of life
with which some of us, I for one, fell in love. We were
given here a new home—not merely a shelter but a true
home.

Hans Krebs MEDICINE, 1953

Speech in 1965 on behalf of ex-German refugees presenting a check
to the presidents of the Royal Society and the British Academy in
gratitude for the welcome they received in Britain

661. It was in Hopkins's laboratory where I saw for the first
time at close quarters some of the characteristics of what
is sometimes referred to as "the British way of life." The
Cambridge laboratory included people of many different
dispositions, convictions, and abilities. I saw them argue
without quarrelling, quarrel without suspecting, suspect
without abusing, criticize without vilifying or ridiculing,
and praise without flattering.

Hans Krebs MEDICINE, 1953

662. I can understand and like the English only after they are dead.

    François Mauriac LITERATURE, 1952

663. It is impossible for an Englishman to open his mouth without making some other Englishman hate or despise him.

    George Bernard Shaw LITERATURE, 1925

664. You've never heard of an English lover. Only an English patient.

    James Watson MEDICINE, 1962

GERMANY AND THE GERMANS

665. In spite of all the horrors of the past, I believe in you. Let us remember the victims and then let us walk together into the future to seek again a new beginning.

    Nelly Sachs LITERATURE, 1966
    On being awarded the German Book Publishers Association Peace Prize, October 1965

666. A good German cannot be a nationalist. A good German knows that he cannot be other than a good European.

    Willy Brandt PEACE, 1971

667. To be anti-German seems to me just as bad as being antisemitic.

    Hans Krebs MEDICINE, 1953

668. I then remarked that we were inflicting damage on ourselves by forcing Jews whose talents we needed to emigrate and that their talents would now be used for the benefit of foreigners. This he [Hitler] did not accept at all

and held forth at great length about quite general matters, ending up by saying: "It is said that I suffer on occasion from weak nerves. That is a slander. I have nerves of steel." With that, he slapped his knee with great force, spoke more and more rapidly and began to shake with such uncontrollable rage that there was nothing I could do but keep silent and take my leave as soon as I decently could.

Max Planck PHYSICS, 1918

RUSSIA AND THE RUSSIANS

669. For a man whose mother tongue is Russian to speak about political evil is as natural as digestion.

Joseph Brodsky LITERATURE, 1987

670. On account of what you are doing to the Russian intelligentsia—demoralizing, annihilating, depraving them—I am ashamed to be called a Russian!

Ivan Pavlov MEDICINE, 1904

671. The guilt of Stalin and his immediate entourage before the Party and the people for the mass repression and lawlessness they committed is enormous and unforgivable.

Mikhail Gorbachev PEACE, 1990

672. Actually, the demands of the hierarchy are very slight. There is only one thing they really want. You should hate what you like and love what you abhor! But this is the most difficult of all.

Boris Pasternak LITERATURE, 1958

673. At the Novosibirsk Transit Prison in 1945 they greeted the prisoners with a roll call based on cases. "So and so! Article 51 and 58-1A, twenty-five years." The chief of the

convoy guard was curious. "What did you get it for?"
"For nothing at all." "You are lying. The sentence for
nothing at all is ten years."
Alexandr Solzhenitsyn LITERATURE, 1970

674. I can say without affectation that I belong to the Russian
convict world no less . . . than I do to Russian literature.
I got my education there, and it will last forever.
Alexandr Solzhenitsyn LITERATURE, 1970

FRANCE AND THE FRENCH

675. One is more foreign in France than in other countries.
Saul Bellow LITERATURE, 1976

676. The Almighty in His infinite wisdom did not see fit to
create Frenchmen in the image of Englishmen.
Winston Churchill LITERATURE, 1953

677. It is unthinkable for a Frenchman to arrive at middle age
without having syphilis and the Cross of the Legion of
Honor.
André Gide LITERATURE, 1947

678. Paris proves that the city—simply a place where many
people live, work and play—can be one of the marvels of
human creativity.
Sheldon Glashow PHYSICS, 1979

679. Paris is very beautiful this fall. It was a fine place to
be quite young in and it is a necessary part of man's
education. We all loved it once and we lie if we say we
didn't. But she is like a mistress who does not grow old
and she has other lovers now.
Ernest Hemingway LITERATURE, 1954

680. If you are lucky enough to have lived in Paris as a young
man, then wherever you go for the rest of your life, it
stays with you, for Paris is a moveable feast.
Ernest Hemingway LITERATURE, 1954

681. Paris . . . the only city besides New York where one feels
what a city truly means—something created by generations
of human beings to be their permanent assertion of
communal pride.
Salvador Luria MEDICINE, 1969

ISRAEL

682. If I am proud of anything, it is that I have been granted
the privilege of living in the land which God promised our
forefathers to give us, as it is written.
Shmuel Agnon LITERATURE, 1966

683. Always I regarded myself as one who was born in
Jerusalem . . . After all my possessions had been burned,
God gave me the wisdom to return to Jerusalem. I returned
to Jerusalem and it is by virtue of Jerusalem that I have
written all that God has put into my heart and into my pen.
Shmuel Agnon LITERATURE, 1966

684. I do not stand here alone, today, on this small rostrum in
Oslo. I am the emissary of generations of Israelis, of the
shepherds of Israel, just as King David was a shepherd, of
the herdsmen and dressers of sycamore trees, as the Prophet
Amos was; of the rebels against the establishment, like the
Prophet Jeremiah, and of men who go down to the sea, like
the prophet Jonah. I am the emissary of the poets and of
those who dreamed of an end to war, like the Prophet
Isaiah . . . I stand here mainly for the generations to come,

so that we may all be deemed worthy of the medallion which you have bestowed on me today. I stand here as the emissary of our neighbors who were our enemies. I stand here as the emissary of the soaring hopes of a people which has endured the worst that history has to offer and nevertheless made its mark—not just on the chronicles of the Jewish people but on all mankind. With me here are five million citizens of Israel—Jews and Arabs, Druze and Circassians—five million hearts beating for peace—and five million pairs of eyes which look to us with such great expectations for peace.

Yitzhak Rabin PEACE, 1994

THE THIRD WORLD

685. When the missionaries came to Africa they had the Bible and we had the land. They said "Let us pray." We closed our eyes. When we opened them we had the Bible and they had the land.

Desmond Tutu PEACE, 1984

686. Asia is not going to be civilised after the methods of the West. There is too much Asia, and she is too old.

Rudyard Kipling LITERATURE, 1907

687. *Now, it is not good for the Christian's health to hustle the Aryan brown,*
For the Christian riles, and the Aryan smiles, and he weareth the Christian down;
And the end of the fight is a tombstone white, with the name of the late deceased,
And the epitaph drear: "A fool lies here who tried to hustle the East."

Rudyard Kipling LITERATURE, 1907

688. The developing countries themselves must restructure
their national psychologies in the direction of greater
responsibility for their own fates. It is time they stopped
blaming their misfortunes on colonialism and neo-
colonialism.

   Andrei Sakharov PEACE, 1975

689. In the name of the Third World: Be not spectators to our
miseries.

   Naguib Mahfouz LITERATURE, 1988

HEAVEN AND HELL

690. Once in Hawaii I was taken to see a Buddhist temple. In
the temple a man said, "I am going to tell you something
that you will never forget." And then he said, "To every
man is given the key to the gates of heaven. The same key
opens the gates of hell."

   Richard Feynman PHYSICS, 1965

691. Many believe that the new discoveries may lead either to
immense progress or to equal catastrophe, to paradise or
to hell. I, however, think that this earth will remain what
it always was; a mixture of heaven and hell, a battlefield of
angels and devils.

   Max Born PHYSICS, 1954

692. The infliction of cruelty with a good conscience is a delight
to moralists. That is why they invented Hell.

   Bertrand Russell LITERATURE, 1950

693. Hell is other people.

   Jean-Paul Sartre LITERATURE, 1964

694. Here as hereafter the alternative to hell is purgatory.
T. S. Eliot LITERATURE, 1948

695. Heaven, as conventionally conceived, is a place so inane, so dull, so useless, so miserable, that nobody has ever ventured to describe a whole day in heaven, though plenty of people have described a day at the seaside.
George Bernard Shaw LITERATURE, 1925

HOME AND THE HOMELAND

696. Everyone ought to have a home to get away from.
Sinclair Lewis LITERATURE, 1930

697. A home from which you can be ejected at any time is no true home.
Shmuel Agnon LITERATURE, 1966

698. No matter under what circumstances you leave it, home does not cease to be home. No matter how you lived there—well or poorly.
Joseph Brodsky LITERATURE, 1987
On leaving the Soviet Union in 1972

699. Wherever I go, wherever I happen to be, I shall always know where I really am. I can never lose my way because I know that I have my living roots there, deep down in the soil of my village, in that land out of which I grew.
Anwar al-Sadat PEACE, 1978

700. It is suicide to be abroad. But what is it to be at home? . . . What is it to be at home? A lingering dissolution.
Samuel Beckett LITERATURE, 1969

701. If my theory of relativity is proven correct, Germany will claim me as a German and France will declare that I am a citizen of the world. Should my theory prove untrue, France will say that I am a German and Germany will declare that I am a Jew.

Albert Einstein PHYSICS, 1921

702. Sweet is the land where one is born. It has no price. All other land is bitter.

Miguel Ángel Asturias LITERATURE, 1967

Politics and Economics

The Nobel awards are a highly political phenomenon. This is most evident in the case of the Peace Prize. Winners of this prize include three U.S. presidents and two vice presidents; presidents of the former Soviet Union, South Africa, Costa Rica, South Korea, Egypt, the Palestine Authority, and Poland; prime ministers of France, Canada, Sweden, Japan, and Israel; two secretaries-general of the United Nations; and numerous ambassadors from various countries.

Because the Peace Prize (and on occasion the Literature Prize) has often honored and encouraged resistance to oppression, it has frequently provoked political controversy. During the Cold War, Nobel selections were periodically attacked as pro-capitalist by the East and pro-communist by the West. Conservatives in the United States denounced the prize as anti-American when it was awarded to domestic critics such as Sinclair Lewis, Linus Pauling, and Martin Luther King, or to foreign critics such as Dario Fo, Elfriede Jelinek, and Harold Pinter.

Much greater controversy arose with the award of the Literature Prize to Boris Pasternak in 1958. His major novel, *Dr. Zhivago*, was still banned in the Soviet Union, and he eventually declined the prize when told that if he went to Sweden to accept it, he would not be permitted to return to the USSR. The experience of Alexandr Solzhenitsyn was similar when he was awarded the Literature Prize in 1970. His Nobel lecture was smuggled to Stockholm by a Swedish friend in 1972. Published by the Nobel Foundation, it caused a sensation; it was in this speech that Solzhenitsyn first used the term *Gulag Archipelago*.

A more vicious campaign against the prize was waged by Adolf Hitler. The führer was enraged when the Peace Prize was awarded in 1935 to Carl von Ossietzky, who was, and remained, in a concentration camp for his opposition to the Nazis. Hitler forbade any German to accept the prize in the future, so a number of German scientists had to wait until after the Second World War to receive their prizes.

POLITICS AND POLITICIANS

703. Politics is a great enemy of love.
Octavio Paz LITERATURE, 1990

704. Ninety percent of politicians give the other ten percent a bad name.
Henry Kissinger PEACE, 1973

705. Politicians think of the next election while statesmen think of the next generation. People elect the best politicians and then are astonished when they discover they have gotten poor statesmen.
Albert Szent-Györgyi MEDICINE, 1937

706. To govern is to educate. A statesman is that person who tells people what people need to know. A politician is that person who tells people what people want to hear.
Oscar Arias Sánchez PEACE, 1987

707. No politician will worry much about anything that can't be photographed.

George Stigler ECONOMICS, 1982

708. I believe . . . that for someone who has read a lot of Dickens, to shoot his like in the name of some idea is more problematic than for someone who has read no Dickens . . . Lenin was literate. Stalin was literate, so was Hitler; as for Mao Zedong, he even wrote verse. What all these men had in common, though, was that their hit list was longer than their reading list.

Joseph Brodsky LITERATURE, 1987

709. Foreign policy is merely domestic policy with its hat on.

Lester Pearson PEACE, 1957

710. No foreign policy—no matter how ingenious—has any chance of success if it is born in the minds of few and carried in the hearts of none.

Henry Kissinger PEACE, 1973

GOVERNMENT

711. Governments never learn. Only people learn.

Milton Friedman ECONOMICS, 1976

712. Thank heavens we do not get all of the government that we are made to pay for.

Milton Friedman ECONOMICS, 1976

713. Nothing is so permanent as a temporary government program.

Milton Friedman ECONOMICS, 1976

714. Almost all government programs are started with good intentions, but when you look at what they actually achieve, there is a general rule. Almost every such program has results that are the opposite of the intentions of the well-meaning people who originally back it.
     Milton Friedman ECONOMICS, 1976

715. If you put the federal government in charge of the Sahara Desert, in five years there'd be a shortage of sand.
     Milton Friedman ECONOMICS, 1976

716. I estimate, in fact, that the federal government is at least 120 times as large as any organization can be and still keep some control over its general operations.
     George Stigler ECONOMICS, 1982

717. The most ineffective government agency is inherently the one most interested in concealing its performance from the public.
     Jimmy Carter PEACE, 2002

718. Governments need enemies to frighten their people with, frightened people being more easy to lead.
     Albert Szent-Györgyi MEDICINE, 1937

719. When they call the roll in the Senate, the Senators do not know whether to answer "Present" or "Not guilty."
     Theodore Roosevelt PEACE, 1906

720. Our government is Hitler's finest weapon.
     Frederick Banting MEDICINE, 1923
     Diary entry, after visiting the Canadian House of Commons, June 3, 1940.

721. The more the state "plans," the more difficult planning becomes for the individual.
     Friedrich von Hayek ECONOMICS, 1974

722. Competition as far as possible, planning as far as necessary.
     Willy Brandt PEACE, 1971

723. There is absolutely nothing to be said for government by a plutocracy.
     Theodore Roosevelt PEACE, 1906

724. Not only does absolute power corrupt absolutely; it delays fantastically.
     George Stigler ECONOMICS, 1982

725. One of the greatest threats to mankind today is that the world may be choked by an explosively pervading but well camouflaged bureaucracy.
     Norman Borlaug PEACE, 1970

726. You have to learn to keep out of corridors because corridors generally lead to committee rooms.
     Thomas Morgan MEDICINE, 1933

727. Avoid trivia.
     George C. Marshall PEACE, 1953
     To George Kennan on appointing him chief of the Policy Planning Staff in 1947

728. There is a connection between fools and power, although seldom between writers and power.
     Günter Grass LITERATURE, 1999

DEMOCRACY

729. Many forms of government have been tried and will be tried in this world of sin and woe. No one pretends that democracy is perfect or all-wise. Indeed, it has been said that democracy is the worst form of government except all those other forms that have been tried from time to time.
Winston Churchill LITERATURE, 1953

730. Modern democracy is the daughter of the rationalism of the 17th and 18th century and is therefore, in a sense, the twin sister of science. It is, by its very origins, committed to rationality, to optimism about the future of mankind, to faith in progress based on factual knowledge of the world.
Salvador Luria MEDICINE, 1969

731. There's nothing more secure than a democratic, accountable, and participatory form of government.
Wole Soyinka LITERATURE, 1986

732. The mistakes made by a democracy in a whole generation do not compare with the mistakes that can be made by a dictatorship in a single day.
Anwar al-Sadat PEACE, 1978

733. It is better to be a total failure in democracy than a martyr or the crème de la crème in tyranny.
Joseph Brodsky LITERATURE, 1987

734. Democracy does not favor continuity. The Englishman will not, except on great occasions, be denied the indulgence of kicking out the Ministers of the Crown whoever they are and of reversing their policy whatever it is.
Winston Churchill LITERATURE, 1953

735. It is very difficult to maintain a genuinely democratic political system in a society where there is a high degree of illiteracy; where most people still live in rural poverty; where most people are uneducated and have little access to modern media. On the other hand, it is almost impossible to have a fully-fledged modern consumer economy without having democratic institutions.
F. W. de Klerk PEACE, 1993

736. Democratic principles do not flourish on empty stomachs.
George C. Marshall PEACE, 1953

737. No substantial famine has ever occurred in any independent and democratic country with a relatively free press.
Amartya Sen ECONOMICS, 1998

738. Building democracy as an imposition from abroad is a form of imperialism.
Lech Walesa PEACE, 1983

TYRANNY AND DICTATORSHIP

739. In dictatorships the beginning may seem easy, but tragedy awaits inescapably at the end.
Giorgos Seferis LITERATURE, 1963

740. Europe's 20th-century totalitarianisms created a completely new type of human being. They forced a person to choose in a way we were never forced to choose before: to become either a victim or a perpetrator. Even surviving involved collaboration, compromises you had to make if you wanted to bring a bigger piece of bread home to your family. This choice has deformed millions of Europeans.
Imre Kertész LITERATURE, 2002

741. Happy is the man who believes in the truth that repudiates tyranny; happy is he who rejects the belief that tyranny is all-powerful.
     Menachem Begin PEACE, 1978

742. It is a dangerous thing in a dictatorship to have a long memory.
     Ernest Hemingway LITERATURE, 1954

743. The man dies in all who keep silent in the face of tyranny.
     Wole Soyinka LITERATURE, 1986

REVOLUTION

744. All modern revolutions have ended in a reinforcement of the power of the State.
     Albert Camus LITERATURE, 1957

745. What is a rebel? A man who says no.
     Albert Camus LITERATURE, 1957

746. What difference does a revolution make when you have experiments to do in the laboratory!
     Ivan Pavlov MEDICINE, 1904
     Attributed remark in 1917 to a colleague who was ten minutes late due to shooting in the streets during the Russian Revolution

747. A love affair, a career, a revolution: these are ventures on which one embarks without knowing their outcome.
     Jean-Paul Sartre LITERATURE, 1964

748. Research in applied science leads to reforms, research in pure science leads to revolutions, and revolutions, whether political or industrial, are exceedingly profitable things if you are on the winning side.
     J. J. Thomson PHYSICS, 1906

749. No matter how valid the ideas that inspire a party, no matter how wise its program, no matter how strong the initial support from the people, sooner or later there will be an inevitable degeneration of a revolutionary party into a conservative party.

Mikhail Gorbachev PEACE, 1990

750. I renounce revolution as a means of solving problems.

Mikhail Gorbachev PEACE, 1990

TERRORISM

751. The difference between the revolutionary and the terrorist lies in the reason for which he fights.

Yasser Arafat PEACE, 1994

752. Frightfulness is not a remedy known to the British pharmacopoeia.

Winston Churchill LITERATURE, 1953

753. If those vested with authority and power practice injustice, resort to torture and killing, is it not inevitable that those who are the victims will react with similar methods?

Seán MacBride PEACE, 1974

754. As long as the more powerful nations exploit the less powerful, they will be repaid by terrorism, hatred, and potential violence. Insofar as our policies are selfish or cynical or short-sighted, there will inevitably be a day of reckoning.

Jimmy Carter PEACE, 2002

755. The first step towards the dethronement of terror is the deflation of its hypocritical self-righteousness.

Wole Soyinka LITERATURE, 1986

FREEDOM

756. So listen to me, children: Put on your marching shoes;
don'cha get weary; though the path ahead may be dark
and dreary; we're walking for freedom, children.
Martin Luther King PEACE, 1964

757. Freedom is not a philosophy, nor is it even an idea.
It is a movement of consciousness that leads us, at
certain moments, to utter one of two monosyllables:
Yes or No.
Octavio Paz LITERATURE, 1990

758. None who have always been free can understand the
terrible fascinating power of the hope of freedom to those
who are not free.
Pearl S. Buck LITERATURE, 1938

759. Peace is indissolubly interwoven with the question of
freedom, for peace without freedom is a mockery.
Albert Lutuli PEACE, 1960

760. For my own part I have made my choice. I will not leave
South Africa, nor will I surrender. Only through hardship,
sacrifice, and militant action can freedom be won. The
struggle is my life. I will continue fighting for freedom
until the end of my days.
Nelson Mandela PEACE, 1993

761. Nothing, not even the most sophisticated weapon, not
even the most brutally efficient policy, no, nothing will
stop people once they are determined to achieve their
freedom and their right to humanness.
Desmond Tutu PEACE, 1984

762. People are not free if they cannot decide where they wish to live; where they wish to work; where and how they wish to educate their children; where and how they wish to worship; what language they wish to speak; to what organisations they wish to belong; or what views they choose to hold. It is precisely because apartheid denied these basic freedoms that it was so unacceptable and had to be dismantled.
F. W. de Klerk PEACE, 1993

763. A society that puts equality . . . ahead of freedom will end up with neither equality or freedom.
Milton Friedman ECONOMICS, 1976

764. Liberty has never come from the government. Liberty has always come from the subjects of it. The history of liberty is a history of resistance.
Woodrow Wilson PEACE, 1919

765. When a nation re-awakens, its finest sons are prepared to give their lives for its liberation. When Empires are threatened with collapse, they are prepared to sacrifice their non-commissioned officers.
Menachem Begin PEACE, 1978

JUSTICE

766. For me, justice is the first condition of humanity.
Wole Soyinka LITERATURE, 1986

767. From the moment that the free-thinkers began to question the existence of God, the problem of justice became of primary importance.
Albert Camus LITERATURE, 1957

768. God help us if our sense of fair play is not the strongest of all our feelings.
Bjørnstjerne Bjørnson LITERATURE, 1903

769. Injustice anywhere is a threat to justice everywhere.
Martin Luther King PEACE, 1964

770. Freedom without social justice is useless, and social justice is useless in the absence of individual freedoms.
Shirin Ebadi PEACE, 2003

771. Any peace not built on justice and on the recognition of the rights of the peoples, would be a structure of sand which would crumble under the first blow.
Anwar al-Sadat PEACE, 1978

772. If I had to choose between justice and disorder, on the one hand, and injustice and order, on the other, I would always choose the latter.
Henry Kissinger PEACE, 1973

773. Power alone is no guarantee of security . . . The only guarantee of security is justice.
Naguib Mahfouz LITERATURE, 1988

774. The whole history of the world is summed up in the fact that, when nations are strong, they are not always just, and when they wish to be just, they are no longer strong.
Winston Churchill LITERATURE, 1953

775. Even those who are fed up with morality ought to realize that it is better to suffer certain injustices than to commit them even to win wars.
Albert Camus LITERATURE, 1957

RACISM

776. Racism is evil—human damnation in the Old Testament
sense, and no compromises, as well as sacrifices, should
be too great in the fight against it.
Nadine Gordimer LITERATURE, 1991

777. No one is born hating another person because of the
colour of his skin or his background, or his religion.
People must learn to hate, and if they can learn to hate,
they can be taught to love, for love comes more naturally
to the human heart than its opposite.
Nelson Mandela PEACE, 1993

778. We don't want apartheid improved—we want it removed,
we want it dismantled. You can't reform apartheid.
Desmond Tutu PEACE, 1984

779. To live anywhere in the world today and be against
equality because of race or color, is like living in Alaska
and being against snow.
William Faulkner LITERATURE, 1949

780. "I know what every colored woman in this country is
doing." "What's that?" "Dying."
Toni Morrison LITERATURE, 1993

781. If Hitler had won the war and established his thousand-year
Reich . . . the first 200 years of that Reich would have been
exactly what that period was in this country for Black people.
Toni Morrison LITERATURE, 1993

782. In this country American means white. Everybody else has
to hyphenate.
Toni Morrison LITERATURE, 1993

783. The less intelligent the white man is, the more stupid he
thinks the black.
André Gide LITERATURE, 1947

MARXISM AND COMMUNISM

784. If people don't like Marxism, they should blame the
British Museum.
Mikhail Gorbachev PEACE, 1990
On a visit to the Reading Room of the British Museum, where Karl
Marx wrote *Das Kapital*

785. Whatever culture it has overlain—whether Russian,
Chinese, or Cuban—Marxism has proven itself economically
unworkable and has perverted its underlying just social
core by showing itself to be infinitely corruptible.
Roald Hoffmann CHEMISTRY, 1981

786. Everyone can see how Communism rots the soul of a
nation; how it makes it abject and hungry in peace, and
proves it base and abominable in war.
Winston Churchill LITERATURE, 1953

787. We are dealing not with the tyranny of an individual but
with the tyranny of a party that simply has put the
production of tyrants on an industrial footing.
Joseph Brodsky LITERATURE, 1987
On the Communist regime

788. From Stettin in the Baltic to Trieste in the Adriatic, an iron
curtain has descended across the Continent.
Winston Churchill LITERATURE, 1953

789. What is called "communism" in developing countries is hunger becoming articulate.

John Boyd Orr PEACE, 1949

790. In spring 1942 I was sent to the front near Witebsk and two months later taken prisoner by the Russians . . . I became tolerably fluent in Russian and got quite friendly with some Russians, mostly doctors. I had the occasion to observe the striking parallels between the psychological effects of Nazi and of Marxist education. It was then that I began to realize the nature of indoctrination as such.

Konrad Lorenz MEDICINE, 1973

791. Human geneticists are particularly vulnerable to the vilification of doctrinaire Marxists because, as scientists, they are in thrall to such bourgeois superstitions as the desirability of telling the truth.

Peter Medawar MEDICINE, 1960

792. This solemn pledge to abstain from truth was called socialist realism.

Alexandr Solzhenitsyn LITERATURE, 1970

793. For us in Russia, communism is a dead dog. For many people in the West, it is still a living lion.

Alexandr Solzhenitsyn LITERATURE, 1970

794. Marxism may be discredited in Eastern Europe, but it still seems to flourish at Harvard.

Max Perutz CHEMISTRY, 1962

795. Marxism became a posture in the 1980s, which enabled very stupid people to pretend they had a coherent view of the world.

V. S. Naipaul LITERATURE, 2001

796. I have often had to smile at the childish nonsense about communism uttered by some leading English physicists, who were sentimentally biased in favor of this doctrine, about the application of which I have had a firsthand knowledge.
Albert Szent-Györgyi MEDICINE, 1937

PATRIOTISM

797. Patriotism kills.
Betty Williams PEACE, 1976

798. Poets sing, orators declaim, and patriots assassinate.
Norman Angell PEACE, 1933

799. You'll never have a quiet world till you knock the patriotism out of the human race.
George Bernard Shaw LITERATURE, 1925

800. Heroism on command, senseless violence, and all the loathsome nonsense that goes by the name of patriotism—how passionately I hate them!
Albert Einstein PHYSICS, 1921

801. I love my country too much to be a nationalist.
Albert Camus LITERATURE, 1957

802. The man who loves other countries as much as his own stands on a level with the man who loves other women as much as he loves his own wife.
Theodore Roosevelt PEACE, 1906

803. A scientist belongs to his country in times of war and to all mankind in times of peace.
Fritz Haber CHEMISTRY, 1918

804. The state is primarily an organization for killing foreigners, that's its main purpose. There are, of course, other things they do. They do a certain amount of educating, but in the course of educating you try very hard to make the young think it is a grand thing to kill foreigners.
Bertrand Russell LITERATURE, 1950

ECONOMICS

805. There's No Such Thing as a Free Lunch.
Milton Friedman ECONOMICS, 1976

806. Nobody spends somebody else's money as carefully as he spends his own. Nobody uses somebody else's resources as carefully as he uses his own. So if you want efficiency and effectiveness, if you want knowledge to be properly utilized, you have to do it through the means of private property.
Milton Friedman ECONOMICS, 1976

807. Economists possess their full share of the common ability to invent and commit errors . . . perhaps their most common error is to believe other economists.
Joseph Stigler ECONOMICS, 1982

808. The single biggest misunderstanding built into the mentality of the popular culture is that one person's gain is another person's loss.
James Heckman ECONOMICS, 2000

809. The only information that is of value in a financial market is information that other people don't have.
Herbert Simon ECONOMICS, 1978

810. Modern high-tech warfare is designed to remove physical contact: dropping bombs from 50,000 feet ensures that one

does not "feel" what one does. Modern economic management is similar: from one's luxury hotel, one can callously impose policies about which one would think twice if one knew the people whose lives one was destroying.
Joseph Stiglitz ECONOMICS, 2001

WEALTH AND POVERTY

811. Unless you're poor, you don't know what poor means. It means you get up in the morning and start killing cockroaches in the bathtub. It means wearing old clothes that make the other kids laugh at you. It means not being able to eat peaches until the end of August . . . To this day, I still feel different. It still hurts a little. Maybe that's why I work so hard for acceptance. I don't like Polish jokes. I don't like people who tease other people. I don't like anything that makes people feel badly about themselves.
Arno Penzias PHYSICS, 1978

812. The uneven division of power and wealth, the wide differences of health and comfort among the nations of mankind, are the sources of discord in the modern world, its major challenge and, unrelieved, its moral doom.
Patrick Blackett PHYSICS, 1948

813. "I'm learnin' one thing good," she said. "Learnin' it all the time and ever' day. If you're in trouble or hurt or need—go to poor people. They're the only ones that'll help—the only ones."
John Steinbeck LITERATURE, 1962

814. The law, in its majestic equality, forbids the rich as well as the poor to sleep under bridges, to beg in the streets, and to steal bread.
Anatole France LITERATURE, 1921

815. It may be that poor people are the only ones who commit crimes, but I do know that they are the only ones who serve prison sentences.
Jimmy Carter PEACE, 2002

816. Peace is inextricably linked to poverty. Poverty is a threat to peace. Ninety-four percent of the world income goes to forty percent of the population while sixty percent of people live on only six percent of world income. Half of the world population lives on two dollars a day. Over one billion people live on less than a dollar a day. This is no formula for peace.
Muhammad Yunus PEACE, 2006

817. People living in poverty and desperation will not hesitate to destroy the environment if they believe that in doing so their needs will be met.
Wangari Maathai PEACE, 2004

818. Since pharmaceutical companies operate for profit then of course people in Africa have another disease called money deficiency disease, and therefore, it's not worthwhile their trying to produce cures for people who can't pay for them.
Sydney Brenner MEDICINE, 2002

819. You cannot help the poor by destroying the rich.
Milton Friedman ECONOMICS, 1976

820. The more I see of the moneyed classes, the more I understand the guillotine.
George Bernard Shaw LITERATURE, 1925

Science and Technology

◇─◇─◇

In 1903, Albert Michelson declared that "the more important fundamental laws and facts of physical science have all been discovered." Twenty-five years later, after learning of the Dirac equation, Max Born asserted that "physics as we know it will be over in six months." Both of these scientists are refuted every October, as new Nobel laureates are announced in Stockholm, and the world grapples with the significance of their discoveries.

Scientists are no more immune than ordinary mortals to the temptation of soothsaying, especially when they step outside their area of specialization. John Strutt, better known as Lord Rayleigh, averred in 1896 that he had "not the smallest molecule of faith in aerial navigation other than ballooning." Ernest Rutherford was one of many scientists who doubted that the atom would ever yield significant power. John Cornforth told Dorothy Hodgkin, "If that's the formula of penicillin, I'll give up chemistry and grow mushrooms." Edward Purcell said in 1952, "All this stuff about traveling around the universe in space suits . . . belongs back where it came from, on the cereal box."

With many controversies, it is possible to count Nobel laureates on both sides: fluoridation of water, atomic energy, Intelligent Design, the big bang, welfare economics, the existence of God. But more significant than their differences are their areas of agreement: in the importance of science and in the freedom to pursue it.

SCIENCE AND SCIENTISTS

821. The sole aim of science is the glory of the human spirit.
Gerhard Herzberg CHEMISTRY, 1971

822. Science is imagination in the service of the verifiable truth.
Gerald Edelman MEDICINE, 1972

823. Let us be clear about it. What science can do, it will do, some time, somewhere, whatever obstacles may be put in its way.
Christian de Duve MEDICINE, 1974

824. The scientific equations we seek are the poetry of nature.
Chen Ning Yang PHYSICS, 1957

825. If you thought that science was certain—well that is just an error on your part.
Richard Feynman PHYSICS, 1965

826. Real science, as opposed to its entrepreneurial image, has a strict taboo against lying. We need this taboo to guard against wasting scarce and valuable resources, such as one's life, on false leads.
Robert Laughlin PHYSICS, 1998

827. I now regard my former belief in the superiority of science over other forms of human thought and behavior as a self-deception . . . In 1921 I believed . . . that science produced an objective knowledge of the world, which is governed by deterministic laws. The scientific method

seemed to me superior to other, more subjective ways of forming a picture of the world—philosophy, poetry and religion; and I even thought the unambiguous language of science to be a step towards a better understanding between human beings. In 1951 I believed in none of these things.

Max Born PHYSICS, 1954

828. I think one could say that a certain modesty toward understanding nature is a precondition to the continued pursuit of science.

Subramanyan Chandrasekhar PHYSICS, 1983

829. Discovery consists in seeing what everyone else has seen and thinking what no one else has thought.

Albert Szent-Györgyi MEDICINE, 1937

830. I'm convinced that a controlled disrespect for authority is essential to a scientist.

Luis Alvarez PHYSICS, 1968

831. Of course scientists have been told to be socially responsible. Of course, I think society ought to be scientifically responsible as well.

Sydney Brenner MEDICINE, 2002

832. You don't need to be bright to be a scientist, you just need to be persistent as hell.

Dudley Herschbach CHEMISTRY, 1986

833. You might have thought I was a strange kid for the things I did. I buried my hamster after it died, then dug it up a while later to see what it looked like.

Linda Buck MEDICINE, 2004

834. You know, most American scientists are duds; they never have read a sensible book.
Salvador Luria MEDICINE, 1969

835. One could not be a successful scientist without realizing that, in contrast to the popular conception supported by newspapers and mothers of scientists, a goodly number of scientists are not only narrow-minded and dull, but also just stupid.
James Watson MEDICINE, 1962

836. Dr. Crick thanks you for your letter but regrets that he is unable to accept your kind invitation to: send an autograph/help you in your project/provide a photograph/read your manuscript/cure your disease/ deliver a lecture/be interviewed/attend a conference/talk on the radio/act as chairman/appear on TV/become an editor/speak after dinner/write a book/give a testimonial/accept an honorary degree.
Francis Crick MEDICINE, 1962

PHYSICS

837. All science is either physics or stamp collecting.
Ernest Rutherford CHEMISTRY, 1908

838. Physics is like sex. Sure, it may give some practical results, but that's not why we do it.
Richard Feynman PHYSICS, 1965

839. Physics is becoming so unbelievably complex that it is taking longer and longer to train a physicist. It is taking so long, in fact, to train a physicist to the place where he

understands the nature of physical problems that he is
already too old to solve them.

Eugene Wigner PHYSICS, 1963

840. We use the wave theory on Mondays, Wednesdays, and
Fridays and the particle theory on Tuesdays, Thursdays,
and Saturdays.

William Henry Bragg PHYSICS, 1915

841. The more precisely the position is determined, the less
precisely the momentum is known, and vice versa.

Werner Heisenberg PHYSICS, 1932

This is the "Heisenberg Uncertainty Principle" regarding subatomic
particles

842. My ambition is to live to see all of physics reduced to a
formula so elegant and simple that it will fit easily on the
front of a T-shirt.

Leon Lederman PHYSICS, 1988

843. The energy produced by the breaking down of the atom is a
poor kind of thing. Anyone who expects a source of power
from transformation of these atoms is talking moonshine.

Ernest Rutherford CHEMISTRY, 1908

844. At Los Alamos I learned that, by and large, physicists were
extraordinary people. The complete intellectual integrity
required in the pursuit of physics carried over into the
personal relationships of physicists.

Val Fitch PHYSICS, 1980

845. When I was young I thought that physics was easy and
relations with women difficult. Now it is just the other way
around.

Wolfgang Pauli PHYSICS, 1945

846. I was lucky enough to look over the good Lord's shoulder while He was at work.

Werner Heisenberg PHYSICS, 1932

THE UNIVERSE

847. Don't let me catch anyone talking about the Universe in my Department.

Ernest Rutherford CHEMISTRY, 1908

848. We have sought for firm ground and found none. The deeper we penetrate, the more restless becomes the universe, and the vaguer and cloudier.

Max Born PHYSICS, 1954

849. What we have found is evidence for the birth of the universe and its evolution . . . If you're religious, it's like looking at God. The order is so beautiful and the symmetry so beautiful that you think there is some design behind it.

George F. Smoot PHYSICS, 2006

850. What really interests me is whether God had any choice in the creation of the world.

Albert Einstein PHYSICS, 1921

851. For every one billion particles of antimatter there were one billion and one particles of matter. And when the mutual annihilation was complete, one billionth remained—and that's our present universe.

Albert Einstein PHYSICS, 1921

852. The very matter of the universe is transient. We're fortunate enough to live in this period when there is matter.

Sheldon Glashow PHYSICS, 1979

853. There is no rational reason to doubt that the universe has existed indefinitely, for an infinite time. It is only myth that attempts to say how the universe came to be, either four thousand or twenty billion years ago.
Hannes Alfvén PHYSICS, 1970

854. Pick a flower on Earth and you move the farthest star.
Paul Dirac PHYSICS, 1933

855. The effort to understand the universe is one of the very few things that lifts human life a little above the level of farce, and gives it some of the grace of tragedy.
Steven Weinberg PHYSICS, 1979

EVOLUTION

856. A curious aspect of the theory of evolution is that everybody thinks he understands it.
Jacques Monod MEDICINE, 1965

857. The purpose of evolution, believe it or not, is beauty.
Joseph Brodsky LITERATURE, 1987

858. The time with which we have to deal is of the order of two billion years. What we regard as impossible on the basis of human experience is meaningless here. Given so much time, the "impossible" becomes possible, the possible probable, and the probable virtually certain. One has only to wait: time itself performs the miracles.
George Wald MEDICINE, 1967

859. One of the elementary rules of nature is that, in the absence of law prohibiting an event or phenomenon it is bound to occur with some degree of probability. To put it

simply and crudely: Anything that *can* happen *does* happen.

Paul Dirac PHYSICS, 1933

860. Any living cell carries with it the experience of a billion years of experimentation by its ancestors.

Max Delbrück MEDICINE, 1969

861. Evolution consists largely of molecular tinkering— producing new objects from old odds and ends.

François Jacob MEDICINE, 1965

862. We are the products of editing, rather than of authorship.

George Wald MEDICINE, 1967

863. Chance alone is the source of every innovation, of all creation in the biosphere. Pure chance, absolutely free, but blind, is at the very root of the stupendous edifice of evolution.

Jacques Monod MEDICINE, 1965

864. Man appears to be the missing link between anthropoid apes and human beings.

Konrad Lorenz MEDICINE, 1973

865. I do not believe that evolution is a well-established fact, but on the contrary, in my view its concepts are largely speculative.

Ernst Chain MEDICINE, 1945

866. For me, faith begins with the realization that a supreme intelligence brought the universe into being and created man. It is not difficult for me to have this faith, for an orderly, intelligent universe testifies to the greatest statement ever uttered: "In the beginning, God."

Arthur Compton PHYSICS, 1927

867. The best data we have are exactly what I would have predicted had I nothing to go on but the five books of Moses, the Psalms, the Bible as a whole, in that the universe appears to have order and purpose.
Arno Penzias PHYSICS, 1978

868. This world is most consistent with purposeful creation.
Arno Penzias PHYSICS, 1978

GENETICS

869. We've discovered the secret of life.
Francis Crick MEDICINE, 1962
Announced by Crick as he entered the Eagle Pub in Cambridge on February 28, 1953

870. DNA, you know, is Midas' gold. Everybody who touches it goes mad.
Maurice Wilkins MEDICINE, 1962

871. It is time for us to take charge of our own evolution.
James Watson MEDICINE, 1962

872. If you really are stupid, I would call that a disease . . . People say it would be terrible if we made all girls pretty. I think it would be great.
James Watson MEDICINE, 1962

873. Some day a child is going to sue its parents for being born. They will say, my life is so awful with these terrible genetic defects and you just callously didn't find out.
James Watson MEDICINE, 1962

874. The controlled injection of the gene for human growth hormone into fertilized human ova could easily lead, in

twenty years, to a Minnesota football team made up
entirely of nine-foot players.
Christian Anfinsen CHEMISTRY, 1972

875. It is just a matter of time until we will be able to clone
human beings. Then, over the long run, it will no longer
be possible to outlaw it.
Eric Wieschaus MEDICINE, 1995

876. Actually we do quite a lot of cloning of persons already.
We do it in institutions called armies, schools; we try to
make everybody a standard issue.
Sydney Brenner MEDICINE, 2002

877. I was asked at a lecture by someone in the audience who
said, why can't I clone myself and keep the copies as spare
parts? And my answer was, be careful, one of the copies
might keep you for spare parts.
Sydney Brenner MEDICINE, 2002

THE ENVIRONMENT

878. The lot of both man and nature could improve if there
were fewer people and more wild animals.
Murray Gell-Mann PHYSICS, 1969

879. The world could get along very well without literature;
it could get along even better without man.
Jean-Paul Sartre LITERATURE, 1964

880. Astronomers say we have another two billion years before
Earth is too hot to live on. If we could begin to engage this
question, we might be guided to a suitable stewardship for
our planet, and it might look a little different from the
plans that are being made today.
John C. Mather PHYSICS, 2006

881. Let there be no doubt about the conclusions of the scientific community: the threat of global warming is very real and action is needed immediately. It is a grave error to believe that we can continue to procrastinate. Scientists do not believe this and no one else should either.

Henry Kendall PHYSICS, 1990

882. Whatever happens, it is clear that the immense, stupid, and suicidal waste of natural resources must come to an immediate end if the human species wishes to survive on this earth.

Octavio Paz LITERATURE, 1990

883. There are many injustices in the world, but there is one of which no one speaks, which is that of climate.

Albert Camus LITERATURE, 1957

884. The urban man is an uprooted tree, he can put out leaves, flowers and grow fruit but what a nostalgia his leaf, flower, and fruit will always have for mother earth!

Juan Ramón Jiménez LITERATURE, 1956

885. The growth of an impersonal concrete jungle directly leads to the psychosis, neuroses, maniacal and freakish behavior evident in the major cities of the so-called developed world.

Wangari Maathai PEACE, 2004

MATHEMATICS

886. God used beautiful mathematics in creating the world.

Paul Dirac PHYSICS, 1933

887. Mathematics is just a tool to guide our intuition.

Arno Penzias PHYSICS, 1978

888. As far as the laws of mathematics refer to reality they are not certain; and as far as they are certain, they do not refer to reality.
Albert Einstein PHYSICS, 1921

889. The physicists defer only to the mathematicians, and the mathematicians defer only to God (though you may be hard pressed to find a mathematician that modest).
Leon Lederman PHYSICS, 1988

890. I have many students in my core course at Harvard who are so afraid of anything to do with mathematics or even just numbers that it's like an allergy. You think dyslexia is a problem? The hidden disease of being unable to deal with numbers is both more prevalent and much more serious.
Sheldon Glashow PHYSICS, 1979

891. The official photographer informed me that I was the 137th Nobel laureate of whom he has had to make a portrait. Certainly all of you know that 137 is a magic, quasi-mystical number in physics. It is equal to the velocity of light times the reduced Planck constant divided by the square of the electron charge! This number governs the size of all objects in the Universe. Some people claim that if this value were to be slightly different life would not be possible.
Georges Charpak PHYSICS, 1992

TECHNOLOGY

892. All our lauded technological progress—our very civilization—is like the axe in the hand of the pathological criminal.
Albert Einstein PHYSICS, 1921

893. Our society is permeated not by science, but by an exploitative distortion of science-based technology, as irrational as the irrational aspects of religion.
Salvador Luria MEDICINE, 1969

894. For a successful technology, reality must take precedence over public relations, for nature cannot be fooled.
Richard Feynman PHYSICS, 1965

895. All the information that man has carefully accumulated in all the books in the world can be written . . . in a cube of material one two-hundredth of an inch wide—which is the barest piece of dust that can be made out by the human eye.
Richard Feynman PHYSICS, 1965

896. Today, we are already working on tiny minicomputers with completely new kinds of chips . . . With these, we might be able to construct devices that work even faster than the fastest computers of today but that are nevertheless so small that we can build them directly into our bodies or our brains.
Gerd Binnig PHYSICS, 1986

897. It is time the American people were told frankly that the present space program is technically impressive, scientifically trivial, culturally misguided, and socially preposterous.
Salvador Luria MEDICINE, 1969

898. The automobile is a peculiarly fertile species that reproduces freely and appears to have no natural enemies sufficiently powerful to hold its growth in check.
Glenn Seaborg CHEMISTRY, 1951

899. You can see the computer age everywhere but in the productivity statistics.
Robert Solow ECONOMICS, 1987

Medicine and Health

The history of the Nobel Prize for Medicine is the history of medical progress since 1900. Before Frederick Banting's work on insulin, diabetics were condemned to slow death. Before antibiotics, doctors could provide only symptomatic treatment for most disease. The work of Edward Thomas on bone marrow transplantation raised leukemia survival rates from zero to 50 percent. That of Peter Medawar, Baruj Benacerraf, Jean Dausset, and Joseph Murray on organ transplants gave new life to innumerable kidney and heart patients.

Two examples may serve to illustrate the quality of commitment that Alfred Nobel sought to honor in his institution of the Nobel prizes. In 1929, Werner Forssmann, then a twenty-five-year-old surgical resident, inserted a cannula into a vein in his arm, advanced a catheter 65 cm until he felt it enter the right ventricle of his heart, walked down to the X-ray room, and had an X-ray taken. This was the first heart catheterization, and when his supervisor learned of it, Forssmann was fired. He had to wait until after World War II, during which he spent harrowing years as a surgeon major in the Wehrmacht, before his discovery was honored with the Nobel Prize.

More recent is the example of Barry Marshall, who won the

prize for Medicine in 2005. Convinced that stomach ulcers were caused by the bacterium *Helicobacter pylori,* he mixed up a growth of some billion bacteria in a petri dish and, to the horror of his lab assistant, swallowed it. His subsequent discomfort, illness, endoscopy, antibiotic treatment, and recovery confirmed his hypothesis.

MEDICINE

900. Advances in medicine and the possibilities of human happiness created by the relief of suffering are a great embarrassment to those determined to think nothing but evil of science and technology.
> *Peter Medawar* MEDICINE, 1960

901. The average patient looks upon the average doctor very much as the non-combatant looks upon the troops fighting on his behalf. The more trained men there are between his body and the enemy the better.
> *Rudyard Kipling* LITERATURE, 1907

902. A good gulp of hot whisky at bedtime—it's not very scientific, but it helps.
> *Alexander Fleming* MEDICINE, 1945
On treatment of the common cold

903. There are people in the world, I think they're probably a minority but they're certainly a substantial minority, who believe that basically health is something you buy. If you have money you can buy health, if you have more money, you can buy greater health. I'm one of the other people who say that health, at least at the most basic level, never mind the trimmings, is something that should be a universal right to everybody. I think it's important for the progress of humanity and indeed all sorts of other things,

the peace of the world and so forth, is underpinned by health care. Now as soon as you take that view, then you have to say and I do, that anything that blocks that cheapest possible point-of-care delivery of health is wrong and we have to find some way not to allow that.

John Sulston MEDICINE, 2002

904. My advice to anybody wanting to be a physician is to love people and like taking care of them.

Joseph Murray MEDICINE, 1990

905. We're losing time now because we're not spending enough money to do research. As a consequence of not acting, we are sentencing people to death when we could help them be treated with new drugs.

Craig C. Mello MEDICINE, 2006

906. Sometimes the best way to predict the doctor's diagnosis is to find out what has just been published in the *Journal of the American Medical Association*.

Herbert Simon ECONOMICS, 1978

907. The microbe that felled one child in a distant continent yesterday can reach yours today and seed a global pandemic tomorrow.

Joshua Lederberg MEDICINE, 1958

FOOD AND HUNGER

908. Hunger makes a thief of any man.

Pearl S. Buck LITERATURE, 1938

909. The first essential component of social justice is adequate food.

Norman Borlaug PEACE, 1970

910. You can't build peace on empty stomachs.
John Boyd Orr PEACE, 1949

911. The science of nutrition is a shambles.
Arthur Kornberg MEDICINE, 1959

912. One thing I can guarantee: you'll get into trouble if you always eat nothing but French fries.
Richard Roberts MEDICINE, 1993

913. Some people eat too much; some people eat too little. Nothing else about diet really matters.
Kary Mullis CHEMISTRY, 1993

914. Yes, I am a vegetarian. I find the thought of stuffing fragments of corpses down my throat quite repulsive, and I am amazed that so many people do it every day.
J. M. Coetzee LITERATURE, 2003

915. I did not become a vegetarian for my health, I did it for the health of the chickens.
Isaac Bashevis Singer LITERATURE, 1978

916. Almost all the food faddists I have ever known, nut-eaters and the like, have died young after a long period of senile decay.
Winston Churchill LITERATURE, 1953

DRINK AND DRUGS

917. A man shouldn't fool with booze until he's fifty; then he's a damn fool if he doesn't.
William Faulkner LITERATURE, 1949

918. Well, between Scotch and nothing, I suppose I'd take Scotch. It's the nearest thing to good moonshine I can find.
William Faulkner LITERATURE, 1949

919. When I was a young subaltern in the South African War, the water was not fit to drink. To make it palatable, we had to add whisky. By diligent effort, I learned to like it.
Winston Churchill LITERATURE, 1953

920. When I was younger I made it a rule never to take a strong drink before lunch. It is now my rule never to do so before breakfast.
Winston Churchill LITERATURE, 1953

921. A man takes to drink, a drink takes another, and the drink takes the man.
Sinclair Lewis LITERATURE, 1930

922. The case for prohibiting drugs is exactly as strong and as weak as the case for prohibiting people from overeating. We all know that overeating causes more deaths than drugs do.
Milton Friedman ECONOMICS, 1976

923. If you look at the drug war from a purely economic point of view, the role of the government is to protect the drug cartel.
Milton Friedman ECONOMICS, 1976

924. I have estimated statistically that the prohibition of drugs produces, on the average, ten thousand homicides a year. It's a moral problem that the government is going around killing ten thousand people.
Milton Friedman ECONOMICS, 1976

925. If you want to lead a miserable life, all you need to do is start smoking cigarettes.
Linus Pauling CHEMISTRY, 1954; PEACE, 1962

War and Peace

The two world wars of the twentieth century left their mark on a large number of the men and women who have won the Nobel Prize.

Considerable numbers of Nobel Prize winners served in the armed forces of the combatant nations in one or both world wars. Anecdotes of their experiences are legion. James Franck, who won the Iron Cross twice in World War I, was famous for ordering his troops, "Come to attention—please!" James Chadwick was a graduate student in Berlin when war broke out in 1914, and passed the four years of war incarcerated in a horse stable. Louis-Victor de Broglie, a French prince, spent the First World War as a radio operator stationed in the Eiffel Tower. Heinrich Böll served on the Eastern Front and was wounded four times. Willy Brandt made daring covert missions from Norway into Germany during World War II. Val Fitch's undergraduate career was interrupted by military service in World War II. He was posted to Los Alamos, where his admiration for the physicists who worked there took him into a career in physics and to the Nobel Prize in 1980. Alexandr Solzhenitsyn's service as a Soviet artillery officer in World War II was cut short when he made a derogatory comment about Stalin in a letter to a friend, for which he served eight years in the Gulag.

The moral ambiguities generated by war are well illustrated by the large number of Nobel laureates who worked in both wars on the invention and improvement of weapons. The history of the development of the atomic bomb at Los Alamos and elsewhere reads like a roll call of Nobel laureates, including Niels Bohr, James Franck, Arthur Compton, Enrico Fermi, Ernest Lawrence, Richard Feynman, and Hans Bethe. Werner Heisenberg headed the German atom bomb project, and Andrei Sakharov led the hydrogen bomb project in the USSR. Other Nobel Prize winners directly affected by the atomic bomb were Luis Alvarez, who as an official observer witnessed the Hiroshima explosion from a U.S. bomber; Joseph Rotblat, who left the project after the defeat of Germany and founded the Pugwash disarmament conferences; and all the Japanese laureates, for whom Hiroshima and Nagasaki were highly traumatic events. Other laureates helped to develop radar. Fritz Haber pioneered the use of poison gas. The rationale seems to have been the same in all these cases of weapons development: to hasten the end of the war.

While some laureates developed weapons of war, others were its victims. Who knows how many future Nobel laureates perished in Nazi concentration camps? A few survived. Georges Charpak and Léon Jouhaux were imprisoned for their activities in the French Resistance. As a child, Roald Hoffmann was smuggled out of a Nazi labor camp by his father, who later died in a breakout attempt. Elie Wiesel was sixteen when he arrived in Auschwitz, where he lost both parents; he was liberated from Buchenwald ten months later. The Hungarian Literature laureate Imre Kertész also survived these two camps.

War, the greatest of human evils, generates notoriety for its protagonists, but those who prevent wars from occurring frequently remain anonymous. History is blind to catastrophes that do not occur, and hence to many peacemakers. But every December, the award of the Peace Prize in Oslo makes that city the focus of human hopes for a more peaceful world.

Few people would have heard of the struggle for human rights in Burma but for the recognition of Aung San Suu Kyi in 1991, or of that in East Timor without the award of the Peace Prize to Carlos Belo and José Ramos-Horta in 1996. Although the Peace Prize has been awarded to two generals, George C. Marshall and Yitzhak Rabin, and to Theodore Roosevelt, the most bellicose of all American presidents, nominees tend to be disqualified if they have advocated violence. Mahatma Gandhi, who had been previously nominated several times, was a front-runner for the prize in 1947, when the Nobel Committee received word that, in the midst of Hindu-Muslim conflict in India, he had renounced his previous opposition to war. This report was later shown to be incorrect, but as a consequence, the 1947 prize went to the Society of Friends, and by the following year Gandhi had been assassinated.

Five Nobel Peace laureates died as martyrs: Carl von Ossietzky perished as a result of brutal treatment in Nazi concentration camps. Dag Hammarskjöld was killed in a plane crash while on a peace mission in the Congo. Martin Luther King, Anwar al-Sadat, and Yitzhak Rabin were all assassinated.

WAR AND CONFLICT

926. If the dead could speak, there would be no more war.
      Heinrich Böll LITERATURE, 1972

927. War may sometimes be a necessary evil. But no matter how necessary, it is always an evil, never a good. We will not learn how to live together in peace by killing each other's children.
      Jimmy Carter PEACE, 2002

928. War almost invariably brings instant popularity to the President.
      Jimmy Carter PEACE, 2002

929. The force which makes for war does not derive its strength from the interested motives of evil men; it

derives its strength from the disinterested motives of good men . . . The world which goes to war is a world usually, genuinely desiring peace. War is the outcome, not mainly of evil intentions, but on the whole, of good intentions which miscarry or are frustrated. It is made, not usually by evil men knowing themselves to be wrong, but is the outcome of policies pursued by good men usually passionately convinced that they are right.

Norman Angell PEACE, 1933

930. The world has had ample evidence that war begets only conditions that beget further war.

Ralph Bunche PEACE, 1950

931. Never, never, never believe any war will be smooth and easy, or that anyone who embarks on the strange voyage can measure the tides and hurricanes he will encounter. The statesman who yields to war ever must realise that once the signal is given, he is no longer the master of policy but the slave of unforeseeable and uncontrollable events.

Winston Churchill LITERATURE, 1953

932. I know war as it is, not through reading about it . . . Supporters of peace have a duty and a task. It is to point out, over and over again, there is nothing heroic in war but that it brings terror and misery to mankind.

Carl von Ossietzky PEACE, 1935

933. Military cemeteries in every corner of the world are silent testimony to the failure of national leaders to sanctify human life.

Yitzhak Rabin PEACE, 1994

934. I find war detestable but even more detestable are those
who praise war without participating in it.
Romain Rolland LITERATURE, 1915

935. When the rich make war, it's the poor who die.
Jean-Paul Sartre LITERATURE, 1964

936. Never think that war, no matter how necessary, nor how
justified, is not a crime. Ask the infantry and the dead.
Ernest Hemingway LITERATURE, 1954

937. It is impossible to defend ourselves unless on occasion we
are prepared to defend others.
Norman Angell PEACE, 1933

938. A sword is needed to conquer a sword.
Albert Camus LITERATURE, 1957

939. Aggression unopposed becomes a contagious disease.
Jimmy Carter PEACE, 2002

940. Moral of the Work. In war: resolution. In defeat: defiance.
In victory: magnanimity. In peace: goodwill.
Winston Churchill LITERATURE, 1953

941. I have always urged fighting wars and other contentions
with might and main till overwhelming victory, and then
offering the hand of friendship to the vanquished. Thus I
have always been against the Pacifists during the quarrel,
and against the Jingoes at its close.
Winston Churchill LITERATURE, 1953

942. We have before us an ordeal of the most grievous kind.
We have before us many, many long months of struggle
and of suffering. You ask, what is our policy? I can say: It

is to wage war, by sea, land and air, with all our might and with all the strength that God can give us; to wage war against a monstrous tyranny, never surpassed in the dark, lamentable catalogue of human crime. That is our policy. You ask, what is our aim? I can answer in one word: It is victory, victory at all costs, victory in spite of all terror, victory, however long and hard the road may be; for without victory, there is no survival.

Winston Churchill LITERATURE, 1953

943. This was a time when it was equally good to live or die.

Winston Churchill LITERATURE, 1953

944. We shall not flag or fail. We shall go on to the end. We shall fight in France, we shall fight on the seas and oceans, we shall fight with growing confidence and growing strength in the air, we shall defend our island, whatever the cost may be. We shall fight on the beaches, we shall fight on the landing grounds, we shall fight in the fields and in the streets, we shall fight in the hills; we shall never surrender.

Winston Churchill LITERATURE, 1953

945. You may have to fight when there is no hope of victory because it is better to perish than to live as slaves.

Winston Churchill LITERATURE, 1953

946. I shall never forget the afternoon of that Christmas Eve. At first there were only a few among us and the English who looked over the parapet of the trenches, which were about fifty metres apart. Then there were more and more, and before long all the soldiers came out of the trenches. We fraternized. The English gave us their good cigarettes, and those among us who had candied fruit gave them some.

We sang songs together, and for the night of 24/25
December the war stopped.

Otto Hahn CHEMISTRY, 1944

Of the 1914 Christmas Truce

947. Don't hit at all if you can help it; don't hit a man if you can
possibly avoid it; but if you do hit him, put him to sleep.

Theodore Roosevelt PEACE, 1906

ARMIES AND ARMAMENTS

948. Of all its inventions, there is none which the human race
has gone to greater lengths to perfect than its means of
mass destruction of its fellow men.

Henri Dunant PEACE, 1901

949. The distinction between offensive and defensive arms
was a very simple one. If you were in front of them, they
were offensive; if you were behind them, they were
defensive.

Lester Pearson PEACE, 1957

950. If sunbeams were weapons of war, we would have had
solar energy centuries ago.

George Porter CHEMISTRY, 1967

951. Peaceful conditions in the world are not welcome to the
arms industry.

Seán MacBride PEACE, 1974

952. No civilization has ever willingly given up its most
powerful weapons.

Mohamed ElBaradei PEACE, 2005

953. The conventional army loses if it does not win. The guerrilla wins if he does not lose.

Henry Kissinger PEACE, 1973

954. The spiritual life of the soldier is more important than his physical equipment.

George C. Marshall PEACE, 1953

NUCLEAR WEAPONS

955. Some recent work by E. Fermi and L. Szilard, which has been communicated to me in manuscript, leads me to expect that the element uranium may be turned into a new and important source of energy in the immediate future. Certain aspects of the situation which has arisen seem to call for watchfulness and if necessary, quick action on the part of the Administration . . . This new phenomenon would also lead to the construction of bombs.

Albert Einstein PHYSICS, 1921

Extract from a letter to President Frankin D. Roosevelt, August 2, 1939. The letter was composed by Leo Szilard and signed by Einstein.

956. I made one mistake in my life—when I signed that letter to President Roosevelt advocating that atom bombs should be built. But perhaps I can be forgiven for that because we all felt that there was a high probability that the Germans were working on this problem and they might have success and use the atomic bomb to become the master race.

Albert Einstein PHYSICS, 1921

957. What was gunpowder? Trivial. What was electricity? Meaningless. This atomic bomb is the Second Coming in Wrath.

Winston Churchill LITERATURE, 1953

958. Our generation has succeeded in stealing the fire of the gods, and it is doomed to live with the horror of its achievement.

Henry Kissinger PEACE, 1973

959. I thank God on bended knees that we did not make the uranium bomb.

Otto Hahn CHEMISTRY, 1944

Remark on learning of the Hiroshima bomb, August 6, 1945, while in British custody with other German physicists

960. It seems to me that the scientists who led the way to the atomic bomb were extremely skilful and ingenious, but not wise men. They delivered the fruits of their discoveries unconditionally into the hands of politicians and soldiers; thus they lost their moral innocence and their intellectual freedom.

Max Born PHYSICS, 1954

961. I remember the spring of 1941 to this day. I realized then that a nuclear bomb was not only possible—it was inevitable . . . I did realize how very, very serious it could be. And I had then to start taking sleeping pills. It was the only remedy. I've never stopped since then.

James Chadwick PHYSICS, 1935

962. We may conclude that the dropping of the atomic bombs was not so much the last military act of the Second World War as the first major operation of the cold diplomatic war with Russia now in progress.

Patrick Blackett PHYSICS, 1948

963. From the moment that I was elected General Secretary of the Communist Party of the Soviet Union and thereby head of the Soviet Nation, the most important question

for me was this: What could be done to put an end to the nuclear arms race?

Mikhail Gorbachev PEACE, 1990

THE HOLOCAUST

964. Never shall I forget that night, the first night in camp, which has turned my life into one long night, seven times cursed and seven times sealed. Never shall I forget that smoke. Never shall I forget the little faces of the children, whose bodies I saw turned into wreaths of smoke beneath a silent blue sky. Never shall I forget those flames which consumed my faith forever. Never shall I forget that nocturnal silence which deprived me, for all eternity, of the desire to live. Never shall I forget those moments which murdered my God and my soul and turned my dreams to dust. Never shall I forget these things, even if I am condemned to live as long as God Himself. Never.

Elie Wiesel PEACE, 1986

965. I remember: it happened yesterday, or eternities ago. A young Jewish boy discovered the Kingdom of Night. I remember his bewilderment, I remember his anguish. It all happened so fast. The ghetto. The deportation. The sealed cattle car. The fiery altar upon which the history of our people and the future of mankind were meant to be sacrificed.

Elie Wiesel PEACE, 1986

966. It seemed as impossible to conceive of Auschwitz with God as to conceive of Auschwitz without God.

Elie Wiesel PEACE, 1986

967. Scientific abstraction, social and economic contention, nationalism, xenophobia, religious fanaticism, racism, mass hysteria. All found their ultimate expression in Auschwitz.
Elie Wiesel PEACE, 1986

968. Auschwitz must have been hanging in the air for a long, long time, centuries, perhaps like a dark fruit slowly ripening in the sparkling rays of innumerable ignominious deeds, waiting to finally drop on one's head.
Imre Kertész LITERATURE, 2002

969. Which writer today is not a writer of the Holocaust?
Imre Kertész LITERATURE, 2002

970. The Holocaust is a value because it has led to immeasurable knowledge through immeasurable suffering, thus creating an immeasurable moral resource.
Imre Kertész LITERATURE, 2002

971. What I discovered in Auschwitz is the human condition, the end point of a great adventure, where the European traveler arrived after his two-thousand-year-old moral and cultural history.
Imre Kertész LITERATURE, 2002

972. I experienced my most radical moments of happiness in the concentration camp. You cannot imagine what it's like to be allowed to lie in the camp's hospital, or to have a 10-minute break from indescribable labor. To be very close to death is also a kind of happiness. Just surviving becomes the greatest freedom of all.
Imre Kertész LITERATURE, 2002

973. I have endeavoured—perhaps it is not sheer self-deception—to perform the existential labour that being an

Auschwitz-survivor has thrust upon me as a kind of obligation. I realize what a privilege has been bestowed on me. I have seen the true visage of this dreadful century, I have gazed into the eye of the Gorgon, and have been able to keep on living. Yet, I knew I would never be able to free myself from the sight; I knew this visage would always hold me captive. And if you now ask me what still keeps me here on this earth, what keeps me alive, then, I would answer without any hesitation: love.

Imre Kertész LITERATURE, 2002

974. If I could not have written, I could not have survived. Death was my teacher.

Nelly Sachs LITERATURE, 1966

975. Jews were required to wear the Star of David and to obey a 6 p.m. curfew. I had gone to play with a Christian friend and had stayed too late. I turned my brown sweater inside out to walk the few blocks home. As I was walking down an empty street, I saw a German soldier approaching. He was wearing the black uniform that I had been told to fear more than others—the one worn by specially recruited SS soldiers. As I came closer to him, trying to walk fast, I noticed that he was looking at me intently. Then he beckoned me over, picked me up, and hugged me. I was terrified that he would notice the star inside my sweater. He was speaking to me with great emotion, in German. When he put me down, he opened his wallet, showed me a picture of a boy, and gave me some money. I went home more certain than ever that my mother was right: people were endlessly complicated and interesting.

Daniel Kahneman ECONOMICS, 2002

PEACE AND PEACEMAKING

976. No more war. No more bloodshed. No more tears. Peace
   unto you. Shalom, salaam, for ever.
   Menachem Begin PEACE, 1978
   At the signing of the peace treaty with Egypt, 1979

977. Today I have come bearing an olive branch and a freedom
   fighter's gun. Do not let the olive branch fall from my hand.
   I repeat: do not let the olive branch fall from my hand.
   Yasser Arafat PEACE, 1994
   Conclusion of speech to the UN, November 13, 1974

978. The time for the healing of the wounds has come. The
   moment to bridge the chasms that divide us has come.
   The time to build is upon us.
   Nelson Mandela PEACE, 1993
   Inaugural Address as President of South Africa, May 10, 1994

979. We, the soldiers who have returned from battles stained
   with blood; we who have seen our relatives and friends
   killed before our eyes; we who have attended their
   funerals and cannot look in the eyes of their parents; we
   who have come from a land where parents bury their
   children; we who have fought against you, the
   Palestinians—we say to you today, in a loud and a clear
   voice: enough of blood and tears. Enough.
   Yitzhak Rabin PEACE, 1994
   Speech at the White House, September 13, 1993, after signing the
   peace agreement

980. We must learn to live together as brothers, or we shall
   perish together as fools.
   Martin Luther King PEACE, 1964

981. We prepare for war like precocious giants and for peace like retarded pygmies.
Lester Pearson PEACE, 1957

982. What we need is Star Peace and not Star Wars.
Mikhail Gorbachev PEACE, 1990

983. If you desire peace, cultivate justice, but at the same time cultivate the fields to produce more bread; otherwise, there will be no peace.
Norman Borlaug PEACE, 1970

984. The struggle for peace and the struggle for human rights are inseparable.
Willy Brandt PEACE, 1971

985. You don't make peace with your friends. You make it with very unsavory enemies.
Yitzhak Rabin PEACE, 1994

986. If man does find the solution for world peace, it will be the most revolutionary reversal of his record we have ever known.
George C. Marshall PEACE, 1953

987. Those who can win a war well can rarely make a good peace, and those who could make a good peace would never have won the war.
Winston Churchill LITERATURE, 1953

988. The desire for peace is the mark of all civilized men and women.
Henry Kissinger PEACE, 1973

989. If history teaches anything it is that there can be no peace without equilibrium and no justice without restraint.
Henry Kissinger PEACE, 1973

990. Whenever peace—conceived as the avoidance of war—has been the primary objective of a power or a group of powers, the international system has been at the mercy of the most ruthless member.
Henry Kissinger PEACE, 1973

991. All works of love are works of peace.
Mother Teresa PEACE, 1979

992. People who are offering revenge, they are just an enemy. But when you offer peace and love that infuriates people. And you get killed for that. That's why Christ is killed, that's why King is shot, that's why Gandhi is killed.
Derek Walcott LITERATURE, 1992

993. My country is a country of teachers. It is therefore a country of peace. We discuss our successes and failures in complete freedom. Because our country is a country of teachers, we closed the army camps and our children go with books under their arms, not with rifles on their shoulders. We believe in dialogue, in agreement, in reaching a consensus. We reject violence. Because my country is a country of teachers, we believe in convincing our opponents, not defeating them. We prefer raising the fallen to crushing them, because we believe that no one possesses the absolute truth. Because mine is a country of teachers, we seek an economy in which men cooperate in a spirit of solidarity, not an economy in which they compete to their own extinction.
Oscar Arias Sánchez PEACE, 1987

Last Words

"Let us now praise famous men," wrote Yeshua Ben Sira in Ecclesiasticus two thousand years ago, in words that might be applied to the men and women who have been awarded the Nobel Prize: "men of mercy, whose righteous deeds have not been forgotten . . . their glory will not be blotted out . . . and their name lives to all generations." The final words of a few may stand for the many laureates who took leave of life with the same grace as they had lived it, and who by their lives and work left the world a better place.

994. Never was there a time in my life when I had so much
to live for—and so much to die for.
Frederick Banting MEDICINE, 1923
Diary entry, January 31, 1941, three weeks before his death.

995. It has been a good journey—well-worth making once.
Winston Churchill LITERATURE, 1953
January 1965, possibly his last recorded utterance

996. I want to go when *I* want. It is tasteless to prolong life
artificially. I have done my share; it is time to go. I will
do it elegantly.
Albert Einstein PHYSICS, 1921
Just before his death

997. I don't know what will happen now. We've got some
difficult days ahead. But it really doesn't matter with me
now, because I've been to the mountaintop. And I don't
mind. Like anybody, I would like to live a long life;
longevity has its place. But I'm not concerned about that
now. I just want to do God's will. And He's allowed me to
go up to the mountain. And I've looked over. And I've
seen—the Promised Land.
Martin Luther King PEACE, 1964
Speech in Memphis, Tennessee, April 3, 1968, the evening before
his death

998. I am seeking to understand.
Jacques Monod MEDICINE, 1965
Last words (*Je cherche à comprendre*)

999. My God, let me grow old and die in my homeland!
Giorgos Seferis LITERATURE, 1963
Last entry in *A Poet's Journal*

1000. It seems to me that I have found what I wanted. When I try to put all into a phrase, I say, "Man can embody truth, but he cannot know it."

William Butler Yeats LITERATURE, 1923

REFERENCES

In the following references the term attributed *is used where the quotation has been ascribed to the laureate by one or more sources, but an authoritative bibliographic reference has not been determined.*

PREFACE

1. Attributed
2. Morley Callaghan, *That Summer in Paris*, 1963
3. Albert Parry, ed., *Peter Kapitsa on Life and Science*, 1968
4. Max Jammer, *Einstein and Religion: Physics and Theology*, 1999

THE QUOTATIONS

1. *Listener*, December 14, 1939
2. Samuel Beckett, *Worstward Ho*, 1983
3. Interview, *Paris Review*, no. 12, Spring 1956
4. Ernest Hemingway, *The Old Man and the Sea*, 1952
5. Boris Pasternak, *Dr. Zhivago*, 1957
6. Attributed
7. Lewis Wolpert and Alison Richards, *Passionate Minds: The Inner World of Scientists*, 1997
8. *New York Times*, March 12, 1944
9. Interview, Lasker Foundation, 1999
10. *Oxford Today*, vol. 14, no. 1, 1991
11. Olga S. Opfell, *The Lady Laureates*, 1986
12. Lloyd Stevenson, *Sir Frederick Banting*, 1946
13. Speech at Harrow School, October 29, 1941, in Robert Rhodes James, ed., *Winston S. Churchill: His Complete Speeches, 1897-1963*, vol. 6, 1974
14. Notebook entry, June 18, 1938, in John Steinbeck, *Working Days*, 1989
15. Letter to his son Hans Albert, January 4, 1937, quoted in Alice Calaprice, ed., *The Quotable Einstein*, 1996
16. Anwar al-Sadat, *In Search of Identity*, 1977
17. W. Sterling Edwards and Peter D. Edwards, *Alexis Carrel: Visionary Surgeon*, 1974
18. Winston Churchill, *Painting as a Pastime*, 1965
19. www.science.utah.edu/cronin.html

20. Nobel lecture, December 10, 1969

21. Labor Day speech in Syracuse, New York, September 7, 1902

22. Interview at meeting of Nobel Prize winners in Lindau, Germany, 2000

23. Riccardo Giacconi, *Johns Hopkins Magazine*, February 2003

24. Sign in Alan MacDiarmid's study, quoted in his Nobel autobiography, 2000

25. Glenn Seaborg, *Adventures in the Atomic Age: From Watts to Washington*, 2001

26. Bertrand Russell, *In Praise of Idleness and Other Essays*, 1932

27. Nobel lecture, December 7, 1996

28. Franco Modigliani, *Adventures of an Economist*, 2001

29. Interview, *Paris Review*, no. 83, 1983

30. William Butler Yeats, *The Choice*, 1933

31. Quoted in Glenn Seaborg, *A Scientist Speaks Out: A Personal Perspective on Science, Society and Change*, 1996

32. Andrew Szanton, *The Recollections of Eugene P. Wigner*, 1992

33. *Newsweek*, October 16, 1978

34. Kary Mullis, *Dancing Naked in the Mind Field*, 1998

35. *Dome*, Johns Hopkins University, November 2003

36. Letter to Sandra Chester, 1965, in Michelle Feynman, ed., *Perfectly Reasonable Deviations: The Letters of Richard P. Feynman*, 2005

37. Teenink.com, June 2003

38. *Boston Globe*, April 25, 1993

39. *Baltimore Sun*, December 10, 2003

40. Nobel acceptance speech, December 10, 1986

41. *Princeton Weekly Bulletin*, March 3, 1997

42. Irwin Abrams, *Reflections on the First Century of the Nobel Peace Prize*, 2000

43. Lecture at the Hoover Institute, January 29, 1977

44. István Hargittai, *Candid Science II: Conversations with Famous Biomedical Scientists*, 2002

45. *Scientist*, April 21, 2003

46. *Harvard Guide*, http://www.news.harvard.edu/guide/faculty/fac8.html

47. Richard Lingeman, *Sinclair Lewis: Rebel from Main Street*, 2002

48. Attributed

49. *Napa Register*, March 25, 2001

50. Christopher Sykes, ed., *No Ordinary Genius: The Illustrated Richard Feynman*, 1994

51. Nofestibel.com interview

52. Response to telegram of congratulations from Caltech students, October 1958

53. Quoted in Gary Taubes, *Nobel Dreams: Power, Deceit, and the Ultimate Experiment*, 1986

54. Nobel acceptance speech, December 10, 1950

55. François Jacob, *Of Flies, Mice, and Men*, 1997

56. *Boston Globe*, October 21, 1995

57. *Life*, January 20, 1962

58. Max Born, *Natural Philosophy of Cause and Chance*, 1951

59. Luis Alvarez, *Adventures of a Physicist*, 1987

60. William Golding, *Fire Down Below*, 1989

61. Francis Crick, *Life Itself: Its Origin and Nature*, 1981

62. G. Gamow, *Thirty Years That Shook Physics*, 1966

63. Pearl S. Buck, *I Believe*, 1939

64. Elie Wiesel, *Ani Maamin* (cantata), 1973

65. François Jacob, *The Statue Within*, 1988

66. Albert Camus, *Resistance, Rebellion, and Death*, 1961

67. Letter, 1962, quoted in Bernard Zeller, *Portrait of Hesse: An Illustrated Biography*, 1971

68. Denis Brian, *The Voice of Genius: Conversations with Nobel Scientists and Other Laureates*, 2001
69. Sign in Einstein's office at Princeton University
70. *New York Times Magazine*, January 29, 1995
71. Jacques Monod, *Chance and Necessity*, 1971
72. Alexandr Solzhenitsyn, *The First Circle*, 1968
73. Nadine Gordimer, *The Essential Gesture: Writing, Politics, and Places*, 1988
74. Horace Engdahl, ed., *Witness Literature: Proceedings of the Nobel Centennial Symposium*, 2002
75. André Gide, *Journal, 1889-1939*, 1939
76. Romain Rolland, *Above the Battle*, 1915
77. István Hargittai, *Candid Science III: More Conversations with Famous Chemists*, 2003
78. Anatole France, *The Gods Are Thirsty*, 1912
79. Max Born, *My Life: Recollections of a Nobel Laureate*, 1975
80. Antony Jay, ed., *The Oxford Dictionary of Political Quotations*, 2001
81. Werner Heisenberg, *Physics and Beyond: Encounters and Conversations*, 1971
82. Juan Ramón Jiménez, *The Complete Perfectionist: A Poetics of Work*, 1997
83. Saul Bellow, *Herzog*, 1965
84. T. S. Eliot, *Four Quartets*, 1935
85. Nobel lecture, December 7, 1991
86. Nobel lecture, December 8, 1980
87. Robert Laughlin, *A Different Universe*, 2005
88. Letter to the Russian Orthodox bishops, 1974
89. Albert Camus, *The Outsider*, 1942
90. V. S. Naipaul, *In a Free State*, 1971
91. *Department of State Bulletin*, vol. 5, no. 129, December 13, 1941
92. Czeslaw Milosz, *The Captive Mind*, 1951
93. C. P. Snow, *Variety of Men*, 1967
94. Quoted in *Alumni Magazine*, University of Toronto, Winter 1986
95. Attributed
96. Bertrand Russell, *A History of Western Philosophy*, 1946
97. Denis Brian, *The Voice of Genius: Conversations with Nobel Scientists and Other Laureates*, 2001
98. John Steinbeck, *Travels with Charley in Search of America*, 1962
99. Robert Jungk, *Brighter than a Thousand Suns*, 1970
100. *Scientist*, August 8, 1988
101. Nobel lecture, December 8, 2003
102. Attributed
103. Quoted by President George H. W. Bush in a speech in Baltimore, Maryland, May 13, 1992
104. Attributed
105. Nobel lecture, December 11, 1950
106. Nobel lecture, April 7, 1948
107. Nobel lecture, December 19, 1922
108. Albert Einstein, *Ideas and Opinions*, 1988
109. Joseph Stiglitz, *Globalization and Its Discontents*, 2002
110. Alexandr Solzhenitsyn, *The Gulag Archipelago*, 1974
111. Jeyifo Biodum, ed., *Conversations with Wole Soyinka*, 2001
112. Horace Engdahl, ed., *Witness Literature: Proceedings of the Nobel Centennial Symposium*, 2002

113. Octavio Paz, *The Other Voice*, 1990
114. Interview, *Die Tagesz*, January 1, 2003
115. *New York Times*, June 18, 1950
116. Quoted by Claude Simon in *Paris Review*, no. 122, Spring 1992
117. Speech in New York City, January 29, 1911
118. Max Perutz, *I Wish I'd Made You Angry Earlier*, 2002
119. T. S. Eliot, *Selected Essays, 1917–1932*, 1932
120. Eugene O'Neill, *The Great God Brown*, 1926
121. Henry Margenau and Roy Varghese, eds., *Cosmos, Bios, Theos*, 1992
122. Commencement address, Middlebury College, May 2000
123. John Eccles, *Evolution of the Brain: Creation of the Self*, 1991
124. T. S. Eliot, *A Dialogue on Dramatic Poetry*, 1928
125. Albert Einstein, *Science, Philosophy and Religion: A Symposium*, 1941
126. Interview, *Macroeconomic Dynamics*, vol. 9, no. 5, 2005
127. Otto Hahn, *My Life: The Autobiography of a Scientist*, 1968
128. Interview of the week, Daystar.org
129. Ronald W. Clark, *The Life of Ernst Chain: Penicillin and Beyond*, 1985
130. Albert Einstein, *My Credo*, quoted in P. A. Schilpp, ed., *Einstein, Philosopher Scientist*, 1931
131. *A Fireside Chat with Walter Kohn*, University of California at Santa Barbara, video, 2003
132. *Washington Times*, October 22, 2001
133. Elias Canetti, *The Secret Heart of the Clock*, 1989
134. *New York Review of Books*, October 21, 1999
135. PBS On-Line News Hour, October 11, 2000
136. Isaac Bashevis Singer, *Conversations with Isaac Bashevis Singer*, 1978
137. Quoted in Martin du Gard, *Recollections of André Gide*, 1953
138. Attributed
139. Quoted in the *Boston Sunday Herald Advertiser*, April 11, 1976
140. Ottar G. Draugsvold, ed., *Nobel Writers on Writing*, 2000
141. Isaac Bashevis Singer, *Conversations with Isaac Bashevis Singer*, 1978
142. Menachem Begin, *White Nights*, 1957
143. Nobel lecture, December 10, 2000
144. Bertrand Russell, *Portraits from Memory*, 1956
145. Paul Samuelson, *Economics*, 1973
146. Anwar al-Sadat, *In Search of Identity*, 1977
147. Patrick White, *Australians in a Nuclear War*, 1983
148. *Daily Telegraph*, December 14, 1988
149. José Saramago, *The Cave*, 2000
150. T. S. Eliot, *The Idea of a Christian Society*, 1939
151. Interview, 1946
152. Albert Camus, *L'envers et l'endroit*, 1958
153. Sermon at Ebenezer Baptist Church, Atlanta, Georgia, February 4, 1968
154. Interview, *Paris Review*, no. 119, Summer 1991
155. Address at Harvard University, June 8, 1978
156. *National Review*, June 6, 2003
157. John Horgan, *The End of Science*, 1996
158. Alice Calaprice, ed., *The Quotable Einstein*, 1996
159. Attributed
160. Nobel acceptance speech, December 10, 1998
161. *New York Times*, October 1, 1972
162. Eugene O'Neill, *Marco Millions*, 1928

163. Albert Camus, *Notebooks, 1935-42*, 1962
164. Nobel lecture, December 8, 1982
165. Albert Schweitzer, *The Ethics of Reverence for Life*, 1936
166. Alexandr Solzhenitsyn, *The First Circle*, 1968
167. Werner Heisenberg, *Physics and Beyond*, 1971
168. Speech in Chicago, April 10, 1899
169. T. S. Eliot, *Four Quartets, Little Gidding*, 1942
170. Leo Esaki, "Innovation and Evolution: Reflections on a Life in Research," speech at the University of Texas, Dallas, February 23, 2002
171. *Nobel Minds*, BBC World TV colloquium, Stockholm, December 2004
172. Anatole France, *Revolt of the Angels*, 1914
173. Samuel Beckett, *Three Occasional Pieces*, 1982
174. Speech at UNESCO Conference, November 6, 1968
175. Nobel acceptance speech, December 10, 1978
176. Attributed
177. William Golding, *The Pyramid*, 1967
178. Winston Churchill, *My Early Life*, 1930
179. Leo Esaki, "Innovation and Evolution: Reflections on a Life in Research," speech at the University of Texas, Dallas, February 23, 2002
180. *Boston Globe*, December 10, 1982
181. Albert Camus, *The Rebel*, 1951
182. George Bernard Shaw, *Man and Superman*, 1903
183. *Time* magazine, October 23, 1950
184. Jimmy Carter, *The Virtues of Aging*, 1998
185. Barbara Shiels, *Winners: Women and Nobel Prize*, 1985
186. Pearl S. Buck, *China, Past and Present*, 1972
187. André Gide, *Further Pretexts*, 1911
188. Samuel Beckett, *Endgame*, 1957
189. *New York Times*, September 21, 1958
190. Address to the Royal Literary Society, July 1926, quoted in Rudyard Kipling, *A Book of Words*, 1928
191. Attributed
192. Gabriel García Márquez, *One Hundred Years of Solitude*, 1970
193. Attributed
194. Todayinliterature.com
195. Richard Feynman, *The Pleasure of Finding Things Out*, 1999
196. Roy Jenkins, *Churchill: A Biography*, 2001
197. Elias Canetti, *The Secret Heart of the Clock*, 1989
198. William Butler Yeats, "Oedipus at Colonus," from *The Tower*, 1928
199. *Guardian*, September 30, 1974
200. Bertrand Russell, *An Inquiry into Meaning and Truth*, 1940
201. Max Born, *Recollections of a Nobel Laureate*, 1975
202. Sheldon Glashow, *Interactions: A Journey Through the Mind of a Particle Physicist and the Matter of This World*, 1988
203. John Galsworthy, *In Chancery*, 1920
204. Nobel lecture, December 7, 1998
205. Quoted by Mrs. King, on ABC's *Turning Point*, June 19, 1997
206. Maurice Maeterlinck, *Our Eternity*, 1913
207. Tyler Wasson, *Nobel Prize Winners*, 1987
208. Charles Richet, *Idiot Man (L'Homme Stupide)*, 1919

209. Testimony before the House Labor, Health and Human Services Appropriations Sub-committee, May 20, 1998
210. Rudyard Kipling, "Epitaphs of the War," in *The Years Between*, 1919
211. Rudyard Kipling, "Epitaphs of the War," in *The Years Between*, 1919
212. Rudyard Kipling, epitaph commissioned for Canadian war memorials
213. Speech in the House of Commons, August 20, 1940
214. Speech in the House of Commons, September 28, 1944
215. Guy Hartcup and T. E. Allibone, *Cockcroft and the Atom*, 1984
216. Nobel lecture, 1994
217. *Observer*, December 15, 1991
218. Obituary in the *Guardian*, January 17, 2002
219. Attributed
220. Quoted by the poet Wilfred Owen in a letter to his mother, August 1918, in Jon Stallworthy, *Wilfred Owen*, 1974
221. Boris Pasternak, *Dr. Zhivago*, 1957
222. William Faulkner, *Requiem for a Nun*, 1951
223. Declaration on the twenty-fifth anniversary of the end of World War II, May 8, 1970
224. Nobel lecture, December 7, 1995
225. Interview, CBS, 1989
226. Attributed
227. Attributed
228. Nobel lecture, December 1994
229. John Galsworthy, "Castles in Spain," in *Candelabra*, 1932
230. *News-Gazette*, December 9, 2003
231. Richard Feynman, *The Meaning of it All: Thoughts of a Citizen-Scientist*, 1998
232. Quoted in Joseph Goldstein, "Medical ramifications," *What Price Designer Genes: The Genetic Revolution, Proceedings of the Philosophical Society of Texas*, 1996
233. *Washington Post*, October 10, 2001
234. *Combat*, no. 27, Fall 1946, reprinted in Albert Camus, *Between Hell and Reason*, 1991
235. *Paris Herald Tribune*, February 23, 1970
236. Attributed
237. Max Delbrück, *Mind from Matter? An Essay on Evolutionary Epistemology*, 1986
238. René Cassin, "The Fight for Human Rights," *World*, January 1969
239. Address at American University, March 18, 2004
240. Nobel lecture, December 12, 1976
241. Alexandr Solzhenitsyn, *The Gulag Archipelago*, 1974
242. Joseph Brodsky, *Less Than One: Selected Essays*, 1986
243. Ernest Hemingway, *A Moveable Feast*, 1964
244. Albert Camus, *Resistance, Rebellion, and Death*, 1961
245. Attributed
246. James C. Humes, *The Wit and Wisdom of Winston Churchill*, 1994
247. Juan Ramón Jiménez, *The Complete Perfectionist: A Poetics of Work*, 1997
248. *Life* magazine, May 2, 1955
249. Samuel Beckett, *Malone Dies*, 1951
250. Jean-Paul Sartre, *Existentialism as Humanism*, 1946
251. Octavio Paz, *The Double Flame*, 1993
252. Anwar al-Sadat, *Those I Have Known*, 1984
253. Ernest Hemingway, *The Old Man and the Sea*, 1952
254. Walter Isaacson, *Kissinger: A Biography*, 1992
255. *Spectator*, April 1, 1995

256. Commencement address, University of Michigan, 1988, reprinted in Joseph Brodsky, *On Grief and Reason*, 1995

257. Albert Lutuli, *Let My People Go: An Autobiography*, 1962

258. Winston Churchill, *Great Contemporaries*, 1937

259. *SAST Report*, January 22, 2002

260. John Harrington, *The Irish Beckett*, 1991

261. *New Yorker*, November 30, 1929

262. Ernest Hemingway, *A Farewell to Arms*, 1929

263. Romain Rolland, *Jean-Christophe*, 1904

264. Irwin Abrams, ed., *The Words of Peace: Selections from the Speeches of the Winners of the Nobel Peace Prize*, 1995

265. Martin Luther King, *Letter from Birmingham Jail*, 1963

266. Jean-Paul Sartre, *Existentialism as Humanism*, 1946

267. Albert Schweitzer, *Out of My life and Thought*, 1933

268. Interview with Studs Terkel, *Perspective on Ideas and the Arts*, May 1963

269. Eleanor Wachtel, *Writers and Company*, 1993

270. *Sechaba*, Third Quarter, 1978

271. Nobel lecture, December 11, 1959

272. Convocation address at Sir George Williams University, May 27, 1961, reprinted in Lester Pearson, *Words and Occasions*, 1970

273. First speech as prime minister in the House of Commons, May 13, 1940

274. Speech in the House of Commons, June 18, 1940

275. *Time*, July 3, 2006

276. SUNY at Fredonia Leader Online, November 12, 2001

277. Tyler Wasson, ed., *Nobel Prize Winners*, 1987

278. Press release, University of Colorado, April 12, 2005

279. Interview, 1985, in Danille Taylor-Guthrie, ed., *Conversations with Toni Morrison*, 1994

280. *New York Times*, June 20, 1932

281. Nadine Gordimer, *Burger's Daughter*, 1979

282. Quoted in M. I. D. Sharma and N. C. Grasset, "History of Achievement of Smallpox 'target zero' in India," *Journal of Communicable Diseases*, vol. 7, August 1973

283. Bertrand Russell, *The Conquest of Happiness*, 1930

284. George Bernard Shaw, *Caesar and Cleopatra*, 1901

285. The Dalai Lama and Howard C. Cutler, *The Art of Happiness*, 1998

286. Richard Feynman, *What Do You Care What Other People Think?* 1988

287. Nobel Centennial Symposium, Oslo, December 7, 2001

288. Bertrand Russell, *The Autobiography of Bertrand Russell*, 1967

289. Attributed

290. Nobel lecture, 1994

291. Alexandr Solzhenitsyn, *One Day in the Life of Ivan Denisovich*, 1962

292. Address on receiving honorary doctor of laws degree at the University of Toronto, February 2000

293. Helena Cobban, ed., *The Moral Architecture of World Peace: Nobel Laureates Discuss Our Global Future*, 2000

294. Nelson Mandela, "Statement of the National Executive Committee of the ANC on the Occasion of the 84th Anniversary of the African National Congress," January 8, 1996

295. *Observer*, August 25, 1996

296. Alan Wood, *The Passionate Sceptic*, 1957

297. *New York Times*, March 13, 1940

298. Friedrich von Hayek, *The Constitution of Liberty*, 1960

299. Robert Conquest, *The Pasternak Affair: Courage of Genius*, 1962
300. George Bernard Shaw, *Caesar and Cleopatra*, 1901
301. Bertrand Russell, *The Autobiography of Bertrand Russell*, 1967
302. A. P. French, *Einstein: A Centenary Volume*, 1979
303. Attributed
304. Fritz Perls, *In and out the Garbage Pail*, 1981
305. Martin Luther King, *Strength to Love*, 1963
306. Paul Theroux, *Sir Vidia's Shadow*, 1998
307. Antony Jay, ed., *The Oxford Dictionary of Political Quotations*, 1996
308. Letter to Maxwell Garnett, November 28, 1931, quoted in Louis Bisceglia, *Norman Angell and Liberal Internationalism in Britain, 1931–1935*, 1982
309. *Time* magazine, May 21, 1979
310. Bertrand Russell, *The Autobiography of Bertrand Russell*, 1967
311. James Watson, "Succeeding in Science: Some Rules of Thumb," *Science*, vol. 261, September 1993
312. Katherine Tupper Marshall, *Together*, 1947
313. Samuel Beckett, *All that Fall*, 1957
314. André Gide, *Fruits of the Earth*, 1897
315. Hermann Hesse, *My Belief: Essays on Life and Art*, 1974
316. Konrad Lorenz, *Civilized Man's Eight Deadly Sins*, 1973
317. Boris Pasternak, *Dr. Zhivago*, 1957
318. Maurice Maeterlinck, *Wisdom and Destiny*, 1898
319. Bertrand Russell, *The Conquest of Happiness*, 1930
320. Sheldon Glashow, *Interactions: A Journey Through the Mind of a Particle Physicist and the Matter of This World*, 1988
321. Ernest Hemingway, *The Garden of Eden*, 1986
322. Marc Abrahams, ed., *The Best of Annals of Improbable Research*, 1998
323. Abraham Pais, *The Genius of Science: A Portrait Gallery of Twentieth-Century Physicists*, 2000
324. Dag Hammarskjöld, *Markings*, 1964
325. Dag Hammarskjöld, *Markings*, 1964
326. Juan Ramón Jiménez, *The Complete Perfectionist: A Poetics of Work*, 1997
327. "The Perils of Indifference," millennium lecture at the White House, April 12, 1999
328. Albert Camus, *The Plague*, 1947
329. Juan Ramón Jiménez, *The Complete Perfectionist: A Poetics of Work*, 1997
330. Hermann Hesse, *Reflections*, 1974
331. Albert Camus, *Notebooks, 1935–42*, 1962
332. Paul Dirac, "The Evolution of the Physicist's Picture of Nature," *Scientific American*, vol. 208, 1963
333. William Faulkner, *The Wild Palms*, 1966
334. Speech in Washington, D.C., August 28, 1963
335. Elaine Steinbeck and Robert Wallsten, eds., *John Steinbeck, A Life in Letters*, 1975
336. *Boston Globe*, March 8, 1980
337. Kary Mullis, *Dancing Naked in the Mind Field*, 1998
338. Pearl S. Buck, *For Spacious Skies*, 1966
339. Anatole France, *The Crime of Sylvester Bonnard*, 1881
340. Quoted in *U.S. Catholic*, July 3, 2003
341. "The Perils of Indifference," millennium lecture at the White House, April 12, 1999
342. *U.S. News and World Report*, October 27, 1986
343. Nobel acceptance speech, December 10, 1986

344. *Combat*, November 30, 1946, reprinted in Albert Camus, *Between Hell and Reason*, 1991
345. François Jacob, *The Possible and the Actual*, 1982
346. Boris Pasternak, *Dr. Zhivago*, 1957
347. Roy Jenkins, *Churchill: A Biography*, 2001
348. Albert Camus, *Summer*, 1954
349. Klas Arnoldson, *Pax Mundi*, 1890
350. Ernest Hemingway, *Across the River and Into the Trees*, 1950
351. Peter Medawar, *The Hope of Progress*, 1973
352. Nobel lecture, December 11, 1959
353. Nobel lecture, December 11, 1986
354. Imre Kertész, *Hungarian Quarterly*, Autumn 2004
355. Attributed
356. Nelson Mandela, *A Long Walk to Freedom*, 1994
357. Aung San Suu Kyi, *Freedom from Fear and Other Writings*, 1991
358. Denis Brian, *The Voice of Genius: Conversations with Nobel Scientists and Other Laureates*, 2001
359. Theodore Roosevelt, *An Autobiography*, 1913
360. Bertrand Russell, *Marriage and Morals*, 1929
361. *Combat*, Fall 1946, reprinted in Albert Camus, *Neither Victims nor Executioners*, 1980
362. Selma Lagerlöf, *Invisible Links*, 1899
363. Attributed
364. Octavio Paz, *The Double Flame*, 1993
365. Octavio Paz, *The Double Flame*, 1993
366. Romain Rolland, *The Enchanted Soul*, 1922–33
367. Bertrand Russell, *The Conquest of Happiness*, 1930
368. Attributed
369. Jane Addams, *Twenty Years at Hull House*, 1910
370. Anwar al-Sadat, *Those I Have Known*, 1984
371. Albert Einstein, *Ideas and Opinions*, 1988
372. Martin Luther King, *Letter from Birmingham Jail*, 1963
373. Nobel lecture, May 2, 1973
374. Albert Camus, *The Plague*, 1947
375. Samuel Beckett, *First Love*, written 1946, published 1970
376. Peter Ackroyd, *T. S. Eliot: A Life*, 1984
377. Ernest Hemingway, *Death in the Afternoon*, 1932
378. John Galsworthy, *The Man of Property*, 1906
379. William Faulkner, "Mississippi," *Holiday*, April 1954
380. Albert Camus, *Notebooks, 1935–42*, 1962
381. George Bernard Shaw, *The Philanderer*, 1893
382. François Mauriac, *Journal*, 1934–51
383. Bertrand Russell, *Marriage and Morals*, 1956
384. Richard Lingeman, *Sinclair Lewis: Rebel from Main Street*, 2002
385. Marc Abrahams, ed., *The Best of Annals of Improbable Research*, 1998
386. *Columns* magazine, University of Washington, March 1998
387. Lillian Hoddeson and Vicki Daitch, *True Genius: The Life and Science of John Bardeen*, 2002
388. A. E. Hotchner, *Papa Hemingway*, 1966
389. Sinclair Lewis, *Ann Vickers*, 1932
390. Letter to Bo Beskow, November 1948, in Elaine Steinbeck and Robert Wallsten, eds., *John Steinbeck, A Life in Letters*, 1975
391. John Galsworthy, *The Man of Property*, 1906

392. William H. Cropper, *Great Physicists*, 2001
393. Attributed
394. François Jacob, *The Possible and the Actual*, 1982
395. François Jacob, *The Possible and the Actual*, 1982
396. Interview, PBS, January 27, 1982
397. Interview, 1997, quoted in obituary, theage.com, April 6, 2005
398. Anatole France, *The Red Lily*, 1894
399. Attributed
400. Videotape speech at NGO Forum on Women, China, September 1995
401. Pearl S. Buck, *Of Men and Women*, 1941
402. Pearl S. Buck, *Of Men and Women*, 1941
403. Pearl S. Buck, *Of Men and Women*, 1941
404. Pearl S. Buck, *Of Men and Women*, 1941
405. Sharon B. McGrayne, *Nobel Prize Women in Science: Their Lives, Struggles, and Momentous Discoveries*, 2001
406. Interview, *Weekly Standard*, November 3, 2003
407. Interview, *Weekly Standard*, November 3, 2003
408. "The Many Faces of Gender Inequality," Radcliffe Institute inaugural lecture, April 2001
409. Message to the International Fund for Agricultural Development, February 21, 2001
410. Rabindranath Tagore, *Stray Birds*, 1916
411. Konrad Lorenz, *Civilized Man's Eight Deadly Sins*, 1973
412. Ernest Hemingway, *True at First Light*, 1999
413. Richard Deutsch, *Mairead Corrigan, Betty Williams*, 1977
414. Remark in 1962, quoted in Allen L. Hammond, ed., *A Passion to Know: 20 Profiles in Science*, 1984
415. Robert Ferguson, *Enigma: The Life of Knut Hamsun*, 1987
416. Nelson Mandela, *A Long Walk to Freedom*, 1994
417. Pearl S. Buck, *My Several Worlds*, 1954
418. Interview, Academy of Achievement, June 27, 1992
419. Interview, 1981, in Danille Taylor-Guthrie, ed., *Conversations with Toni Morrison*, 1994
420. *Time* magazine, May 22, 1989
421. *New York Times*, June 9, 1963
422. Address at enthronement as Anglican archbishop of Cape Town, September 7, 1986
423. André Gide, *New Fruits of the Earth*, 1935
424. Letter to her sister Bronia in 1932, quoted in Susan Quinn, *Marie Curie: A Life*, 1995
425. Hermann Hesse, *Reflections*, 1974
426. William Butler Yeats, *The Municipal Gallery Re-visited*, 1939
427. Rudyard Kipling, *The Thousandth Man, in Rewards and Fairies*, 1910
428. Octavio Paz, *The Double Flame*, 1993
429. Matti Golan, *Shimon Peres: A Biography*, 1982
430. Attributed
431. Albert Camus, *Notebooks, 1935-42*, 1962
432. Remark made at award of honorary doctorate by the University of the Philippines, July 1999
433. Albert Einstein, *Out of My Later Years*, 1950
434. Theodore F. Harris, *Pearl S. Buck: A Biography*, 1969
435. Maurice Maeterlinck, *The Double Garden*, 1904
436. Eugene O'Neill, *Lazarus Laughed*, 1927
437. E. H. Craigie and W. C. Gibson, eds., *The World of Ramón Y. Cajal*, 1968
438. *Commonweal*, December 19, 1997

439. Dag Hammarskjöld, *Diaries*, 1951
440. Bertrand Russell, *The Autobiography of Bertrand Russell*, 1967
441. Abraham Pais, *Einstein Lived Here*, 1994
442. Attributed
443. Max Perutz, *I Wish I'd Made You Angry Earlier*, 1998
444. Henri Bergson, *Ecrits et Paroles*, 1957
445. Quoted in Antony Flew, *Thinking about Thinking*, 1975
446. Nobel autobiography, 1997
447. Abraham Pais, *The Genius of Science: A Portrait Gallery of Twentieth-century Physicists*, 2000
448. Bertrand Russell, *Unpopular Essays*, 1950
449. CBC TV, August 19, 1974
450. E. T. Bell, *Mathematics, Queen and Servant of the Sciences*, 1952
451. István Hargittai, *Candid Science II: Conversations with Famous Biomedical Scientists*, 2002
452. Albert Szent-Györgyi, *Science, Ethics, and Politics*, 1963
453. Peter Medawar, *Pluto's Republic*, 1982
454. Albert Camus, *Resistance, Rebellion, and Death*, 1961
455. Nobel address to university students in Stockholm, December 10, 1954
456. Richard Feynman, *The Character of Physical Law*, 1967
457. Samuel Beckett, *Waiting for Godot*, 1952
458. Attributed
459. Eugene O'Neill, *The Iceman Cometh*, 1946
460. Bertrand Russell, *The Conquest of Happiness*, 1930
461. Kary Mullis, *Dancing Naked in the Mind Field*, 1998
462. John Horgan, *The End of Science*, 1996
463. Bertrand Russell, *Unpopular Essays*, 1950
464. Theodor Mommsen, *History of Rome*, 1908
465. J. Michael Bishop, *How to Win the Nobel Prize*, 2003
466. Pearl S. Buck, *For Spacious Skies*, 1966
467. Saul Bellow, *Herzog*, 1964
468. Attributed
469. Quoted in Baruch S. Blumberg, *Hepatitis B, The Hunt for a Killer Virus*, 2002
470. James Gleick, *Genius: The Life and Science of Richard Feynman*, 1992
471. Interview, *Saturday Evening Post*, October 26, 1929
472. "A Life in Economics," in Arnold Heertje, ed., *The Makers of Modern Economics*, vol. 2, 1995
473. Saul Bellow. *Mr. Sammler's Planet*, 1970
474. Heinrich Böll, *Die Fahigkeit zu trauern: Schriften und Reden*, 1983–85
475. Willy Brandt, *My Road to Berlin*, 1960
476. Günter Grass, *Warning: Political Speeches and Essays, 1965–1976*, 1978
477. Juan Ramón Jiménez, *The Complete Perfectionist: A Poetics of Work*, 1997
478. Robert Ferguson, *Enigma: The Life of Knut Hamsun*, 1987
479. Maurice Maeterlinck, *Wisdom and Destiny*, 1898
480. François Mauriac, *Bloc-notes, 1952–57*, 1958
481. Pablo Neruda, "Saddest Poem," in *Love: Ten Poems*, 1995
482. Romain Rolland, *Jean-Christophe*, 1904
483. Nobel acceptance speech, December 10, 1986
484. Nobel lecture, December 11, 1986
485. Andrew Szanton, *The Recollections of Eugene P. Wigner*, 1992
486. Attributed

487. Luigi Pirandello, *The Rules of the Game*, 1918
488. Elias Canetti, *The Human Province*, 1978
489. William Golding, *Pincher Martin*, 1956
490. Associated Press report, December 2002
491. George Bernard Shaw, *Back to Methuselah*, 1921
492. Pearl S. Buck, *The Patriot*, 1939
493. Nobel lecture, December 1994
494. Speech in Washington, D.C., August 28, 1963
495. Octavio Paz, *The Double Flame*, 1993
496. Christopher Sykes, ed., *No Ordinary Genius: The Illustrated Richard Feynman*, 1994
497. Bertrand Russell, *The Philosophy of Logical Atomism*, 1959
498. Bertrand Russell, *Bertrand Russell Speaks His Mind*, 1960
499. Abraham Pais, *Niels Bohr's Times*, 1991
500. Boris Pasternak, *Dr. Zhivago*, 1957
501. Albert Camus, *The Myth of Sisyphus*, 1942
502. Albert Camus, *Notebooks, 1935–42*, 1962
503. Letter, 1950, in Helen Dukas and Benesh Hoffmann, eds., *Albert Einstein; The Human Side*, 1979
504. Franco Modigliani, *Adventures of an Economist*, 2001
505. T. S. Eliot, *Murder in the Cathedral*, 1935
506. *Inter Se*, Singapore, November–December 2003
507. Remark in the House of Commons on November 27, 1914
508. *Kansas City Star*, May 7, 1918
509. Nobel lecture, December 12, 1930
510. John Kenneth Galbraith, introduction to *The Affluent Society*, 1978
511. André Gide, *Fruits of the Earth*, 1897
512. T. S. Eliot, *The Rock*, 1934
513. The *Times* (London), June 8, 1989
514. Attributed
515. Theodore Roosevelt, *National Strength and International Duty*, 1917
516. Letter to Dorothy Wellesley, December 21, 1935
517. Robert Franciosi, ed., *Elie Wiesel: Conversations*, 2002
518. Isaac Bashevis Singer, *Conversations with Isaac Bashevis Singer*, 1978
519. Interview with Shahram Mostarshed, October 12, 2003
520. Friedrich von Hayek, *The Road to Serfdom*, 1944
521. Wole Soyinka, "Climate of Fear," the 2004 Reith lectures
522. Nobel lecture, December 10, 1998
523. *New York Times*, July 5, 1954
524. Attributed
525. George Bernard Shaw, "A Treatise on Parents and Children," preface to *Misalliance*, 1909
526. Albert Einstein, "Autobiographical Notes," in Paul Schilpp, ed., *Albert Einstein: Philosopher-Scientist*, 1951
527. Paul Webster, "Madame Curie and Her Lively Classroom," *Guardian Weekly*, September 4, 2003
528. Rabindranath Tagore, *Talks in China: Lectures Delivered in April and May 1924*, 1925
529. Winston Churchill, *My Early Life*, 1930
530. J. Michael Bishop, *How to Win the Nobel Prize*, 2003
531. Laurie M. Brown and John S. Rigden, eds., *Most of the Good Stuff: Memories of Richard Feynman*, 1993
532. Herbert Simon, *Models of My Life*, 1991

533. Interview, Academy of Achievement, April 5, 2001
534. Leon Lederman, *The God Particle*, 1993
535. George Stigler, *The Intellectual and the Marketplace*, 1984
536. George Stigler, *The Intellectual and the Marketplace*, 1984
537. Interview, *Saturday Telegraph*, September 23, 1979
538. Letter to Conrad Aiken, December 1914
539. Ronald Clark, *Sir Edward Appleton*, 1971
540. Trevor I. Williams, *Howard Florey: Penicillin and After*, 1984
541. Max Perutz, *I Wish I'd Made You Angry Earlier*, 1998
542. J. J. Thomson, *Recollections and Reflections*, 1936
543. Toni Morrison, *Song of Solomon*, 1977
544. *San Francisco Chronicle*, August 13, 2001
545. Interview, Academy of Achievement, January 31, 1991
546. Walter Isaacson, *Kissinger: A Biography*, 1992
547. Robert Marc Friedman, "Balancing Act: The Historian as Playwright," lecture at a symposium in Copenhagen, September 1999
548. Hermann Hesse, *Reflections*, 1974
549. Essay, 1914, quoted in Bernard Zeller, *Portrait of Hesse: An Illustrated Biography*, 1971
550. Nobel lecture, May 2, 1973
551. Nobel lecture, December 8, 1987
552. Albert Camus, *Notebooks, 1935-42*, 1962
553. Albert Camus, *The Guest*, 1957
554. Address to the plenum of the Union of Writers, quoted in Robert Conquest, *The Pasternak Affair: Courage of Genius*, 1962
555. Jacinto Benavente, *Lo Cursi*, 1901
556. André Gide, *Return from the USSR*, 1937
557. Romain Rolland, *Jean Christophe*, 1904
558. Attributed
559. Nobel lecture, December 8, 1987
560. Ottar G. Draugsvold, ed., *Nobel Writers on Writing*, 2000
561. Nobel acceptance speech, December 10, 1989
562. Nobel lecture, December 7, 1999
563. Review of Sartre's *La Nausée* in *Alger Republicain*, October 20, 1938, quoted in Philip Thody, ed., *Camus: Selected Essays and Notebooks*, 1970
564. Elias Canetti, *The Human Province*, 1978
565. *New York Times*, September 15, 1974
566. James C. Humes, *The Wit and Wisdom of Winston Churchill*, 1994
567. Interview with Richard Burgin, *New York Times Magazine*, November 26, 1978
568. Answer to questionnaire, 1965, in Saint-John Perse, *Letters*, 1979
569. Nobel acceptance speech, December 10, 1950
570. Ernest Hemingway, "Old Newsman Writes: A Letter from Cuba," *Esquire*, December 1934
571. Nobel lecture, December 12, 1967
572. William Golding, *A Moving Target*, 1982
573. Charles Juliet, *Conversations with Samuel Beckett and Bram van Velde*, 1995
574. John Steinbeck, "Critics—from a Writer's Viewpoint," in *America and Americans and Selected Nonfiction*, 2002
575. Ernest Hemingway, *A Moveable Feast*, 1964
576. Press release, Swedish Academy, October 13, 1988
577. Deirdre Bair, *Samuel Beckett, A Biography*, 1978

578. Interview, *Paris Review*, no. 12, Spring 1956

579. Interview, *Paris Review*, no. 18, Spring 1958

580. Nobel acceptance speech, December 10, 1954

581. *Newsweek*, December 24, 1962

582. Interview with Richard Burgin, *New York Times Magazine*, November 26, 1978

583. Albert Camus, *Notebooks, 1935–42*, 1962

584. Nobel lecture, December 8, 2006

585. Interview, *Paris Review*, no. 12, Spring 1956

586. Attributed

587. Konrad Lorenz, *Civilized Man's Eight Deadly Sins*, 1973

588. *New York Times*, June 30, 1985

589. Interview, 1982, in William Baer, ed., *Conversations with Derek Walcott*, 1996

590. James Knowlson, *Damned to Fame: The Life of Samuel Beckett*, 1996

591. Attributed

592. Attributed

593. Cissie Dore Hill, "Remembering Joseph Brodsky," Hoover Institute Archives

594. Nobel lecture, December 7, 1992

595. Joseph Brodsky, *On Grief and Reason*, 1995

596. Albert Parry, ed., *Peter Kapitsa on Life and Science*, 1968

597. Naguib Mahfouz, *Reflections of a Nobel Laureate*, 2001

598. *Newsweek*, May 15, 1986

599. William Butler Yeats, *Per Amica Silentia Lunae*, 1917

600. Joseph Brodsky, *On Grief and Reason*, 1995

601. T. S. Eliot, *Dante*, 1920

602. Octavio Paz, *The Double Flame*, 1993

603. Juan Ramón Jiménez, *Selected Writings*, 1957

604. T. S. Eliot, *Dante*, 1920

605. Pablo Neruda, *Caballo Verde para La Poesía*, no. 1, October 1935

606. Pablo Neruda, *Memoirs*, 1977

607. Peter Ackroyd, *T. S. Eliot: A Life*, 1984

608. T. S. Eliot, *The Sacred Wood: Essays on Poetry and Criticism*, 1922

609. *New Statesman*, March 3, 1917

610. Interview with Christopher Bigsby, BBC radio, October 2, 1990

611. Salvador Luria, *A Slot Machine, A Broken Test Tube: An Autobiography*, 1984

612. Tyler Wasson, ed., *Nobel Prize Winners*, 1987

613. Interview, *Paris Review*, no. 139, Summer 1996

614. Anders Hallengren, "Grazia Deledda, Voice of Sardinia," Nobel Museum (nobelprize.org)

615. T. S. Eliot, *The Use of Poetry and the Use of Criticism*, 1933. When asked in 1959, in an interview by Donald Hall, whether he felt the same at seventy, he said, "There may be honest poets who do feel sure, I don't" (*Paris Review*, no. 21, Spring-Summer 1959)

616. T. S. Eliot, *Alternating Current*, 1967

617. Interview, *Paris Review*, no. 119, Summer 1991

618. Interview, *Paris Review*, no. 50, Fall 1970

619. Nobel lecture, December 7, 1996

620. Alan Hodgkin, *Chance and Design: Reminiscences of Science in Peace and War*, 1992

621. Attributed

622. Attributed

623. Wislawa Szymborska, *Nonrequired Reading*, 2002

624. Press conference, Washington, D.C., on acceptance of U.S. poet laureateship, quoted in the *Independent on Sunday*, London, May 19, 1991

625. Anatole France, *The Literary Life*, 1888

626. Anatole France, *The Crime of Sylvester Bonnard*, 1881

627. Paul Theroux, *Sir Vidia's Shadow*, 1998

628. Octavio Paz, *The Other Voice*, 1990

629. Octavio Paz, *The Other Voice*, 1990

630. Remark in June 1959, quoted in http://www.psych.uni-goettingen.de

631. Interview with Dawn Engle and Ivan Suvanjieff, Houston, Texas, July 4, 1995

632. Elias Canetti, *The Secret Heart of the Clock*, 1989

633. Attributed

634. Nobel lecture, December 8, 2003

635. Interview, Homeschool.com

636. Romanes lecture, Oxford, May 10, 1990, in Saul Bellow, *It All Adds Up*, 1994

637. *Financial Times*, January 31, 1995

638. Quoted in Hoover Institution press release, September 27, 2000

639. Quoted in Arthur Compton, *Atomic Quest*, 1956

640. Remarks at farewell dinner as secretary of state, December 1976, quoted in Walter Isaac-
    son, *Kissinger: A Biography*, 1992

641. Czeslaw Milosz, *Native Realm: A Search for Self-definition*, 1968

642. Nobel autobiography, 1930

643. Speech, 1947

644. Saul Bellow, *Humboldt's Gift*, 1975

645. Interview, Berlin, December 29, 1930

646. Interview, Academy of Achievement, October 22, 1991

647. Gunnar Myrdal, *Challenge to Affluence*, 1962

648. Graduation speech, West Point, May 31, 1942, quoted in Katherine Tupper Marshall,
    Together, 1947

649. Ernest Hemingway, introduction to Ben Raeburn, ed., *Treasury for the Free World*, 1946

650. "Beyond Vietnam," lecture, 1968

651. Interview, *Red Cross International Review*, January 2005

652. Nobel lecture, December 7, 2005

653. Lawrence Martin, *The Presidents and the Prime Ministers*, 1981

654. Henryk Sienkiewicz, *Portrait of America*, 1959

655. Abraham Pais, *The Genius of Science: A Portrait Gallery of Twentieth-Century Physicists*,
    2000

656. Helge Kragh, *Dirac: A Scientific Biography*, 1990

657. Andrew Szanton, *The Recollections of Eugene P. Wigner*, 1992

658. Franco Modigliani, *Adventures of an Economist*, 2001

659. François Jacob, *The Statue Within*, 1988

660. Mortimore Wheeler, *The British Academy, 1949–1968*, 1970

661. Hans Krebs, *Reminiscences and Reflections*, 1981

662. François Mauriac, *Second Thoughts: Reflections on Literature and on Life*, 1961

663. George Bernard Shaw, *Pygmalion*, 1916

664. *San Francisco Chronicle*, November 13, 2000

665. www.Britannica.com

666. Nobel lecture, December 11, 1971

667. Hans Krebs, *Reminiscences and Reflections*, 1981

668. Benno Muller-Hill, *Murderous Science*, 1998

669. Nobel lecture, December 8, 1987

670. Letter to Stalin in 1927, quoted in *Discover*, January 2000

671. Speech on the Seventieth Anniversary of the Russian Revolution, November 2, 1987

672. *Daily Mail*, October 24, 1958
673. Alexandr Solzhenitsyn, *The Gulag Archipelago*, 1974
674. Alexandr Solzhenitsyn, *The Oak and the Calf*, 1980
675. Saul Bellow, *It All Adds Up*, 1994
676. Speech in the House of Commons, December 10, 1942
677. Attributed
678. Sheldon Glashow, *Interactions: A Journey Through the Mind of a Particle Physicist and the Matter of This World*, 1988
679. Ernest Hemingway, *Esquire*, February 1934
680. Ernest Hemingway, epigraph, *A Moveable Feast*, 1964
681. Salvador Luria, *A Slot Machine, a Broken Test Tube: An Autobiography*, 1984
682. Nobel acceptance speech, December 10, 1966
683. Nobel acceptance speech, December 10, 1966
684. Nobel lecture, December 1994
685. *Observer*, December 16, 1984
686. Rudyard Kipling, "The Man Who Was," in *Life's Handicap*, 1891
687. Rudyard Kipling, *The Naulahka, A Story of West and East*, 1892
688. Andrei Sakharov, *My Country and the World*, 1975
689. Nobel lecture, December 8, 1988
690. Richard Feynman, *The Meaning of it All: Thoughts of a Citizen-Scientist*, 1998
691. Max Born, *Physics in My Generation*, 1969
692. Bertrand Russell, *Sceptical Essays*, 1928
693. Jean-Paul Sartre, *No Exit*, 1944
694. T. S. Eliot, *The Idea of a Christian Society*, 1939
695. George Bernard Shaw, *Misalliance*, 1914
696. Richard Lingeman, *Sinclair Lewis: Rebel from Main Street*, 2002
697. Attributed
698. *New York Times*, October 1, 1972
699. Anwar al-Sadat, *In Search of Identity*, 1977
700. Samuel Beckett, *All that Fall*, 1957
701. Address at the Sorbonne, quoted in the *New York Times*, February 16, 1930
702. Miguel Ángel Asturias, *The Green Pope*, 1971
703. Octavio Paz, *The Double Flame*, 1993
704. Antony Jay, ed., *The Oxford Dictionary of Political Quotations*, 1996
705. Albert Szent-Györgyi, *The Crazy Ape*, 1970
706. Jeffrey Hopkins, ed., *The Art of Peace*, 2000
707. Dialogue between George Stigler and Paul Samuelson at Swarthmore College, 1963, in Graduate School of Business, University of Chicago, Selected Papers No. 7
708. Nobel lecture, December 8, 1987
709. *Toronto Star*, October 23, 1975
710. Speech to the International Platform Association, August 2, 1973
711. Milton Friedman, *Free to Choose*, PBS, 1980
712. Quoted by Lord Harris in the House of Lords, November 24, 1994
713. Milton Friedman, *Capitalism and Freedom*, 1962
714. Interview, Academy of Achievement, January 31, 1991
715. *International Herald Tribune*, August 15, 1994
716. Dialogue between George Stigler and Paul Samuelson at Swarthmore College, 1963, in Graduate School of Business, University of Chicago, Selected Papers No. 7
717. Jimmy Carter, *Why Not the Best?* 1975
718. Albert Szent-Györgyi, *The Crazy Ape*, 1970

719. Attributed

720. Michael Bliss, *Banting: A Biography*, 1984

721. Friedrich von Hayek, *The Road to Serfdom*, 1944

722. Platform of the German Social Democratic Party, in Willy Brandt, *My Road to Berlin*, 1960

723. Letter to Sir Edward Grey, November 15, 1913

724. Dialogue between George Stigler and Paul Samuelson at Swarthmore College, 1963, in Graduate School of Business, University of Chicago, Selected Papers No. 7

725. Interview, *Reason*, April 2000

726. Ian Shine and Sylvia Wrobel, *Thomas Hunt Morgan: Pioneer of Genetics*, 1976

727. George Kennan, *Memoirs, 1925–1950*, 1967

728. Günter Grass, "On Writers as Court Jesters and on Non-Existent Courts," address at Princeton University, April 1966. Quoted in *Speak Out!* 1968

729. Speech in the House of Commons, November 11, 1947

730. Salvador Luria, *Bulletin of Atomic Scientists*, May 1977

731. Interview with Harry Kriesler, University of California, Berkeley, April 16, 1998

732. Anwar al-Sadat, *Those I Have Known*, 1984

733. Nobel lecture, December 8, 1987

734. Winston Churchill, *My Early Life*, 1930

735. "Reform in Practice," speech to the Universidad Tecnológica de México, Mexico City, November 17, 2002

736. Nobel lecture, December 11, 1953

737. *Le Monde Diplomatique*, November 1998

738. The *Times* (London), August 30, 2005

739. Attributed

740. Interview, *Newsweek*, December 2002

741. Menachem Begin, *White Nights*, 1957

742. Ernest Hemingway, *Esquire*, January 1936

743. Wole Soyinka, *The Man Died*, 1972

744. Albert Camus, *The Rebel*, 1951

745. Albert Camus, *The Rebel*, 1951

746. Attributed

747. Attributed

748. Lord Rayleigh, *The Life of Sir J. J. Thomson*, 1942

749. Mikhail Gorbachev, *Memoirs*, 1995

750. Public declaration as general secretary of the Central Committee of the Communist Party of the Soviet Union. Mikhail Gorbachev, *On My Country and the World*, 2000

751. Speech before the UN General Assembly, November 13, 1974

752. Speech in the House of Commons, July 8, 1920

753. Nobel lecture, December 12, 1974

754. Speech to the Foreign Policy Association, New York, June 23, 1976. Reprinted in Jimmy Carter, *A Government as Good as its People*, 1977

755. *Observer*, March 28, 2004

756. Speech in Albany, Georgia, 1962

757. Octavio Paz, *The Other Voice*, 1990

758. Pearl S. Buck, *What America Means to Me*, 1942

759. Message to the National Peace Convention, Johannesburg, October 1956

760. Press statement, June 26, 1961. Reprinted in Nelson Mandela, *The Struggle Is My Life*, 1978

761. Speech in Cupertino, California, March 8, 1999. *Los Altos Town Crier*, March 15, 1999

762. Speech, September 30, 2002, quoted in fwdklerk.org.za

763. Milton Friedman, *Capitalism and Freedom*, 1962

764. Address to the New York Press Club, New York City, September 9, 1912

765. Menachem Begin, *The Revolt*, 1964

766. Wole Soyinka, *The Man Died*, 1972

767. Albert Camus, *The Rebel*, 1951

768. Ottar G. Draugsvold, ed., *Nobel Writers on Writing*, 2000

769. Martin Luther King, *Letter from Birmingham Jail*, 1963

770. Interview, *Asia Source*, June 10, 2004

771. Nobel lecture, December 10, 1978

772. Paraphrasing Goethe, quoted in Walter Isaacson, *Kissinger: A Biography*, 1992

773. Naguib Mahfouz, *Reflections of a Nobel Laureate*, 2001

774. Speech in the House of Commons, March 26, 1936. In Winston Churchill, *Arms and the Covenant*, 1938

775. Albert Camus, *Resistance, Rebellion, and Death*, 1961

776. Nadine Gordimer, *Writing and Being*, 1995

777. Nelson Mandela, *A Long Walk to Freedom*, 1994

778. Speech at the Commonwealth Club of California, San Francisco, January 22, 1986

779. William Faulkner, "On Fear: Deep South in Labor: Mississippi," *Harper's*, June 1956

780. Toni Morrison, *Sula*, 1973

781. Interview, 1987, in Danille Taylor-Guthrie, ed., *Conversations with Toni Morrison*, 1994

782. *Guardian*, January 29, 1992

783. André Gide, *Travels in the Congo*, 1927

784. *New York Times*, December 16, 1984

785. Roald Hoffmann, *The Same and Not the Same*, 1995

786. Speech in the House of Commons, January 20, 1940

787. Joseph Brodsky, *A Part of Speech*, 1980

788. Speech at Westminster College, Fulton, Missouri, March 5, 1946

789. John Boyd Orr, *As I Recall*, 1967

790. Nobel autobiography, 1973

791. Peter Medawar, *Pluto's Republic*, 1982

792. Alexandr Solzhenitsyn, *The Oak and the Calf*, 1980

793. *Listener*, February 15, 1979

794. Max Perutz, *I Wish I'd Made You Angry Earlier*, 2002

795. Interview, *Independent on Sunday*, August 16, 1992

796. Albert Szent-Györgyi, *Science, Ethics, and Politics*, 1963

797. Interview with Dawn Engle and Ivan Suvanjieff, Houston, Texas, July 4, 1995

798. Quoted in Mortimer Lipsky, *Quest for Peace: The Story of the Nobel Award*, 1966

799. George Bernard Shaw, *Misalliance*, 1910

800. Albert Einstein, *Ideas and Opinions*, 1988

801. Albert Camus, *Resistance, Rebellion, and Death*, 1961

802. Theodore Roosevelt, speech in New York City, September 6, 1918

803. Morris Goran, "The Present-day Significance of Fritz Haber," *American Scientist*, vol. 35, no. 3, July 1947

804. Bertrand Russell, *Bertrand Russell Speaks His Mind*, 1960

805. Milton Friedman, *There's No Such Thing as a Free Lunch*, 1975

806. Interview, PBS, November 1, 2000

807. Joseph Stigler, *The Intellectual and the Marketplace*, 1984

808. James Heckman, "Conversations with Nobel Prize Winners," Forbes.com, November 3, 2003

809. Herbert Simon, *Models of My Life*, 1991

810. Joseph Stiglitz, *Globalization and Its Discontents*, 2002

811. *Boston Globe*, February 5, 1989

812. Bernard Lovell, *P.M.S. Blackett: A Biographical Memoir*, 1976

813. John Steinbeck, *The Grapes of Wrath*, 1939

814. Anatole France, *The Red Lily*, 1894

815. Speech in Atlanta, May 4, 1974, quoted in Bill Adler, ed., *The Wit and Wisdom of Jimmy Carter*, 1977

816. Nobel lecture, December 10, 2006

817. Wangari Maathai, *The Green Belt Movement*, 2004

818. "Persons and Genomes—Genetics and the Human Sciences," lecture at the London School of Economics, June 19, 2003

819. Interview, *Right Wing News*, 2003

820. Attributed

821. *Toronto Star*, November 6, 1982

822. Nobel acceptance speech, December 10, 1972

823. Christian de Duve, *Life Evolving*, 2002

824. Bill Moyers, *A World of Ideas*, 1989

825. Richard Feynman, *The Character of Physical Law*, 1967

826. Robert Laughlin, *A Different Universe*, 2005

827. Max Born, *Physics in My Generation*, 1969

828. Allen L. Hammond, ed., *A Passion to Know: 20 Profiles in Science*, 1984

829. Irving John Good, ed., *The Scientist Speculates*, 1962

830. Luis Alvarez, *Adventures of a Physicist*, 1987

831. Sydney Brenner, "Persons and Genomes—Genetics and the Human Sciences," lecture at the London School of Economics, June 19, 2003

832. Speech at Cal State, quoted in the *Daily 49er*, March 28, 2000

833. *Seattle Post-Intelligencer*, October 5, 2004

834. Quoted in Horace Freeland Judson, *The Eighth Day of Creation*, 1979

835. James Watson, *The Double Helix*, 1968

836. Quoted in Peter Medawar, *Memoirs of a Thinking Radish*, 1986

837. J. B. Birks, ed., *Rutherford at Manchester*, 1963

838. Commencement address, Caltech 1974, quoted in Richard Feynman, *Surely You're Joking, Mr. Feynman*, 1985

839. Attributed

840. W. C. and M. Dampier-Whetham, *History of Science*, 1929

841. "Uber den anschaulichen Inhalt der quantentheoretische Kinematik und Mechanik," *Zeitschrift fur Physik*, vol. 43, 1927

842. Leon Lederman, *The God Particle*, 1993

843. *New York Herald Tribune*, September 12, 1933

844. Val Fitch, "Soldier in the Ranks," in Jane Wilson, ed., *All in Our Time*, 1974

845. Abraham Pais, *The Genius of Science: A Portrait Gallery of Twentieth-Century Physicists*, 2000

846. Quoted in Subramanyan Chandrasekhar, *Truth and Beauty*, 1987

847. Attributed

848. Max Born, *The Restless Universe*, 1951

849. *Los Angeles Times*, April 4, 1992

850. Allen L. Hammond, ed., *A Passion to Know: 20 Profiles in Science*, 1984

851. Attributed

852. *Boston Globe*, December 10, 1982

853. Anthony L. Peratt, "Dean of the Plasma Dissidents" in *The World and I* (supplement to the *Washington Times*), May 1988.

854. Attributed

855. *Boston Globe*, December 10, 1982

856. Jacques Monod, *On the Molecular Theory of Evolution*, 1974

857. Joseph Brodsky, *On Grief and Reason*, 1995

858. George Wald, "The Origin of Life," in *Scientific American, The Physics and Chemistry of Life*, 1955

859. Helge Kragh, *Dirac: A Scientific Biography*, 1990

860. Max Delbrück, *A Physicist Looks at Biology*, 1949

861. François Jacob, "Molecular Tinkering and Evolution," in D. S. Bendall, ed., *Evolution from Molecules to Men*, 1983

862. George Wald, "The Origin of Optical Activity," *Annals of the New York Academy of Sciences*, vol. 69, 1957

863. Jacques Monod, *Chance and Necessity*, 1971

864. *New York Times*, April 11, 1965

865. Ronald W. Clark, *The Life of Ernst Chain: Penicillin and Beyond*, 1985

866. *Chicago Daily News*, 1936

867. Denis Brian, *The Voice of Genius: Conversations with Nobel Scientists and Other Laureates*, 2001

868. Denis Brian, *The Voice of Genius: Conversations with Nobel Scientists and Other Laureates*, 2001

869. Quoted in James Watson, *The Double Helix*, 1968

870. Horace Freeland Judson, *The Eighth Day of Creation*, 1979

871. Quoted in Ralph Brave, "James Watson Wants to Build a Better Human," Alternet.com, May 29, 2003

872. "Nobel Laureate Flags Cure for Stupidity," *Sun-Herald*, Sydney, March 2, 2003

873. *Sunday Telegraph*, February 16, 1997

874. Address at Nobel conference, at Gustavus Adolphus College, St. Peter, Minnesota, October 19, 1983

875. "Will I Soon Have a Clone?" in Bettina Stiekel, ed., *The Nobel Book of Answers*, 2003

876. "Persons and Genomes—Genetics and the Human Sciences," lecture at the London School of Economics, June 19, 2003

877. "Persons and Genomes—Genetics and the Human Sciences," lecture at the London School of Economics, June 19, 2003

878. Ralph Gunther, *The Magic Zone: Sketches of the Nobel Laureates*, 2003

879. Jean-Paul Sartre, *Situations I*, 1947

880. International Society for Optical Engineering newsroom, 2006

881. News release, Union of Concerned Scientists, February 10, 1997

882. Octavio Paz, *The Other Voice*, 1990

883. Albert Camus, *Betwixt and Between*, 1937

884. Juan Ramón Jiménez, *Selected Writings*, 1957

885. *Guardian Weekly*, October 15-21, 2004

886. Quoted in J. E. Avron, D. Osadchy, and R. Seiler, *Topological Quantum Numbers in the Hall Effect*, Department of Mathematics, Technical University of Berlin, 2003

887. Denis Brian, *The Voice of Genius: Conversations with Nobel Scientists and Other Laureates*, 2001

888. Albert Einstein, *Sidelights on Relativity*, 1920

889. Leon Lederman, *The God Particle*, 1993

890. Allen L. Hammond, ed., *A Passion to Know: 20 Profiles in Science*, 1984

891. Nobel acceptance speech, December 10, 1992
892. Remark in 1917, quoted in Allen L. Hammond, ed., *A Passion to Know: 20 Profiles in Science*, 1984
893. Salvador Luria, *A Slot Machine, a Broken Test Tube: An Autobiography*, 1984
894. "Personal Observations on the Reliability of the Shuttle," appendix F to the President's Commission to Investigate the Challenger Disaster, 1986. Reprinted in Richard Feynman, *Classic Feynman*, 2006
895. Richard Feynman, *The Pleasure of Finding Things Out*, 1999
896. "How Does the Telephone Work?" in Bettina Stiekel, ed., *The Nobel Book of Answers*, 2003
897. Letter to the *New York Times* composed September 17, 1969
898. Glenn Seaborg, *A Scientist Speaks Out: A Personal Perspective on Science, Society and Change*, 1996
899. *New York Times*, July 12, 1987
900. Peter Medawar, *The Threat and the Glory: Reflections of Science and Scientists*, 1990
901. Address at Middlesex Hospital, October 1908, reprinted in Rudyard Kipling, *A Book of Words*, 1928
902. News summaries, March 22, 1954
903. Interview with Jonathan Holms, Australian Broadcasting Corporation, July 9, 2003
904. Marc Abrahams, ed., *Annals of Improbable Research*, vol. 1, 2003
905. *Worcester State College News*, November 13, 2006
906. Herbert Simon, "Decision Making: Rational, Nonrational, and Irrational," *Educational Administration Quarterly*, vol. 29, 1993
907. P. F. Harrison and J. Lederberg, *Antimicrobial Resistance: Issues and Options*, 1998
908. Pearl S. Buck, *The Good Earth*, 1933
909. Inaugural lecture in the Norman Borlaug Lecture Series in Ames, Iowa, 2002
910. Quoted by Norman Borlaug in Nobel lecture, December 11, 1970
911. Arthur Kornberg, *For the Love of Enzymes: The Odyssey of a Biochemist*, 1989
912. "Why Can't I Live on French Fries?" in Bettina Stiekel, ed., *The Nobel Book of Answers*, 2003
913. Kary Mullis, *Dancing Naked in the Mind Field*, 1998
914. http://www.satyamag.com/may04/coetzee.html
915. Attributed
916. Roy Jenkins, *Churchill: A Biography*, 2001
917. James M. Webb and A. Wigfall Green, *William Faulkner of Oxford*, 1965
918. *National Observer*, February 3, 1964
919. Remark at Silver Spring, Maryland, February 1947
920. James C. Humes, *The Wit and Wisdom of Winston Churchill*, 1994
921. Vincent Sheean, *Dorothy and Red*, 1963
922. Interview, PBS, 1991
923. Interview, PBS, 1991
924. Interview, PBS, 1991
925. Interview, Academy of Achievement, November 11, 1990
926. Heinrich Böll, *A Soldier's Legacy*, 1985
927. Nobel lecture, December 10, 2002
928. Jimmy Carter, *Living Faith*, 1996
929. Nobel lecture June 12, 1935
930. Nobel lecture, December 11, 1950
931. Winston Churchill, *My Early Life*, 1930
932. Tyler Wasson, ed., *Nobel Prize Winners*, 1987
933. Nobel lecture, 1994

934. Romain Rolland, *Above the Battle*, 1915

935. Jean-Paul Sartre, *Lucifer and the Lord*, 1951

936. Ernest Hemingway, introduction to Ben Raeburn, ed., *Treasury for the Free World*, 1946

937. Norman Angell, *The Steep Places*, 1947

938. *Combat*, August 30, 1944, reprinted in *Between Hell and Reason*, 1991

939. Address to the nation on the Soviet intervention in Afghanistan, January 4, 1980

940. Winston Churchill, epigraph to *The Second World War*, vol. 1, *The Gathering Storm*, 1948

941. Winston Churchill, *My Early Life*, 1930

942. First speech in the House of Commons as prime minister, May 13, 1940

943. Winston Churchill, *The Second World War*, vol. 2, *Their Finest Hour*, 1949

944. Speech in the House of Commons, June 4, 1940

945. Winston Churchill, *The Second World War*, vol. 1, *The Gathering Storm*, 1948

946. Otto Hahn, *My Life: The Autobiography of a Scientist*, 1968

947. Speech in New York City, February 17, 1899

948. Pam Brown, *Henry Dunant*, 1988

949. Lester Pearson, "Peace in the Family of Man," the 1968 Reith lectures

950. *Observer*, August 26, 1973

951. Nobel lecture, December 12, 1974

952. Nobel lecture, December 10, 2005

953. Henry Kissinger, *Foreign Affairs*, January 13, 1969

954. Quoted in *ACLU v. Prayer at Virginia Military Institute*, 2002

955. Alice Calaprice, ed., *The Quotable Einstein*, 1996

956. Letter to Linus Pauling, quoted in Alice Calaprice, ed., *The Quotable Einstein*, 1996

957. Lansing Lamont, *Day of Trinity*, 1965

958. Henry Kissinger, *Nuclear Weapons and Foreign Policy*, 1957

959. Jeremy Bernstein, *Hitler's Uranium Club: The Secret Recordings at Farm Hall*, 1996

960. Max Born, *The Restless Universe*, 1951

961. Interview in 1969, quoted in Andrew Brown, *The Neutron and the Bomb: A Biography of Sir James Chadwick*, 1997

962. Patrick Blackett, *Fear, War, and the Bomb*, 1949

963. "How Do I Win the Nobel Prize?" in Bettina Stiekel, ed., *The Nobel Book of Answers*, 2003

964. Elie Wiesel, *Night*, 1958

965. Nobel acceptance speech, December 10, 1986

966. Nobel lecture, December 11, 1986

967. Nobel lecture, December 11, 1986

968. Imre Kertész, *Kaddish for a Child not Born*, 1990

969. Nobel lecture, December 7, 2002

970. Remark in 1997, quoted in www.juedisches-leben-in-breisach.de

971. Nobel lecture, December 7, 2002

972. Interview, *Newsweek*, December 2002

973. Nobel acceptance speech, December 10, 2002

974. Nelly Sachs, quoted in www.raquelpartnoy.tripod.com.ve

975. Nobel autobiography, 2002

976. Israel Ministry of Foreign Affairs, 2004

977. BBC, 2006

978. www.anc.org.za/ancdocs/history/mandela/1994/inaugpta.html

979. *New York Times*, September 14, 1993

980. Speech in St. Louis, March 22, 1964

981. Nobel lecture, December 11, 1957

982. Speech to the Parliament of India, New Delhi, November 28, 1986, quoted in *Time*, December 8, 1986

983. Nobel lecture, December 11, 1970

984. Speech in Stockholm, December 12, 1971

985. *New York Times*, September 10, 1993

986. George C. Marshall, *Biennial Report of the Chief of Staff, United States Army*, September 1, 1945

987. Winston Churchill, *My Early Life*, 1930

988. Address at the Royal Institute of International Affairs, London, May 10, 1982; reprinted in Henry Kissinger, *Observations: Selected Speeches and Essays, 1982–1984*, 1985

989. Henry Kissinger, *White House Years*, 1979

990. Henry Kissinger, *A World Restored: Metternich, Castelreagh, and the Problems of Peace, 1812–22*, 1957

991. Olga S. Opfell, *The Lady Laureates*, 1986

992. William Baer, ed., *Conversations with Derek Walcott*, 1996

993. Nobel lecture, December 11, 1987

994. Michael Bliss, *Banting: A Biography*, 1984

995. James C. Humes, *The Wit and Wisdom of Winston Churchill*, 1994

996. Alice Calaprice, ed., *The Quotable Einstein*, 1996

997. Speech in Memphis, Tennessee, April 3, 1968

998. Tyler Wasson, ed., *Nobel Prize Winners*, 1987

999. Giorgos Seferis, *A Poet's Journal*, 1974

1000. Alan Wade, ed., *The Letters of W. B. Yeats*, 1954

ALFRED NOBEL AND THE NOBEL PRIZES

Alfred Nobel was born in 1833 in Sweden, but he grew up in Russia, where his father was engaged in the manufacture of explosives. Nobel traveled widely; he spent four years in the United States, lived most of his life in France, and died in Italy. Like his father, he was primarily a manufacturer of explosives. Nitroglycerin, which was highly unstable, blew up one of his factories in 1864, killing one of his brothers and several employees. Nobel discovered ways of mixing nitroglycerin with other substances to produce the much safer dynamite, which he patented in 1867. He expressed the belief that the destructive force of his explosives would be such as to render future wars unthinkable. The rapid adoption of dynamite in construction and mining made Nobel very wealthy. Dynamite was not his only invention; during his lifetime, he took out over 350 patents, including those for artificial silk and artificial leather. Reclusive and ascetic, a lifelong bachelor, prone to depression but gracious to other people, Nobel spoke and wrote fluent Swedish, French, English, German, and Russian. An avid reader, he also wrote novels, plays, and poetry.

In 1895, the year before his death, Nobel drew up his will. He directed that the bulk of his fortune should be invested in a fund, the annual interest from which should be divided in five equal parts, to be awarded as follows:

> One part to the person who shall have made the most important discovery or invention within the field of physics; one part to the person who shall have made the most important chemical discovery or improvement; one part to the person who shall have made the most important discovery within the domain of physiology or medicine; one part to the person who shall have produced in the field of literature the most outstanding work of an idealistic tendency; and one part to the person who shall have done the most or the best work for fraternity among nations, for the abolition or reduction of standing armies, and for the holding and promotion of peace congresses.

Nobel added, "It is my express wish that in awarding the prizes no consideration whatever shall be given to the nationality of the candidates." Each prize could be shared by a maximum of three persons. A sixth prize was added in 1969, when, on its tercentenary, the Bank of Sweden established the "Bank of Sweden Prize in Economic Sciences in Memory of Alfred Nobel." The names of the prizes are typically abbreviated to Chemistry, Economics, Literature, Medicine, Peace, and Physics.

The Nobel prizes are awarded by committees established by four institutions. The Royal Swedish Academy of Science is responsible for the prizes in Physics, Chemistry, and Economics. The Prize in Medicine is awarded by the Karolinska Institutet in Stockholm. The Prize for Literature is the responsibility of the Swedish Academy. And the Peace Prize is awarded by a committee of the Norwegian parliament.

At the time of Nobel's death in 1896, his industrial empire included ninety factories in twenty countries, and his fortune totaled over 30 million Swedish kronor. The first prizes were worth about $20,000 in today's values, and with inflation the real value of the prizes did not pass this amount for many decades.

The exemption of the Nobel Foundation from taxes in 1946 and the liberalization of the foundation's investment rules in 1953 resulted in a rapid growth in its capital. In 2006 the value of each prize stood at 10 million Swedish kronor, or about $1.457 million.

Those authorized to nominate people for the prize include previous laureates, members of the Swedish academies and the Norwegian parliament, and members of scientific institutions throughout the world. The processes of nomination and selection are conducted in strict secrecy, and the files remain closed for fifty years. Nominations must be received by February 1. Names of the laureates are normally announced during the first half of October, and the awards are presented each year in Stockholm and Oslo on December 10, the anniversary of Alfred Nobel's death. Award ceremonies are conducted with great pomp and dignity, in the presence of the royal families of Sweden and Norway. At the formal banquet on December 10, each prize winner makes a brief acceptance speech; in the case of multiple recipients of one prize, one of the winners does so. Each laureate is also required to deliver a lecture, which is normally given a few days before or after the prize ceremony. The events constitute a weeklong party for the citizens of Oslo and Stockholm in the middle of the dark Scandinavian winter. On Lucia Day, December 13, the laureate is woken by a choir, led by a girl wearing a crown of lighted candles. Many Nobel laureates have remarked that the experience was for themselves and their families like living in a fairy tale.

In its first 106 years, the Nobel Prize was awarded to 768 individuals; in addition, nineteen organizations received the Peace Prize. Four people have won two prizes: Marie Curie (Physics and Chemistry), Linus Pauling (Chemistry and Peace), Frederick Sanger (both in Chemistry), and John Bardeen (both in Physics). The Red Cross has been awarded the Peace Prize three times, and it has been given twice to the Office of the United Nations High Commission for Refugees.

BIOGRAPHIES OF
NOBEL LAUREATES QUOTED
◇◦◇◦◇◦◇

 ADDAMS, JANE (USA, 1860–1935). Peace, 1931. A pioneer social worker, feminist, pacifist, and internationalist, Addams founded a famous settlement house, Hull House, in Chicago. She was the moving spirit of the National American Woman Suffrage Association, president of the Women's International League for Peace and Freedom, and a founding member of the American Civil Liberties Union.

AGNON, SHMUEL (Poland, Israel; 1888–1970). Literature, 1966. Born to a Yiddish-speaking family in eastern Galicia, then part of the Austrian Empire, Agnon emigrated to Palestine in 1907, returning for long sojourns in Europe. His novels and stories, written in Hebrew, deal with the decline of Jewry in Galicia and with Jewish life in Palestine.

 AGRE, PETER (USA, born 1949). Chemistry, 2003. Peter Agre, a professor at Johns Hopkins School of Medicine, was honored for his work on "water channels," showing how water enters and is utilized by cells. When Agre was a child in Minnesota, his father predicted that he would one day win a Nobel Prize. Agre started his career in medicine before he switched to biological research.

ALEIXANDRE, VICENTE (Spain, 1898–1984). Literature, 1977. Aleixandre devoted his life to poetry. He spent the Spanish Civil War in the

Republican zone, following which he was silenced by the Franco government for four years. The Swedish Academy cited his "creative poetic writing which illuminates man's condition in the cosmos and in present-day society."

ALFVÉN, HANNES (Sweden, 1908–1995). Physics, 1970. Both of Alfvén's parents were physicians, his mother one of the first women doctors in Sweden. He discovered antimatter and was much ahead of his time in his work on plasma physics and the evolution of the solar system; consequently, his discoveries usually took years to be accepted. He was one of the few scientists to be a member of both the American and the Soviet academies of science.

AL-SADAT, ANWAR (Egypt, 1918–1981). Peace, 1978. Sadat shared the Peace Prize with Menachem Begin for the Camp David agreement between Egypt and Israel. An army officer, imprisoned for his opposition to British rule in Egypt, Sadat helped overthrow the Farouk monarchy and became president of Egypt in 1970. He was assassinated in 1981 by Muslim extremists.

ALTMAN, SIDNEY (Canada, USA; born 1939). Chemistry, 1989. Born in Montreal, Altman worked as a screenwriter and poetry editor before spending "four years of overstimulation" at MIT and a period of "scientific heaven" working with Francis Crick in Cambridge. In 1971, he moved to Yale, where he became dean of Yale College. Altman started as a physicist, ended as a biologist, and won his Nobel Prize in chemistry for his studies of RNA.

ALVAREZ, LUIS (USA, 1911–1988). Physics, 1968. A classic type A personality, Alvarez was a pioneer in many areas, ranging from designing the detonators for the atomic bomb to inventing the ground control approach system for blind aircraft landing. He flew as an observer of the Hiroshima bomb. He worked in optics, cosmic rays, radar, high-energy physics, and elementary particle physics, for which he won the Nobel Prize. He later proposed the asteroid theory of the extinction of the dinosaurs.

ANDERSON, PHILIP (USA, born 1923). Physics, 1977. Anderson interrupted his studies at Harvard to serve in the U.S. Navy in World War II and afterward spent most of his career at Bell Laboratories; he also taught at Princeton, Cambridge, and Kyoto. His areas of research included crystals, superconductors, and low-temperature physics. He shared the Nobel Prize for "investigations of the electronic structure of magnetic and disordered systems." He spoke out frequently against both the Vietnam War and "Star Wars."

ANFINSEN, CHRISTIAN (USA, 1916-1995). Chemistry, 1972. A pioneer in the study of enzymes and the genetic basis of protein organization, Anfinsen was awarded the Nobel Prize for his work on ribonuclease. He subsequently pioneered research in interferon. Anfinsen spent his career at the National Institutes of Health, with visiting appointments in Denmark, Sweden, and Britain. In 1981, as chair of the National Academy of Sciences Committee on Human Rights, he led a delegation to Argentina to free twelve scientists imprisoned by the Videla dictatorship.

ANGELL, NORMAN (Britain, 1872-1967). Peace, 1933. Born in England, Angell spent several years working as a cowboy and at other jobs in California. He then moved to Paris as a journalist, correspondent, and editor. His 1910 antiwar book, *The Great Illusion*, sold 2 million copies. Thereafter, Angell divided his time between Britain and the United States, writing a book a year, opposing the policy of appeasement, and promoting peace, European unity, and international control of atomic energy.

APPLETON, EDWARD (Britain, 1892-1965). Physics, 1947. Son of a Yorkshire mill worker, Appleton became an atmospheric physicist, proved the existence of the ionosphere, and contributed to the development of radar and cathode ray oscillography. An officer in the Royal Engineers in World War I, in World War II he was administrative head of the British atom bomb project. After professorships at London and Cambridge, he became vice-chancellor of the University of Edinburgh.

ARAFAT, YASSER (Palestine, 1929-2004). Peace, 1994. Born in Cairo, Arafat fought in the 1947 Arab-Israel War and in 1958 founded Al Fatah, an armed underground network, which absorbed the Palestine Liberation Organization in 1969. In 1988, he renounced terrorism and recognized Israel's right to exist. He shared the Nobel Prize with Yitzhak Rabin and Shimon Peres for their work toward the 1993 Oslo Accords on the development of Palestinian self-rule. The award to Arafat was controversial, and one member of the Nobel Committee resigned in protest. In 1996, Arafat was elected president of the Palestine Authority.

ARIAS SÁNCHEZ, OSCAR (Costa Rica, born 1941). Peace, 1987. After taking a doctorate in Britain, Arias Sánchez entered politics in Costa Rica, becoming head of the National Liberation Party in 1979 and president of Costa Rica from 1986 to 1990. He received the Nobel Prize for negotiating peace in 1987 among Costa Rica, El Salvador, Honduras, and Nicaragua.

ARNOLDSON, KLAS PONTUS (Sweden, 1844–1916). Peace, 1908. Arnoldson spent twenty years working for the Swedish railways before devoting himself to journalism and the cause of peace. He won election to parliament, where he worked for religious toleration, arms reduction, Swedish neutrality, and widening the suffrage. Arnoldson was honored for his work toward the peaceful separation of Norway and Sweden, the permanent neutrality of Sweden, and the founding of the Swedish Peace and Arbitration Society.

ASTURIAS, MIGUEL ÁNGEL (Guatemala, 1899–1967). Literature, 1967. The works of Asturias reflected his interest in the South American Indian tradition and his support for the underdog. He wrote his best-known novel, *El Señor Presidente,* during ten years in Paris. His career rose and fell with Guatemalan politics: an ambassador under left-wing governments, an exile under right-wing dictators.

AUMANN, ROBERT (Israel, USA; born 1930). Economics, 2005. Born in Germany, Aumann's family left for the United States in 1938. He studied at City College, New York, then earned a Ph.D. in algebraic topology at MIT. He moved to Israel in 1956. Controversial for his conservative views, Aumann won the Nobel Prize for "having enhanced our understanding of conflict and cooperation through game-theory analysis."

AUNG SAN SUU KYI (Burma, born 1945). Peace, 1991. The daughter of an assassinated general who was a hero of the Burmese independence movement, Suu Kyi studied at Oxford and worked in the UN Secretariat. On returning to Burma in 1988, she assumed leadership of the National League for Democracy, which won 82 percent of the vote in 1990. The military junta refused to relinquish power and placed Suu Kyi under house arrest. Since then she has spent more than ten years in detention.

BALCH, EMILY (USA, 1867–1961). Peace, 1946. Educated at Bryn Mawr, Harvard, and in Chicago, Paris, and Berlin, Balch was a lifelong campaigner for peace, justice, and the rights of minorities, women, and children. A delegate to the International Congress of Women during World War I, and subsequently secretary to the Women's International League for Peace and Freedom, she was dismissed from Wellesley College in 1918 for her pacifist views.

BALTIMORE, DAVID (USA, born 1938). Medicine, 1975. A leader in biomedical research, Baltimore worked on the polio and leukemia viruses, and was appointed head of the National Institutes of Health AIDS Vaccine Committee in 1996. An outspoken advocate for science-based public policy, he became president of Caltech in 1997. He won the Nobel Prize for "discoveries concerning the interaction between tumor viruses and the genetic material of the cell."

BANTING, FREDERICK (Canada, 1891–1941). Medicine, 1923. The son of a farmer, Banting served with the Canadian Army Medical Corps in France, where he was wounded and won the Military Cross. He received the Nobel Prize for his discovery of insulin at the University of Toronto in 1921. When his student and fellow investigator Charles Best was not given the prize as well, Banting split his award money with him. An unpretentious man and gifted amateur painter, Banting died in a plane crash in Newfoundland while on a wartime medical mission to England.

BARDEEN, JOHN (USA, 1908–1991). Physics, 1956; Physics, 1972. After studying electrical engineering and geophysics in Wisconsin, Bardeen completed a doctorate in mathematical physics at Princeton. He worked during World War II in the Naval Ordnance Laboratory and spent the next six years at Bell Laboratories, where he was codiscoverer of the transistor, for which he won his first Nobel Prize. The last twenty-five years of his career he spent at the University of Illinois, winning his second Nobel for research in the theory of superconductivity.

BEADLE, GEORGE (USA, 1903–1989). Medicine, 1958. The son of a Nebraska farmer, Beadle attended agriculture college and became a specialist on corn genetics. He taught at Caltech, Harvard, and Stanford, and became chancellor and president of the University of Chicago. His award was for work on the genes that specify proteins.

BECKETT, SAMUEL (Ireland, France; 1906–1989). Literature, 1969. Born in Ireland, Beckett moved to France in 1938. During the Second World War, he worked for the Resistance. In 1945, he embarked on his full-time career as an author, writing in both French and English. His works, of which the most famous is the play *Waiting for Godot*, depict humanity struggling to live in a world that appears bleak and absurd.

BEGIN, MENACHEM (Poland, Israel; 1913–1992). Peace, 1978. Born in Poland, Begin learned nine languages and trained as a lawyer. The leader of a militant Zionist youth organization, he was imprisoned first by the Poles and then in Siberia by the Russians. His parents died in the Holocaust. Arriving in Israel in 1942, he became commander of the Irgun underground military group fighting British rule. As prime minister, he signed the peace treaty with Egypt at Camp David in 1979.

BELLOW, SAUL (USA, 1915–2005). Literature, 1976. Born in Quebec, Bellow served in the Merchant Marine in World War II and as a war correspondent in the 1967 Arab-Israeli War. A Chicagoan from age ten, Bellow spoke four languages and was married five times. The Swedish Academy praised him "for the human understanding and subtle analysis of contemporary culture that are combined in his work."

BENAVENTE, JACINTO (Spain, 1866–1954) Literature, 1922. Benavente was honored for his plays, of which he wrote more than 170. Celebrated for his witty dialogue, he was influential in the development of Spanish theater. His later work, and his support of Franco after the Spanish Civil War, diminished his reputation.

BERG, PAUL (USA, born 1926). Chemistry, 1980. The son of Yiddish-speaking immigrants, Berg grew up in Brooklyn, New York, and served two years in the U.S. Navy at the end of World War II. Like several other science laureates, he was originally attracted to science by Paul de Kruif's book *Microbe Hunters*. A professor at Stanford, he has been called "the father of genetic engineering." He was awarded the Nobel Prize for his work on recombinant DNA.

BERGSON, HENRI (France, 1859-1941). Literature, 1927. Born in Britain, Bergson was professor of philosophy at the Collège de France. Widely influential through his books on philosophy, psychology, and religion, he championed intuition and spirituality over intellect and materialism. Jewish by birth but Catholic in outlook, in 1941 he refused an offered exemption from the Vichy racial laws and stood in line to register as a Jew. He died of pneumonia a few days later.

BINNIG, GERD (Germany, Switzerland; born 1947). Physics, 1986. As a teenager, Binnig was an active athlete and sang, played the violin, and played guitar in a rock band. He has spent most of his career at the IBM Research Laboratory in Zurich. He received the Nobel Prize for his design of the scanning tunnel electron microscope, which can resolve vertical features one tenth the diameter of a hydrogen atom. He regards parenthood of his two children as the highlight of his life.

 BISHOP, J. MICHAEL (USA, born 1936). Medicine, 1989. Son of a Lutheran minister, Bishop spent more than thirty years at the University of California at San Francisco. He shared the Nobel Prize for the "discovery of the cellular origin of retroviral oncogenes." A pianist, he once said that if he were reincarnated, he would choose to be a musician in a string quartet.

BJØRNSON, BJØRNSTJERNE (Norway, 1832-1910). Literature, 1903. Son of a pastor, Bjørnson grew up in rural Norway. He wrote historical and realistic plays, dramatic sagas, peasant stories, rustic novels, lyric poetry, and literary criticism. Themes of morality and religion are prominent in his work. He worked as a theater manager and traveled widely in Europe. He was politically active in liberal causes. A vigorous patriot, he composed the lyrics to the Norwegian national anthem.

BLACKETT, PATRICK (Britain, 1897-1974). Physics, 1948. Blackett trained as a regular navy officer and served in the Royal Navy through World War I. In World War II, he was a senior adviser in various war departments. He was awarded the Nobel Prize "for his development of the Wilson cloud chamber method, and his discoveries therewith in the fields of nuclear physics and cosmic radiation." A lifelong socialist, Blackett was an outspoken opponent of nuclear weapons.

BOHR, NIELS (Denmark, 1885-1962). Physics, 1922. Bohr was honored for his work on the structure of the atom. At his institute in Copenhagen, he became a much-loved father figure to many future Nobel physicists and assisted many Jewish scientists fleeing Nazi Germany. Warned of his imminent arrest in 1942, he was spirited out of occupied Denmark and joined the atom bomb project at Los Alamos. He met with both Roosevelt and Churchill to urge, unsuccessfully, the international control of atomic energy.

BÖLL, HEINRICH (Germany, 1917-1985). Literature, 1972. Böll served in the Wehrmacht through World War II in France and on the Eastern Front, and was wounded four times. In some forty books of fiction and essays, he expressed compassion for the victims of society and condemned both contemporary materialism and the forces that led to the catastrophes of the twentieth century.

BORLAUG, NORMAN (USA, born 1914). Peace, 1970. Born on a farm in Iowa, Borlaug became a plant pathologist. While working in Mexico from 1944 to 1960, he developed a high-yield, hardy, disease-resistant strain of wheat, which tripled Mexican wheat production. He was honored for his leadership of the "Green Revolution."

 BORN, MAX (Germany, Britain; 1882-1970) Physics, 1954. Born studied at Göttingen and Cambridge. During World War I, he conducted military research and worked at the University of Berlin, where his friendship with Albert Einstein began. He returned to Göttingen for its golden age, 1921-1933. He left Germany in 1933 and in 1935 became a professor at Edinburgh. Born won the Nobel Prize for his statistical interpretation of quantum theory. He refused to work on poison gas in World War I and on the atomic bomb in World War II. After retiring to Germany, he was active in the campaign against nuclear weapons.

BOYER, PAUL (USA, born 1918). Chemistry, 1997. Boyer was born and grew up in Utah. He was high school valedictorian at sixteen, and served in the U.S. Navy at the end of World War II. He spent his career at the University of Minnesota and at UCLA. He was awarded the Nobel Prize for his work on enzymes.

BRAGG, WILLIAM HENRY (Britain, 1862-1942). Physics, 1915. After leaving Cambridge, Bragg taught in Australia for eighteen years. He did not begin serious research until 1904, when he quickly made major findings on alpha particles. He left sunny Adelaide in 1909 to take a position in rainy, smoky Leeds in England. During World War I, he headed submarine detection research; his younger son was killed in France. Bragg shared the Nobel Prize with his son Lawrence Bragg, for their X-ray analysis of crystal structure.

BRANDT, WILLY (Germany, Norway; 1913-1992). Peace, 1971. A Social Democratic journalist, anti-Nazi, and anti-Communist, Brandt went into exile in Norway and Sweden during the Nazi era, making covert missions back into Germany during the war. He was mayor of West Berlin in 1957-1966 and chancellor of West Germany in 1969-1974, in which office he worked to normalize relations between West and East.

BRENNER, SYDNEY (South Africa, Britain; born 1927). Medicine, 2002. Born in South Africa, the son of a multilingual but illiterate Lithuanian cobbler, Brenner entered the University of Witwatersrand at fifteen, and qualified as a doctor before moving to Oxford and then Cambridge, where he spent most of his career. His prize was awarded for work in genetics.

BRIDGMAN, PERCY (USA 1882-1961). Physics, 1946. During his forty years at Harvard, Bridgman never attended a faculty meeting, which enabled him to write 260 papers and thirteen books. He worked on sonar in World War I and on plutonium in World War II. Bridgman won the Nobel Prize for his work in high-pressure physics, leading to advances in thermodynamics, crystallography, and the production of synthetic diamonds.

BRODSKY, JOSEPH (USSR, USA; 1940-1996). Literature, 1987. Brodsky was a gifted translator of English poetry into Russian. He worked at many occupations while writing poetry that circulated in underground samizdat publications. In 1964, he was sentenced to exile with hard labor in Siberia for "social parasitism." In 1972, he emigrated to the United States. The Swedish Academy praised the "clarity of thought and poetic intensity" of his prose and poetry.

BUCK, LINDA (USA, born 1947). Medicine, 2004. Buck grew up in Seattle, the daughter of an electrical engineer. She explored various career possibilities before entering graduate school at twenty-eight in microbiology. Buck won the Nobel with Richard Axel for their research on the sense of smell.

BUCK, PEARL S. (USA, 1892–1973). Literature, 1938. Pearl Buck spent forty years in China, where her parents were missionaries. She spoke Chinese before English, and many of her eighty works were set in China. A woman of immense energy and drive, she adopted many children. With her literary earnings of more than $7 million, she endowed the Pearl S. Buck Foundation, founded to aid Asian children of U.S. servicemen.

BUNCHE, RALPH (USA, 1904–1971). Peace, 1950. The great-grandson of a slave, Bunche was the first African American to win the Nobel Prize. A brilliant student and athlete, he earned a Ph.D. from Harvard in 1934. A prodigious worker, active in the civil rights movement, Bunche spent most of his career as an international troubleshooter at the United Nations. He received the Nobel Prize for his mediation of an armistice between Israel and the Arab states in 1949.

CAMUS, ALBERT (France, 1913–1960). Literature, 1957. Camus's father was killed in World War I, and Albert grew up in poverty in Algeria. At twenty-five, he moved to Paris, where he worked in the theater as a producer and playwright. During the German occupation, he contributed articles to the Resistance newspaper *Combat*. An opponent of both fascist and Marxist ideology, he wrote about the problem of justice and the need to create personal meaning in an unfeeling and absurd universe. Camus died in a car crash at the age of forty-seven.

CANETTI, ELIAS (Bulgaria, Britain; 1905–1994). Literature, 1981. Canetti was born in Bulgaria to a Sephardic family; his first language was Ladino. He earned a doctorate in chemistry from the University of Vienna. With the intensification of Nazi anti-Semitism, Canetti moved permanently to London in 1938. He wrote in German, his fourth language. A playwright, critic, and novelist, he is the author of the multidisciplinary *Crowds and Power*, his magnum opus.

CARREL, ALEXIS (France, 1873-1944). Medicine, 1912. Carrel left France in 1904 and spent almost forty years at Rockefeller University. He returned to serve in the French Army Medical Corps during World War I. His Nobel Prize was "for his work on vascular suturing, and on the grafting of blood vessels and organs." Carrel's reputation was clouded by his acceptance in 1944 of the directorship of the Carrel Foundation for the Study of Human Problems under the Vichy government.

CARTER, JIMMY (USA, born 1924). Peace, 2002. A graduate of the U.S. Naval Academy, Carter served seven years as a nuclear specialist and submarine officer. He became governor of Georgia in 1971 and the thirty-ninth president of the United States in 1976. He helped bring about the Panama Canal Treaty, the Camp David Accords between Israel and Egypt, and the SALT (Strategic Arms Limitation Talks) II Treaty. In 1982, he founded the Carter Center, which works to resolve conflicts, enhance freedom, and improve health around the world.

CASSIN, RENÉ (France, 1887-1976). Peace, 1968. Severely wounded in World War I, Cassin founded the French Federation of Disabled War Veterans. In World War II, he held a senior position under General Charles de Gaulle. A jurist, professor of law, humanitarian, and internationalist, Cassin worked throughout his life for human rights and gender equality. As chair of the UN Commission on Human Rights, he was largely responsible for drafting the Declaration of Human Rights.

CELA, CAMILO JOSÉ (Spain, 1916-2002). Literature, 1989. Although Cela fought and was wounded on the Franco side in the Spanish Civil War, his books, marked by violent language and brutal action, were censored by the Franco government. In 1954, he moved to Mallorca, where he established an antifascist journal. He authored ten novels and sixty other works of essays, short stories, and poetry.

CHADWICK, JAMES (Britain, 1891-1974). Physics, 1935. Chadwick was a graduate student in Berlin when war broke out in 1914, and he spent the war interned in a horse stable. On his release, he was invited by

Ernest Rutherford to the Cavendish Laboratory at Cambridge. There he discovered the neutron, which led to the development of nuclear fission, and for which he won the Nobel Prize. During World War II, he led the British mission attached to the Manhattan Project. He later became master of Gonville and Caius College, Cambridge.

CHAIN, ERNST (Germany, Britain; 1906-1979). Medicine, 1945. Born in Berlin, the son of an industrial chemist, Chain first considered a career as a concert pianist. He moved to Britain when Hitler became chancellor of Germany; the rest of his family perished. Chain worked with Howard Florey to purify and test penicillin, for which they shared the Nobel Prize with Alexander Fleming. He had a distinguished career in Britain and Italy, ending as professor of biochemistry at London.

CHANDRASEKHAR, SUBRAMANYAN (India, USA; 1910-1995). Physics, 1983. Born in Lahore, a nephew of the Nobel laureate Venkata Raman, Chandrasekhar won a scholarship to Cambridge, where, at twenty, he did fundamental work on black holes. When he presented his findings at the Royal Astronomical Society, they were derided by Sir Arthur Eddington, the leading astronomer of the day. Devastated, Chandrasekhar left Britain and taught at the University of Chicago for fifty years. His ideas were vindicated long before he was awarded the Nobel Prize.

CHARPAK, GEORGES (Poland, France; born 1924). Physics, 1992. Born in Poland, Charpak's family moved to France in 1931. During World War II, Charpak served in the French Resistance and was arrested and deported to Dachau. Honored "for his invention and development of particle detectors," he worked for thirty years at the Centre Européen pour la Recherche Nucléaire (CERN). He is also noted for his work in support of scientists in repressive countries.

CHURCHILL, WINSTON (Britain, 1874-1965). Literature, 1953. In his youth, Churchill was a dashing cavalry officer and war correspondent, seeing action in India, the Sudan, and South Africa. He published many books and was a gifted painter. But he is mainly known as the indomitable prime minister of Britain during World War II, whose defiant speeches and determined leadership did much to save Britain from defeat.

COCKCROFT, JOHN (Britain, 1897-1967). Physics, 1951. Born to a family of Lancashire cotton manufacturers, Cockcroft served in the Royal Artillery during World War I, then took degrees in electrical engineering and mathematics. He directed the Canadian Atomic Energy Project during World War II and subsequently the Atomic Energy Research Establishment at Harwell in England. He was awarded the Nobel Prize for his "discovery of the transmutations of atomic nuclei by artificially accelerated particles."

COETZEE, J. M. (South Africa, born 1940). Literature, 2003. Of Boer and English descent, Coetzee spent his twenties in England and his thirties in the United States, before returning to South Africa as a professor at Cape Town. In 2002, he was appointed to the University of Adelaide; he also holds a position at the University of Chicago. Coetzee is the author of more than eighteen books and has twice won the Booker Prize.

COMPTON, ARTHUR (USA, 1892-1962). Physics, 1927. Compton shared the Nobel Prize "for his discovery of the effect named after him." (The Compton effect refers to the increase in wavelength of X-rays caused by the scattering of the incident radiation by electrons.) Compton held senior positions in several universities and scientific associations. During World War II, he directed the atom bomb project at the University of Chicago.

CORNELL, ERIC (USA, born 1961). Physics, 2001. The son of an engineering professor at MIT, as a teenager Cornell built model rockets powered by gunpowder. He interrupted his university studies to spend a year teaching English in Taiwan and traveling in China. A professor at the University of Colorado, he shared the Nobel Prize for work on Bose-Einstein condensation. In 2004, he lost his left arm and shoulder to necrotizing fasciitis.

CORRIGAN, MAIREAD (Northern Ireland, born 1944). Peace, 1976. Corrigan shared the Nobel Prize with Betty Williams for their work for peace in Northern Ireland. They founded the group Peace People after three of Corrigan's nieces and nephews were killed by a car driven by a terrorist who had been shot. In 1981, she married Jackie Maguire, the widower of her sister Anne, who never recovered from the tragic loss of her children and died in January 1980.

CRICK, FRANCIS (Britain, USA; 1916–2004). Medicine, 1962. Originally a physicist, Crick worked as a scientist in the British Admiralty during World War II. He shared the Nobel award with James Watson and Maurice Wilkins for their discovery of the structure of DNA. In 1977, Crick moved to the Salk Institute, where he specialized in neurobiology.

CRONIN, JAMES (USA, born 1931). Physics, 1980. The son of a professor of classical languages, Cronin worked at Princeton and then moved to the University of Chicago, where he conducted much experimental work in elementary particle physics at Fermilab. He was awarded the Nobel Prize for studies of K-mesons.

CURIE, MARIE (Poland, France; 1867–1934). Physics, 1903; Chemistry, 1911. Born in Poland, Marie Curie moved to France to attend the Sorbonne. She and her husband, Pierre, working under difficult physical conditions, isolated radium, for which they shared the Nobel Prize. She was the first woman laureate and the first person to win two Nobels. Like her daughter Irène, who won the Nobel Prize for Chemistry in 1935, Marie Curie died of leukemia, probably due to radiation exposure.

DAE-JUNG, KIM (Korea, born 1925). Peace, 2000. Kim Dae-jung, the leader of the New Democratic Party, ran for the presidency of South Korea in 1971. Imprisoned many times by a series of military governments, he was once sentenced to death, and he survived five assassination attempts. He was elected president in 1997 and won the Nobel Prize for his efforts to normalize relations with North Korea. He is the first Korean laureate.

DALAI LAMA, THE FOURTEENTH (Tibet, born 1935). Peace, 1989. Chosen as Dalai Lama at age five, and considered the reincarnation of the Buddha of Compassion, he is the spiritual and secular head of the Tibetan people. He went into exile in 1959 after the Chinese occupation of Tibet. He received the Nobel Prize for his consistent advocacy of tolerance and nonviolence in the solution of human and international problems, especially those of Tibet.

DE DUVE, CHRISTIAN (Belgium, born 1917). Medicine, 1974. Born in London to Belgian refugees, de Duve took his medical degree at Louvain.

Briefly in the army in 1940, and then in a prison camp, from which he escaped, he returned to Louvain to take a doctorate in chemistry. From 1962 he held joint appointments at Louvain and Rockefeller University. He shared the Nobel Prize for research on the structure and function of cells.

DE KLERK, F. W. (South Africa, born 1936). Peace, 1993. The son of a conservative Afrikaner senator, de Klerk practiced law and was elected to parliament in 1972. Becoming president in 1989, he called for a democratic, nonracist South Africa, lifted the ban on the African National Congress, and released Nelson Mandela from prison. His actions initiated the end of apartheid and the transition to democracy.

DELBRÜCK, MAX (Germany, USA; 1906-1981). Medicine, 1969. Delbrück grew up in Berlin, the son of a professor of history, and studied at Göttingen. He left Germany in 1937 on a Rockefeller scholarship and spent most of his career at Caltech. Interested in music and philosophy, he was an expert on the poet Rilke. He was awarded the Nobel Prize for "discoveries concerning the replication mechanism and the genetic structure of viruses."

 DELEDDA, GRAZIA (Italy, 1871-1936). Literature, 1926. Deledda was born in a village of Sardinia so remote that the local language was a variant of Latin. She published her first story at fifteen and her first novel at twenty-two, and produced a book a year for thirty years. Little read today, her early fiction focused on life in Sardinia, her later work on the theme of redemption through love.

DIRAC, PAUL (Britain, 1902-1984). Physics, 1933. Dirac became Lucasian Professor at Cambridge at the age of thirty. The author of over two hundred papers, in 1928 he formulated a relativistic quantum mechanical wave equation since known as the Dirac equation. Famously reticent and exact, a keen mountain climber, he traveled widely, making a journey around the world with Werner Heisenberg in 1929. Niels Bohr said of him, "Of all physicists, Dirac has the purest soul." After retirement from Cambridge, he joined the faculty at the University of Florida at Tallahassee.

DUNANT, HENRI (Switzerland, 1828-1910). Peace, 1901. The first winner of the Nobel Peace Prize, Dunant founded the Red Cross after witnessing, and helping to relieve, the suffering of the wounded at the Battle of Solferino in 1859. In his dedicated work organizing the Geneva Conventions, Dunant neglected his business interests, went bankrupt, was forgotten, and lived in poverty for many years before his rediscovery and winning of the Nobel Prize. He spent none of the prize money and bequeathed it to charity.

EBADI, SHIRIN (Iran, born 1947). Peace, 2003. Appointed one of Iran's first female judges in 1975, Ebadi was forced to resign after the revolution in 1979 and was subsequently imprisoned on numerous occasions for her advocacy of democracy and human rights, especially those of women and children, and for her defense of victims of conservative attack and repression.

ECCLES, JOHN (Australia, Britain, USA, Switzerland; 1903–1997). Medicine, 1963. Eccles spent his research career in Australia, New Zealand, Britain, and the United States; after retirement in 1975, he settled in Switzerland. The research for which he won the Nobel Prize was on nerve cells; his later research focused on the brain and consciousness. He also wrote a number of books on the relation of science and religion.

EDELMAN, GERALD (USA, born 1929). Medicine, 1972. Originally trained as a concert violinist, after he obtained his medical degree Edelman was drafted into the U.S. Army in 1955 and served as a surgeon at European Command Headquarters in Paris. He spent almost fifty years at Rockefeller University. He was awarded the Nobel Prize for his research on the chemical structure of antibodies. His subsequent work focused on the issue of consciousness.

EINSTEIN, ALBERT (Germany, Switzerland, USA; 1879–1955). Physics, 1921. The outstanding physicist of the twentieth century, Einstein saw his prize delayed for a decade because the Nobel committee chairman thought he was "just writing formulas." Although Einstein is known for his theory of relativity, the prize was awarded for his work on the photoelectric effect. Einstein left Europe for the United States in 1933 and spent the rest of his life at the Institute for Advanced Study at Princeton. He declined an invitation to become president of Israel.

ElBaradei, Mohamed (Egypt, born 1942). Peace, 2005. The International Atomic Energy Agency (IAEA) and its director general, ElBaradei, shared the Peace Prize "for their efforts to prevent nuclear energy from being used for military purposes and to ensure that nuclear energy for peaceful purposes is used in the safest possible way." ElBaradei received a doctorate in international law from New York University. He joined the Egyptian diplomatic service, moving to the UN in 1980, and to the IAEA Secretariat in 1984, being appointed director in 1997.

Eliot, T. S. (USA, Britain; 1888-1965). Literature, 1948. The most revolutionary poet of the early twentieth century, Eliot was a social and political conservative. Unlike the ninety laureates who became American, Eliot was an American who became British. He settled in England in 1914 and adopted English dress, manners, speech, churchmanship, and prejudices. As a poet and critic, editor of the magazine *Criterion*, and a director of Faber & Faber publishers, he was enormously influential in shaping literary trends. He is best known for his 1922 poem, *The Waste Land*.

Esaki, Leo (Japan, born 1925). Physics, 1973. After working for Sony in Japan, Esaki spent thirty years with IBM in the United States before returning to Japan as president of the University of Tsukuba. He was awarded the Nobel Prize for his research in tunneling phenomena in semiconductors. The Esaki diode contributed to the development of high-speed computer circuits.

Faulkner, William (USA, 1897-1962). Literature, 1949. A lifelong resident of Mississippi, Faulkner served in the Royal Canadian Air Force at the end of World War I. His early novels were not commercially successful, and he worked at many different jobs, including several stints in Hollywood as a screenwriter. His novels are marked by literary experiment, psychological insight, and a preoccupation with issues of white racial guilt in the Deep South.

Feynman, Richard (USA, 1918-1988). Physics, 1965. Considered by many the greatest American physicist, Feynman was honored for his work on quantum electrodynamics. Despite his youth, he was a group leader on the Los Alamos atom bomb project. He was an energetic and popular teacher, and his lectures on physics became a major textbook. A lifelong opponent of formality and pomposity, he was known for his attachment to bongo drums, Las Vegas, and opening locked safes.

FITCH, VAL (USA, born 1923). Physics, 1980. Born on a cattle ranch in Nebraska, Fitch had to interrupt his undergraduate career when World War II began. The U.S. Army assigned him to Los Alamos for three years, and the experience of working in proximity to many of the world's greatest physicists impelled him into a career in physics. A professor at Princeton for fifty years, he was awarded the Nobel Prize for his studies of K-mesons.

FLEMING, ALEXANDER (Britain, 1881–1945). Medicine, 1945. Born on a remote farm in Scotland, Fleming spent four years as a shipping clerk in London before entering medical school. He joined a Scottish regiment during the Boer War but was not sent overseas. In 1928, he discovered and named penicillin, but it aroused little interest, and the elaborate process of isolation of the active substance was achieved by Howard Florey, Ernst Chain, and others during World War II.

FLOREY, HOWARD (Australia, Britain; 1898–1968). Medicine, 1945. A native of Australia, Florey went to Oxford as a Rhodes Scholar and took his Ph.D. at Cambridge. He spent most of his career at Oxford, becoming provost of Queen's College in 1962 and president of the Royal Society in 1960. He shared the Nobel Prize for the development of penicillin.

FRANCE, ANATOLE (France, 1844–1924). Literature, 1921. France's real name was Jacques-Anatole-François Thibault. For fifty years an enormously prolific writer of novels, criticism, and essays, he was awarded the Nobel Prize "in recognition of his brilliant literary achievements, characterized as they are by a nobility of style, a profound human sympathy, grace, and a true Gallic temperament."

FRANCK, JAMES (Germany, USA; 1882–1964). Physics, 1925. Franck served on the Russian front during World War I and twice won the Iron Cross. While a professor at Göttingen, he received the Nobel Prize for his "discovery of the laws governing the impact of an electron upon an atom." In 1935, he moved to Johns Hopkins University. During World War II he worked on the Manhattan Project. He was an author of the "Franck Report," urging an open demonstration of the atom bomb in some uninhabited locality of Japan.

FRIEDMAN, MILTON (USA, 1912–2006). Economics, 1976. The son of immigrants from central Europe, Friedman worked his way through university to become a leading member of the "Chicago School." His conservative economics were enormously influential, particularly on the economic policies of Prime Minister Margaret Thatcher and Presidents Richard Nixon and Ronald Reagan.

GAJDUSEK, CARLETON (USA, born 1923). Medicine, 1976. A multilingual pediatrician and virologist of wide interests, Gajdusek won the Nobel Prize for his work on slow-virus diseases, especially kuru, scrapie, and Creutzfeldt-Jakob disease. He traveled extensively, studying tropical diseases in isolated communities, and adopted some fifty boys from Stone Age cultures in New Guinea and Micronesia. Charges of pedophilia led to a year's imprisonment in 1997, after which Gajdusek moved to Europe.

GALSWORTHY, JOHN (Britain, 1867–1933). Literature, 1932. Galsworthy took a law degree at Oxford but did not practice. He traveled widely, met Joseph Conrad on board a ship in the South Pacific, and began to write on his return. *The Man of Property*, the first volume of his *Forsyte Saga*, was published in 1906. Galsworthy was critical of inequalities of wealth and interested in questions of justice. His play *Justice* stimulated prison reform in Britain.

GARCÍA MÁRQUEZ, GABRIEL (Colombia, born 1928). Literature, 1982. García Márquez has spent most of his life in voluntary or involuntary exile in Latin America and Europe. The author of novels, stories, and journalism, and a central figure in the magic realism movement, he writes with a blend of surrealism, myth, comedy, and compassion for the oppressed. His most celebrated work is *One Hundred Years of Solitude*.

GELL-MANN, MURRAY (USA, born 1929). Physics, 1969. Gell-Mann entered Yale at fifteen and earned his Ph.D. from MIT at twenty-two. A professor at Caltech for almost forty years, he won the Nobel Prize for his theoretical work on elementary particles, which subsequently led to the discovery of quarks. His other interests include conservation, cultural evolution, languages, and Peruvian artifacts.

GIACCONI, RICCARDO (Italy, USA; born 1931). Physics, 2002. Giacconi grew up in Milan and first went to the United States on a Fulbright fellowship. An astrophysicist, he worked on rocket and satellite pay-loads, and on the Hubble telescope. He received the Nobel Prize "for pioneering contributions to astrophysics, which have led to the discovery of cosmic X-ray sources."

GIDE, ANDRÉ (France, 1869–1951) Literature, 1947. Financial independence allowed Gide to spend his entire life as a writer. He published over fifty works, including novels, plays, poetry, criticism, and translation. He was a communist for a few years, until disillusioned by a visit to the Soviet Union. He was also one of the first major writers to openly acknowledge his homosexuality. Gide's writing is marked by criticism of conventional morality and a commitment to personal authenticity.

GILBERT, WALTER (USA, born 1932). Chemistry, 1980. Gilbert grew up in Washington, D.C., and spent much of his high school career playing truant in order to read in the Library of Congress. He did his doctorate at Cambridge and spent the rest of his career at Harvard. Originally a physicist, ultimately an evolutionary biologist, he received the Nobel Prize for work on DNA.

GILMAN, ALFRED (USA, born 1941). Medicine, 1994. Gilman's father was a professor of pharmacology; both his parents were musicians. With doctorates in medicine and chemistry, Gilman started and ended his career at Yale. He shared the Nobel Prize for discovering G proteins and the role of these proteins in signal transduction in cells.

GLASHOW, SHELDON (USA, born 1932). Physics, 1979. Glashow's father was a Russian immigrant plumber; his two brothers became a doctor and a dentist. A graduate of the Bronx High School of Science, where another future laureate, Steven Weinberg, was a schoolmate, Glashow attended Cornell and Harvard, did postdoctoral work at the Niels Bohr Institute in Copenhagen, and taught at Stanford, Berkeley, and Harvard. His Nobel Prize was awarded for discoveries in elementary particle research.

GOLDING, WILLIAM (Britain, 1911–1993). Literature, 1983. Golding worked for many years as a schoolteacher and saw considerable action as a Royal Navy officer in World War II. Both of these experiences influenced his fiction, which is marked by a belief in the human capacity for evil; his best-known work is the dystopian novel *Lord of the Flies*.

GORBACHEV, MIKHAIL (USSR, born 1931). Peace, 1990. Born in the Caucasus to a peasant family, Gorbachev is the only person to have received both the Order of Lenin and the Ronald Reagan Freedom Award. As president of the USSR, he inaugurated policies of glasnost (openness) and perestroika (economic liberalization). Intended to reform the Soviet system, they led to the repudiation of communism and the breakup of the Soviet Union.

GORDIMER, NADINE (South Africa, born 1923). Literature, 1991. Prevented by the faulty diagnosis of a bad heart from becoming a dancer, Gordimer began to write, and published her first story at fourteen. A committed and active liberal in the police state that was apartheid South Africa, Gordimer wrote novels that uncompromisingly portrayed the destructive effects of racial segregation on individuals and their relationships. In 1987, she helped found the Congress of South African Writers, most of whose members are black.

GRASS, GÜNTER (Germany, born 1927). Literature, 1999. During World War II, Grass served in a Waffen SS tank division and was captured by the Americans. After the war he worked as a sculptor in Paris and Berlin, and began to write. He was active in Willy Brandt's Social Democratic Party. Success as a writer came with his 1959 *The Tin Drum*, which, like his other works, probes the traumatic history of Germany, especially under the Nazis.

GULLSTRAND, ALLVAR (Sweden, 1862–1930). Medicine, 1911. Self-taught in optics, Gullstrand became professor of opthalmology at Uppsala in 1894 and is considered the founder of modern ophthalmology. His work led to improved eyeglasses and to the invention of other optical instruments. His Nobel Prize was awarded for his research in the physiology of the eye.

HABER, FRITZ (Germany, 1868–1934). Chemistry, 1918. Haber's method of fixing atmospheric nitrogen was crucial to the German munitions industry in World War I. During this conflict, Haber directed German chemical warfare and was responsible for the development and first use of poison gas as a weapon. When he ignored his wife's entreaties to give up this work, she killed herself with his service revolver. The Allies named him a war criminal. As director of the Kaiser Wilhelm Institute in

1933, he refused to dismiss his fellow Jews. He resigned, went into exile, and died the following year.

HAHN, OTTO (Germany, 1879-1968). Chemistry, 1944. During World War I, Hahn served first in the infantry and then in the German gas warfare service. He was the discoverer of nuclear fission, for which he won the Nobel Prize. Hahn refused to join the Nazi Party and took a courageous stand against Nazi science policy. Following the war, he became director of the prestigious Max Planck Society. He was a strong opponent of German acquisition of nuclear weapons. He was a dedicated long-distance runner into his sixties.

HAMMARSKJÖLD, DAG (Sweden, 1905-1961). Peace, 1961. The son of a prime minister of Sweden, Hammarskjöld was an exceptionally conscientious and reflective diplomat, and secretary general of the United Nations from 1953 until his death. In this capacity he mediated many international conflicts. He died in a plane crash while working for peace in the Congo.

HAMSUN, KURT (Norway, 1859-1952). Literature, 1920. Hamsun spent his youth in poverty in Europe and the United States, achieving a breakthrough with his 1890 novel, *Hunger*. A lifelong Germanophile, Anglophobe, and antidemocrat, he supported the Nazi cause and was received by Hitler and Goebbels during the war. Tried for treason after the war, he was heavily fined and died in poverty.

HAYEK, FRIEDRICH VON (Austria, Britain, USA; 1899-1992). Economics, 1974. Von Hayek served in the Austrian army during World War I, then earned doctorates in law and economics. He moved to London in 1931 and to Chicago in 1950. An influential leader in free-market economics, Hayek became famous for his 1944 book, *The Road to Serfdom*, predicting that the welfare state would lead to totalitarianism and slavery.

HEANEY, SEAMUS (Northern Ireland, born 1939). Literature, 1995. The eldest of nine children, Heaney was born on a farm in County Derry, which remained his "country of the mind." Since 1982 he has taught part-time at Harvard, and from 1989 to 1994 was professor of poetry at Oxford. A prolific poet, Heaney received the Nobel Prize "for works of lyrical beauty and ethical depth, which exalt everyday miracles and the living past."

HECKMAN, JAMES (USA, born 1944). Economics, 2000. Born in Chicago, Heckman returned there for part of his graduate work and for most of his career, though he went to high school in Colorado, where he was taught physics by Robert Oppenheimer's brother Frank. He has a major interest in the development of human resources through education. Heckman was awarded the Nobel Prize for his work on sampling in microeconomics.

HEISENBERG, WERNER (Germany, 1901–1976). Physics, 1932. The son of a professor of Greek, Heisenberg published his theory of quantum mechanics, for which he won the Nobel Prize, when he was twenty-three. An accomplished pianist, he is best known today for his uncertainty principle, which posits that it is impossible simultaneously to determine the position and the momentum of a particle. In World War II, he headed German atomic research; historians still debate how committed he was to this project, which failed even to build a reactor.

HEMINGWAY, ERNEST (USA, 1899–1961). Literature, 1954. Hemingway, who saw action in both World Wars as well as the Spanish Civil War, was a boxer, big-game hunter, fisherman, and bullfight aficionado. His reputation rests on a few novels, in which a theme is that if life ends in inevitable failure, the human task is to fail with dignity. His unadorned literary style was greatly influential. He was married four times and maintained homes in Cuba, Key West, and Idaho. Mentally unbalanced in his last years, he died by suicide.

HERSCHBACH, DUDLEY (USA, born 1932). Chemistry, 1986. The first of six children of a rabbit breeder, Herschbach grew up in rural California, where he was a high school football star. After undergraduate work at Stanford, he spent the rest of his career at Harvard, where he pioneered "Chem Zen," a popular science course for liberal arts students. He won the Nobel Prize for studies of chemical reactions.

HERZBERG, GERHARD (Germany, Canada; 1904–1999). Chemistry, 1971. Deprived of his professorship because his wife was Jewish, Herzberg left Germany for Canada in 1934, where he found a position at the University of Saskatchewan. Subsequently, he worked at the National Research Council in Ottawa into his nineties. An unaffected man with a fine singing voice, Herzberg was known as "the father of modern molecular spectroscopy." He was honored for his discoveries in the structure of molecules.

HESSE, HERMAN (Germany, Switzerland; 1877–1962). Literature, 1946. Hesse left school at sixteen and was apprenticed first to a clockmaker, then to a book dealer. He moved to Switzerland in 1912. During World War I, his pacifism made him unpopular in Germany. This, together with the stress of his wife's mental illness, produced a mental crisis that took Hesse into therapy with a disciple of Jung. His books were banned by the Nazis. Hesse's prolific works largely deal with the search for spiritual truth and the essential self.

HITCHINGS, GEORGE (USA, 1905–1998). Medicine, 1988. A researcher at Burroughs Wellcome, Hitchings was for forty years the mentor of and collaborator with Gertrude Elion, with whom he shared the Nobel Prize for designing drugs that operated selectively against various diseases, including leukemia and malaria.

HOFFMANN, ROALD (Poland, USA; born 1937). Chemistry, 1981. Born in what is now Ukraine, Hoffmann lost most of his family in the Holocaust. He spent World War II in a ghetto, a labor camp, and in hiding. His father, who smuggled Hoffmann and his mother out of the camp, died in a breakout attempt. After three years in a camp for displaced persons, Hoffmann emigrated to the United States. Multilingual and a published poet, Hoffmann won the Nobel Prize for his studies of orbital symmetry in chemical reactions.

 HULL, CORDELL (USA, 1871–1955). Peace, 1945. Born in a log cabin in Tennessee, Hull was successively a state legislator, an infantry captain, a judge, a U.S. congressman, a U.S. senator, and secretary of state. He was honored for his work in international relations and specifically for his role in the establishment of the United Nations.

JACOB, FRANÇOIS (France, born 1920). Medicine, 1965. Jacob was the grandson of the first Jewish four-star general in the French army. He joined the Free French Forces in 1940, served as a medical officer in central and north Africa, and participated in the invasion of Normandy. Serious wounds from a fragmentation bomb prevented him from realizing his long-cherished ambition to be a surgeon. He shared the Nobel Prize with colleagues at the Pasteur Institute "for their discoveries concerning genetic control of enzyme and virus synthesis."

JIMÉNEZ, JUAN RAMÓN (Spain, United States; 1881–1958). Literature, 1956. The son of a banker, Jiménez abandoned law studies for poetry. At the outbreak of the Spanish Civil War, the Republican government sent him to the United States as cultural attaché. After Franco's victory, Jiménez stayed in the United States and in 1951 settled in Puerto Rico. Periodically hospitalized for depression, he dealt in his poetry with the experience of beauty as a means to struggle against nothingness.

KAHNEMAN, DANIEL (Israel, USA; born 1934). Economics, 2002. Kahneman survived World War II in occupied France and then emigrated to Palestine, graduating in psychology from the Hebrew University of Jerusalem. Drafted into the Israeli Defense Force in 1954, he worked on the assessment of officer candidates. He moved to the University of California at Berkeley in 1958. Kahneman received the Nobel Prize "for having integrated insights from psychological research into economic science."

KAPITSA, PYOTR (Russia, 1894–1984). Physics, 1978. The son of a czarist general, Kapitsa was born in St. Petersburg. One of his daughters died of scarlet fever, and his other daughter, his father, and his wife perished during the 1920 influenza epidemic. In 1921, he went to Cambridge to work with Ernest Rutherford. Visiting Russia in 1934, he was prevented from leaving on Stalin's orders. He continued his research in low-temperature physics in Moscow, for which he later won the Nobel Prize. During the war, he worked on large-scale production of oxygen for the steel industry but was later disgraced for refusing to work on nuclear weapons.

KENDALL, HENRY (USA, 1926–1999). Physics, 1990. Kendall joined the Merchant Marines in the summer of 1945, resigning to attend Amherst College in 1946, afterward spending forty years at MIT. For many years the head of the Union of Concerned Scientists, he was honored for his work on subatomic particles, which confirmed the existence of quarks. A keen photographer, mountaineer, and diver, Kendall died while scuba diving on a National Geographic Society expedition in Florida.

KERTÉSZ, IMRE (Hungary, born 1929). Literature, 2002. Born in Budapest, as a teenager Kertész survived both Auschwitz and Buchenwald.

Dismissed by the Communist government from his newspaper position, he shared a one-room flat with his wife and worked as a translator. The Nobel presentation speech cited Kertész "for writing that upholds the fragile experience of the individual against the barbarian arbitrariness of history."

KING, MARTIN LUTHER (USA, 1929–1968). Peace, 1964. A Baptist minister, King became the eloquent voice of the American civil rights movement. Deeply influenced by Gandhi, he advocated nonviolent resistance to injustice. He was assassinated in Memphis, Tennessee, at the age of thirty-nine. He was the youngest recipient of the Peace Prize and the only laureate to die before the age of forty.

KIPLING, RUDYARD (Britain, 1865–1936). Literature, 1907. Born in India, Kipling spoke Hindustani before learning English. He experienced great cruelty during his schooling in England. He returned to India for some years as an adult, and India was frequently the setting for his poetry, novels, and stories for adults and children. He was deeply affected by the loss of a daughter to pneumonia and of his only son in World War I. A superb literary craftsman, he held conservative and imperialist views, which made his reputation controversial.

KISSINGER, HENRY (Germany, USA; born 1923). Peace, 1973. Kissinger's immediate family immigrated from Germany to the United States in 1938; thirteen other relatives perished in the Holocaust. He served in army counterintelligence during World War II and taught at Harvard University from 1954 to 1969. He was an adviser to five presidents, and secretary of state under Presidents Richard Nixon and Gerald Ford. He shared the Nobel award with Le Duc Tho of North Vietnam (who refused it) for their attempts to negotiate an end to the Vietnam War. The award was controversial, and two of the five members of the Norwegian Nobel Committee resigned in protest.

KOHN, WALTER (Austria, Canada, USA; born 1923). Chemistry, 1998. Kohn was rescued from Austria by the Kindertransport to Britain; the rest of his family perished in the Holocaust. In Britain, he was interned as an enemy alien and then sent to Canada. He studied at Toronto and Harvard. Most of his career was spent at the University of California. He won the Nobel Prize "for his development of the density-functional theory."

KORNBERG, ARTHUR (USA, born 1918). Medicine, 1959. Kornberg graduated from high school at fifteen and, like eight other Nobel laureates, attended the tuition-free City College of New York. He served as an officer in the U.S. Public Health Service and as a ship's doctor in the navy, and taught at Washington University, St. Louis, and Stanford. A world authority on enzymes, Kornberg was awarded the Nobel Prize for his studies of RNA and DNA.

KREBS, HANS (Germany, Britain; 1900-1981). Medicine, 1953. Krebs served in the German army in 1918. Dismissed by the Nazis from his professorship at the University of Freiberg in 1934, he emigrated to Britain, where he taught at the universities of Sheffield, Cambridge, and Oxford. His Nobel was awarded for his discovery of the citric acid cycle, now known as the Krebs cycle.

LAGERLÖF, SELMA (Sweden, 1858-1940). Literature, 1909. An educator, novelist, story writer, poet, biographer, and dramatist, Lagerlöf was a leading figure in the romantic revival in Swedish literature. In her last days, she saved the life of the German poet Nellie Sachs by endorsing her application for a visa to Sweden. In her writing, she was influenced by Greek tragedy, the Old Testament, and Icelandic sagas.

LAUGHLIN, ROBERT (USA, 1950-2007). Physics, 1998. Laughlin attended the University of California at Berkeley during the days of Vietnam War protests and was then drafted into the military, spending much of his tour of duty in Germany. He subsequently worked at MIT, Bell Labs, the Livermore Lab, and Stanford University. His Nobel-winning work explained how electrons in a powerful magnetic field can condense to form a kind of quantum fluid.

LAUTERBUR, PAUL (USA, 1929-2007). Medicine, 2003. A professor of medicine at the College of Medicine at Illinois from 1985 until his death, Lauterbur was honored for "discoveries concerning Magnetic Resonance Imaging" which led to the widespread development and use of MRI in medical diagnosis.

LEDERBERG, JOSHUA (USA, born 1925). Medicine, 1958. Lederberg's parents immigrated to the United States from Palestine. He earned his B.A. at nineteen and trained as a doctor in the navy during World War II. He was a consultant to the World Health Organization and NASA, and president of Rockefeller University for twelve years. Lederberg won the Nobel Prize "for his discoveries concerning genetic recombination and the organization of the genetic material of bacteria."

LEDERMAN, LEON (USA, born 1922). Physics, 1988. Born and educated in New York, Lederman served three years in the U.S. Army in World War II. During his twenty-eight years at Columbia, he had fifty Ph.D. students. ("None, to my knowledge is in jail," he reports.) He was awarded the Nobel Prize for his discovery of neutrinos.

LEHN, JEAN-MARIE (France, born 1939). Chemistry, 1987. Born in Alsace, Lehn studied the classics, philosophy, and science in high school. Lehn spent his entire career in France, at the National Center for Scientific Research, the University of Strasbourg, Université Louis Pasteur, and the Collège de France. He was awarded the Nobel Prize for his part in "development and use of molecules with structure-specific interactions of high selectivity."

LEONTIEF, WASSILY (Russia, USA; 1906–1999). Economics, 1973. Born in St. Petersburg, where his father was a professor of economics, as a boy Leontief witnessed Lenin addressing a mass rally at the Winter Palace. He took his B.A. at Leningrad and earned his Ph.D. at Berlin at twenty-two. Leontief moved to the United States in 1931 and spent forty-four years at Harvard. The Swedish Academy of Sciences cited his "development of the input-output method of economic analysis," which became a standard technique in the economic planning of many countries.

 LEWIS, ARTHUR (St. Lucia, West Indies, 1915–1991). Economics, 1979. With Derek Walcott, Lewis was one of two Nobel laureates from the tiny island of St. Lucia. The son of teachers, he graduated from high school at fourteen. He studied at the London School of Economics and was one of the first blacks to be appointed to a university lectureship in Britain. He worked for the UN for several years, mainly in Africa. He was honored for his work on poverty, growth, and development in Third World countries.

LEWIS, SINCLAIR (USA, 1885–1951). Literature, 1930. The first American to win the Nobel Prize for Literature, Lewis achieved fame with *Main Street* (1920), a satirical view of the hypocrisy of Middle America, which sold five hundred thousand copies. Attacked for his critical treatment of American life, Lewis in turn rejected the Pulitzer Prize. An alcoholic and perpetual nomad, Lewis died in Rome.

 LORENZ, KONRAD (Austria, 1903–1989). Medicine, 1973. A dedicated naturalist from early childhood, this son of a surgeon earned an M.D. but was working as a professor of psychology in 1941 when he was drafted into the Wehrmacht as a medical officer. Captured on the Armenian front in 1944, he served as a doctor in Soviet prison camps until his release in 1948. The founder of modern ethology, Lorenz was awarded the Nobel Prize for his discoveries "concerning organization and elicitation of individual and social behavior patterns."

LUCAS, ROBERT (USA, born 1937). Economics, 1995. Lucas grew up in Seattle and attended the University of Chicago, where he was a student of Milton Friedman. He returned to teach at Chicago in 1974. He was awarded the Nobel Prize "for having developed and applied the hypothesis of rational expectations, and thereby having transformed macroeconomic analysis."

LURIA, SALVADOR (Italy, USA; 1912–1991). Medicine, 1969. Luria served as a medical officer in the Italian army before leaving Italy for Paris, emigrating to the United States in 1940. An active socialist, he opposed the Vietnam War and was deprived of his passport in the McCarthy era. He founded and directed the Center for Cancer Research at MIT, where he also taught a course on world literature. He won the Nobel Prize for his work on the genetic structure of viruses.

 LUTULI, ALBERT (South Africa, 1898–1967). Peace, 1960. Lutuli was a teacher and lay preacher who was elected chief of the Zulu Abasemakholweni tribe and later became president of the African National Congress. He spent much of his life in internal exile under a ban by the government of South Africa. He was honored for his leadership of nonviolent resistance to apartheid.

 MAATHAI, WANGARI (Kenya, born 1940). Peace, 2004. Maathai studied in Germany and earned her doctorate at the University of Nairobi, where she became chair of the Department of Veterinary Anatomy. She also headed the Kenyan National Council of Women. She founded the Green Belt Movement, whose members (mostly women) have planted over 20 million trees. In 2002, she was elected to the Kenyan parliament and served as assistant minister of environment, natural resources, and wildlife.

MACBRIDE, SEÁN (Ireland, 1904-1988). Peace, 1974. Macbride was the son of the Irish nationalists Maud Gonne, a muse of William Butler Yeats, and John Macbride, who was executed after the Easter Rising in 1916. Macbride served in the IRA for twenty years. He subsequently became an expert trial lawyer and Irish minister for external affairs. He worked with several international human rights organizations and was chairman of Amnesty International from 1961 to 1974.

MACDIARMID, ALAN (New Zealand, USA; 1927-2007). Chemistry, 2000. During the depression in New Zealand, MacDiarmid went to his two-room school barefoot and had an early morning milk round. He left school at sixteen and became a lab boy and janitor at the university. He studied part-time and won a Fulbright fellowship to the United States, where he spent forty-five years at the University of Pennsylvania. MacDiarmid shared the Nobel Prize for the discovery that modified plastics can conduct electricity.

MACKINNON, RODERICK (USA, born 1956). Chemistry, 2003. After completing his M.D. at Tufts University and his residency at Harvard Medical School, MacKinnon decided to embark on postdoctoral studies in basic research. Later, he gave up a tenured professorship at Harvard to move to Rockefeller University, where he continued the research on ion channels for which he won the Nobel Prize.

 MAETERLINCK, MAURICE (Belgium, 1862-1949). Literature, 1911. Maeterlinck trained as a lawyer but practiced only briefly. A prolific writer of poems and essays, he was primarily a dramatist. He moved from symbolism and fantasy in his early writings to more realistic works addressing moral and philosophical issues. The king of Belgium named him a count in 1932. An opponent of totalitarianism, Maeterlinck spent World War II in Portugal and the United States.

MAHFOUZ, NAGUIB (Egypt, 1911-2006). Literature, 1988. The author of over forty novels and one hundred short stories, as well as plays and screenplays, Mahfouz is widely recognized as the foremost exponent of

234

the Arab novel. His 1957 Cairo Trilogy made him famous throughout the Arab world, but he continued working as a cultural officer in the Egyptian civil service until the age of sixty. In 1994, he survived a near-fatal assassination attempt.

MANDELA, NELSON (South Africa, born 1918). Peace, 1993. The son of a cattle owner of the Xhosa royal family and one of his five wives, Mandela was an amateur boxer in his youth. He became an activist lawyer and helped organize the guerrilla army of the African National Congress. He was convicted of treason and sentenced to life imprisonment in 1964. In 1991, a year after his release, he was elected president of the newly democratic South Africa.

MANN, THOMAS (Germany, Switzerland, USA; 1875–1955). Literature, 1929. The Swedish Academy cited *Buddenbrooks* (1901), which sold a million copies, but several of Mann's other novels are also regarded as classics of European literature. An outspoken opponent of Nazism, Mann left Germany in 1933 for Switzerland and lived in California from 1941 to 1952. He refused to return to Germany and spent his last years in Switzerland.

MARSHALL, GEORGE C. (USA, 1880–1959). Peace, 1953. A career officer, Marshall served in the Philippines and in France. Between the wars he served three years in China, where he learned Chinese. As chief of staff of the U.S. Army in World War II, Marshall proved an outstanding administrator and strategist. A model public servant, he became secretary of state and secretary of defense under President Harry Truman. Marshall was recognized for his leadership in creating the "Marshall Plan" for the postwar reconstruction of Europe.

MATHER, JOHN C. (USA, born 1946). Physics, 2006. A graduate of Swarthmore and Berkeley, Mather is a senior astrophysicist at NASA's Goddard Space Center. He coordinated the work of the huge team that developed the Cosmic Background Explorer satellite. He and George F. Smoot were honored for research that revealed the black body form of the microwave background radiation. Their work threw new light on the nature of the universe immediately after the big bang.

MAURIAC, FRANÇOIS (France, 1885–1970). Literature, 1952. Mauriac was a left-wing Catholic and prolific writer in many genres. He supported the Republicans in the Spanish Civil War. During the occupation, though at first a Pétain supporter, he soon began to produce underground writing for the Resistance. The Swedish Academy praised "the deep spiritual insight and the artistic intensity with which he has in his novels penetrated the drama of human life."

McFADDEN, DANIEL (USA, born 1937). Economics, 2000. McFadden grew up on the family farm deep in rural North Carolina. He earned his B.S. at nineteen and taught at MIT, Chicago, and Caltech. He bought a small vineyard and farm in the Napa Valley, to grow grapes and olives, and raise ducks and chickens. He won the Nobel Prize for his theory of "discrete choice," which predicts how a majority will behave if given a limited number of options.

 MEDAWAR, PETER (Britain, 1915–1987). Medicine, 1960. Medawar was born in Brazil, but spent most of his life in Britain at the universities of Oxford and London. During the Second World War, he worked on wound and burn healing, and his investigations of graft rejection led to the award of the Nobel Prize for his discovery of acquired immunological tolerance. He wrote widely on scientific subjects, with a particularly acid pen when dealing with anything he considered pseudoscience.

MELLO, CRAIG C. (USA, born 1960). Medicine, 2006. A graduate of Brown and Harvard universities, Mello is professor of molecular medicine at the University of Massachusetts Medical School. He and Andrew Z. Fire were awarded the Nobel Prize for their discovery of RNA interference, adding another dimension to the understanding of life and providing new tools for medicine.

MILOSZ, CZESLAW (Poland, USA; 1911–2004). Literature, 1980. Born in Lithuania, Milosz was educated in the classics and law. He published his first book of verse at twenty-one. During the Nazi occupation of Poland, he wrote clandestine works for the Resistance. He was appointed cultural attaché to Washington by the Communist government but sought asylum in France in 1951 and emigrated to the United States in 1960, where he taught at Berkeley. He was honored for work of "uncompromising clear-sightedness."

MISTRAL, GABRIELA (Chile, 1889–1957). Literature, 1945. Mistral's father abandoned his family when she was three. She started her teaching career in a village school at sixteen and began to write poetry after the suicide of a former lover in 1909. Mistral left Chile in 1922 and lived in Mexico, Brazil, Europe, and the United States, often serving as an honorary Chilean consul. Her poetry, lyrical and passionate, deals with themes of love, faith, childhood, and death.

MODIGLIANI, FRANCO (Italy, USA; 1918–2003). Economics, 1985. Modigliani received a doctor of law degree from the University of Rome but left Italy in 1938 after Mussolini promulgated his racial laws. He earned a Ph.D. in economics at the New School of Social Research in New York and spent most of his career at MIT, consulting with the Federal Reserve Bank and with the government of Italy. He was awarded the Nobel Prize for theories of personal saving and corporate finance.

 MOMMSEN, THEODOR (Denmark, Germany; 1817–1903). Literature, 1902. Mommsen, a professor at the University of Berlin for forty-two years, had sixteen children. A liberal and outspoken opponent of German anti-Semitism, he was a gifted and prolific writer; his magnum opus was *History of Rome*. He also produced major works on Latin inscriptions and on Roman law. Mommsen, who was chosen for the Nobel Prize over Tolstoy, was the earliest-born of all the laureates, as well as the first Nobel laureate to die.

MONOD, JACQUES (France, 1910–1976). Medicine, 1965. Monod was the son of a French painter and an American mother. During the German occupation, he was a major figure in the Resistance; he was once captured by the Gestapo but escaped. A classic French rationalist, a cellist and director of a Bach choir, a friend of Camus, Monod was a man of great charm and character. He shared the prize with François Jacob and André Lwoff, colleagues at the Pasteur Institute, "for their discoveries concerning genetic control of enzyme and virus synthesis."

MONTALE, EUGENIO (Italy, 1896–1981). Literature, 1975. Montale served as an infantry officer in World War I and trained in opera before turning to poetry. He became the director of a prestigious library in Florence but was dismissed in 1938 for his refusal to join the Fascist Party; he withdrew from public life for many years to write and translate. In 1967, he was made a senator. The Swedish Academy praised his poetry, which "interpreted human values under the sign of an outlook on life with no illusions."

MORGAN, THOMAS (USA, 1866-1945). Medicine, 1933. A professor at Columbia and Caltech, Morgan was at the beginning and end of his career a marine biologist. But his major life's work was in genetics, in which his studies of drosophilae, fruit flies, led to greater understanding of the function of the chromosome in heredity.

MORRISON, TONI (USA, born 1931). Literature, 1993. A writer, editor, lecturer, and academic, Morrison was born to a working-class family in Ohio. She taught at Texas Southern, Howard, Yale, and Princeton universities. Her fiction and criticism focus on the black experience in America, especially the life of black women. Her best-known book is *Beloved*.

MULLIS, KARY (USA, born 1944). Chemistry, 1993. A native of South Carolina, subsequently a dedicated California surfer with unconventional ideas and lifestyle, Mullis was awarded the Nobel Prize for devising the technique of polymerase chain reaction, which allowed duplication of a single gene fragment. Mullis worked mainly as a researcher and consultant in the chemical and pharmacological industry. His autobiography, *Dancing Naked in the Mind Field,* became a best seller.

MURRAY, JOSEPH (USA, born 1919). Medicine, 1990. Murray was one of very few practicing physicians to receive the Nobel Prize for Medicine. A pioneering transplant and plastic surgeon, he applied his experience from skin grafts on badly burned soldiers in World War II, performing the first kidney transplant between identical twins in 1954, between fraternal twins in 1959, and from an unrelated cadaver in 1962. The principles he developed were subsequently used in the general practice of organ transplants.

MYRDAL, ALVA (Sweden, 1902-1986). Peace, 1982. Alva Myrdal was a Swedish educator and public servant. She worked for the UN and UNESCO, was a member of parliament and cabinet minister, and Swedish ambassador to India. As Sweden's ambassador for disarmament to the United Nations, she worked for nuclear disarmament with great perseverance and in the face of constant discouragement.

MYRDAL, GUNNAR (Sweden, 1898–1987). Economics, 1974. Husband of Alva Myrdal, Gunnar Myrdal became widely known for his 1944 *An American Dilemma: The Negro Problem and Modern Democracy*. He was honored for his work on money, economic fluctuations, and the interdependence of economic, social, and institutional phenomena. A professor at the University of Stockholm, he served as minister of commerce and was active in the United Nations.

NAIPAUL, V. S. (Trinidad, Britain; born 1932). Literature, 2001. Naipaul left Trinidad at eighteen for Oxford University and thereafter lived in England, with long periods of world travel. The first of his many books to achieve celebrity was *A House of Mr. Biswas* (1961). The Swedish Academy praised him for "having united perceptive narrative and incorruptible scrutiny in works that compel us to see the presence of suppressed histories."

NANSEN, FRIDTJOF (Norway, 1861–1922). Peace, 1922. Nansen made three voyages of exploration to the Arctic and was the first to cross the Greenland ice cap on skis. He wrote works on zoology, oceanography, and anthropology. He was active in the peaceful separation of Norway from Sweden in 1905 and in the League of Nations. After World War I, he organized the repatriation of four hundred thousand prisoners of war and helped save millions of Russians from starvation.

NERUDA, PABLO (Chile, 1904–1973). Literature, 1971. Neruda's 1924 book, *Twenty Love Poems and A Song of Despair*, sold 2 million copies and made him famous throughout Latin America. He was honorary consul for Chile to many countries, including Burma, Indonesia, and Spain. He joined the Communist Party, and became a senator in 1945, but was forced into exile in 1948. Appointed ambassador to France by President Salvador Allende, Neruda died a few days after Allende's death in the 1973 military coup.

NOEL-BAKER, PHILIP (Britain, 1889–1982). Peace, 1959. Noel-Baker competed as a runner in three Olympic games. The son of Canadian Quakers, he served in an ambulance unit during World War I and was decorated several times. Fluent in seven languages, he was a Labor member of

Parliament for thirty-five years and a cabinet minister for sixteen. Noel-Baker helped draft the UN charter and campaigned widely for peace through multilateral disarmament.

OE, KENZABURO (Japan, born 1935). Literature, 1994. Oe was born to a clan of storytellers. His father died in the Pacific war when Kenzaburo was nine. Oe's life and his writing were deeply influenced by the war, Hiroshima, the American occupation, his commitment to democracy, and his fatherhood of a brain-damaged son. The latter is the subject of his best-known work, *A Personal Matter*.

O'NEILL, EUGENE (USA, 1888–1953). Literature, 1936. O'Neill's father was a touring actor, his mother a morphine addict. After expulsion from Princeton, he spent some years as a sailor, actor, reporter, gold prospector, and derelict. He became malarial, tubercular, and alcoholic. He began to write plays, cofounded the Playwrights' Theater, and had his first Broadway play produced in 1920. His powerful and tragic drama owes much to Greek theater; *A Long Day's Journey into Night* is considered his masterpiece.

ORR, JOHN BOYD (Britain, 1880–1971). Peace, 1949. Trained in medicine and physiology, Orr was a decorated medical officer in both the army and the navy during World War I. He built the Nutrition Institute in Aberdeen, helped formulate national food policy in World War II, and became the first director of the UN Food and Agriculture Organization. He was awarded the Nobel Prize for his efforts to eliminate world hunger and to promote global unity.

OSSIETZKY, CARL VON (Germany, 1889–1938). Peace, 1935. Ossietzky's experiences as a soldier in World War I reinforced his pacifist views. His writings against militarism resulted in frequent arrests and imprisonment. In 1933, the Nazis sent Ossietzky to Oranienburg concentration camp, where he suffered severe ill-treatment and eventually died. His Nobel award, the result of an international campaign, so infuriated Hitler that he prohibited any future German from accepting a Nobel Prize.

PAMUK, ORHAN (Turkey, born 1952). Literature, 2006. Born into a prosperous secular family in Istanbul, Pamuk originally wanted to become a painter. He studied architecture and journalism and has spent his entire working life as a writer. He was the first author in the Muslim world to publicly condemn the fatwa against Salman Rushdie. After referring in an interview to the genocide of a million Armenians in Turkey, he was charged with insulting the state, but charges were dropped after international protests. His books have been translated into over forty languages.

PASTERNAK, BORIS (Russia, 1890-1960). Literature, 1958. Originally a musician, Pasternak became the preeminent poet and translator in the Soviet Union. He fell into disfavor when his only novel, *Dr. Zhivago*, considered by the authorities to be critical of Soviet communism, was published abroad in 1957. He was forced to refuse the prize and was expelled from the Writers Union. Continuing pressure on him and those close to him is thought to have hastened his death.

PAULI, WOLFGANG (Austria, Switzerland; 1900-1958). Physics, 1945. Pauli won the Nobel Prize for his discovery of the exclusion principle, also known as the Pauli principle, which posits that no two electrons in the same atom can exist in the same state. At age twenty, he wrote a book on relativity that was praised by Einstein, who later nominated him for the Nobel Prize. At thirty, he postulated the existence of the neutrino. It was claimed that if Pauli was nearby, experimental equipment would break spontaneously; this became known as the Pauli effect.

PAULING, LINUS (USA, 1901-1994). Chemistry, 1954; Peace, 1962. Popularly known for his advocacy of vitamin C, Pauling is widely considered the most outstanding American chemist of the twentieth century. He was the first person to receive two unshared Nobels in different fields. His prize in chemistry was awarded for work on chemical bonds and molecular structure, and in peace for his warnings on nuclear weapons. His opposition to nuclear testing resulted in withdrawal of his passport in the 1950s.

PAVLOV, IVAN (Russia, 1849-1946). Medicine, 1904. Born in central Russia, the son of a priest, Pavlov studied theology before switching to medicine. An expert anatomist and surgeon, a pioneer in the study of the circulatory and digestive systems, he is best remembered for the concept of the conditioned reflex. Pavlov was unique in escaping punishment for his open criticism of the Soviet government.

PAZ, OCTAVIO (Mexico, 1914–1998). Literature, 1990. Paz was a political commentator, essayist, poet, and novelist of great eloquence and erudition. He entered the diplomatic service in 1945 and was for six years ambassador to India, resigning to protest his government's massacre of student demonstrators at the 1968 Olympic Games.

PEARSON, LESTER (Canada, 1897–1972). Peace, 1957. Pearson served as an officer in the Royal Flying Corps during World War I, then became a history professor, and entered the Canadian foreign service in 1928. He was ambassador to the United States and to the United Nations, chairman of the North Atlantic Treaty Organization, and president of the UN General Assembly in 1952–1953. He was prime minister of Canada in 1963–1968. He won the Nobel Prize for his work in negotiating a resolution of the Suez crisis of 1956.

PENZIAS, ARNO (Germany, USA; born 1933). Physics, 1978. Penzias's family escaped from Germany in 1939. After graduating from City College, spending two years in the Army Signal Corps, and earning a doctorate at Columbia University, Penzias took a job in radio astronomy at Bell Laboratories, where he remained for thirty-four years. He shared the Nobel Prize for the detection of microwave background radiation, which supported the big bang theory of the origin of the universe.

PERES, SHIMON (Poland, Israel; born 1923). Peace, 1994. In 1947, Peres joined the Haganah, led by David Ben-Gurion, who, when he became prime minister, appointed him head of the Israeli navy at the age of twenty-seven. As foreign minister, Peres shared the Nobel Prize with Yitzhak Rabin and Yasser Arafat for their work toward agreement on the development of Palestinian self-rule. He became prime minister of Israel after the assassination of Rabin in 1995.

PERSE, SAINT-JOHN (France, 1887–1975). Literature, 1960. Saint-John Perse was born on Saint-Leger-les-Feuilles, a tiny coral islet off Guadeloupe. He was a diplomat in France until 1940, when he escaped to the United States, where he worked at the Library of Congress and stayed until 1957. Not well known even in France, Perse's poetry is relatively difficult, and his oeuvre is limited by the destruction of his manuscripts during the Second World War.

PERUTZ, MAX (Austria, Britain; 1914–2002). Chemistry, 1962. Perutz left Vienna for Cambridge in 1936. During World War II, he was interned as an enemy alien in Canada but released to work on secret scientific projects. With fellow laureate John Kendrew, he founded the Cambridge Laboratory of Molecular Biology. He was honored for his X-ray diffraction analysis of the structure of hemoglobin. A keen skier and mountaineer, Perutz also studied the crystal structure and flow mechanism of glaciers.

PHELPS, EDMUND (USA, born 1933). Economics, 2006. A graduate of Amherst and Yale, Phelps worked at RAND, the University of Pennsylvania, and Yale, and is now professor of Economics at Columbia. He is known for his work on savings and on unemployment. He received the Nobel Prize "for his analysis of intertemporal tradeoffs in macroeconomic policy," which "deepened understanding of the relation between short-run and long-run effects of economic policy."

PHILLIPS, WILLIAM (USA, born 1948). Physics, 1997. Both of Phillips's parents were social workers. A scientist at the National Institute of Standards and Technology, he shared the Nobel Prize for his development of a method to use laser light to trap atoms by chilling them to very low temperatures.

PINTER, HAROLD (Britain, born 1930). Literature, 2005. The son of a tailor in London's East End, Pinter published his first book of poems at twenty. As a pacifist, he was prosecuted for refusing to undergo military service. He trained and worked as an actor. The first of his many plays was produced in 1957. His work, which deals with themes of violence, family hatred, and obsessive jealousy, uses silence, understatement, and cryptic small talk to evoke a sense of nameless menace. He has also written a number of screenplays for major films. Since the 1970s, Pinter has been an outspoken advocate of human rights.

PIRANDELLO, LUIGI (Italy, 1867–1936). Literature, 1934. Born in Sicily, Pirandello wrote poetry, short stories, novels, criticism, and drama. His famous play, *Six Characters in Search of an Author*, opened in Paris in 1923; like much of his work, it deals with illusion and reality. Pirandello was deeply affected by financial misfortune and by his wife's insanity, for which she was eventually institutionalized. He joined Mussolini's Fascist Party, but it is uncertain whether this was a matter of conviction or of expediency.

PIRE, GEORGES (Belgium, 1910–1969). Peace, 1958. Pire entered the Dominican order at Huy, Belgium, at eighteen and earned his doctorate of theology in Rome. He received many decorations for his work with the Resistance in World War II. His family had been refugees in World War I, and in 1949, Pire began his work with refugees, founding "European villages" and organizing sponsorship. After winning the Nobel Prize, he founded the University of Peace in Huy.

 PLANCK, MAX (Germany, 1858–1947). Physics, 1918. Planck chose physics over music, at which he excelled, and earned his doctorate at twenty-one. The founder of modern physics, he introduced quantum theory in 1900. Planck went directly to Hitler to protest the dismissal of Jewish professors. His wife died after twenty-two years of marriage, he lost his two daughters in childbirth, and his elder son was killed in World War I. The execution of his younger son after the 1944 bomb plot against Hitler was a blow from which he did not recover.

 POLANYI, JOHN (Germany, Britain, Canada; born 1929). Chemistry, 1986. Polanyi was born in Berlin, the son of the eminent Hungarian scientist and philosopher Michael Polanyi. He was educated in Britain and spent almost fifty years at the University of Toronto. A leading figure in the promotion of science in Canada, he was awarded the Nobel Prize for work on the dynamics of chemical elementary processes.

PORTER, GEORGE (Britain, 1920–2002). Chemistry, 1967. The son of a Yorkshire Methodist minister, Porter first attended a "tin hut school." He served as a naval radar officer during World War II and took his doctorate at Cambridge. An advocate for science education, he made a successful film series, *The Laws of Disorder*, for television. In 1990, he was created Lord Porter of Luddenham for services to science. He shared the Nobel Prize for his development of flash photolysis to study chemical reactions lasting one billionth of a second.

PRIGOGINE, ILYA (Russia, Belgium; 1917–2003). Chemistry, 1977. Prigogine's family left Russia after the revolution. His first specializations were classics and music. For many years, he held dual appointments at the Universities of Brussels and Texas. He received the Nobel Prize "for contributions to non-equilibrium thermodynamics." Much of his later work focused on "the arrow of time" in physics. He was created a Belgian viscount, and five international institutes bear his name.

QUASIMODO, SALVATORE (Italy, 1901-1968). Literature, 1959. Born in Sicily, Quasimodo trained and worked as an engineer for ten years before becoming a writer, editor, and professor of literature. During World War II, he was briefly imprisoned for his antifascist sympathies. He joined the Communists in 1945 but resigned when the party insisted he write political poems. He was honored "for his lyrical poetry, which with classical fire expresses the tragic experience of life in our times."

RABIN, YITZHAK (Israel, 1922-1995). Peace, 1994. Rabin rose from the ranks of the Haganah to be chief of staff of the Israeli army and ambassador to the United States. In 1992, he became the first native-born prime minister of Israel. Rabin shared the Nobel Prize with Shimon Peres and Yasser Arafat for their work toward agreement on Palestinian self-rule. Six years later, Rabin was assassinated by an Israeli student who opposed his policies of giving up land for peace.

RAMÓN Y CAJAL, SANTIAGO (Spain, 1852-1934). Medicine, 1906. Cajal's father had risen from poor barber-surgeon to professor of anatomy. Ramón rebelled against his father's desire to make him a doctor. He was a fine draftsman and photographer, and wanted to be an artist. His father apprenticed him to a barber, then to a cobbler; Cajal eventually entered the field of medicine. In 1874-1875, he served as an army doctor in Cuba, where he contracted malaria and TB. He was awarded the Nobel Prize for his work on the structure of the nervous system.

RICHET, CHARLES (France, 1850-1935). Medicine, 1913. Richet was a professor of medicine, as were his father, son, and grandson. His wide interests included hypnosis, telepathy, aeronautics, playwriting, and pacifism. He received the Nobel Prize for his work on anaphylaxis. His misanthropic book, *L'Homme Stupide*, was published in 1919.

ROBERTS, RICHARD (Britain, USA; born 1943). Medicine, 1993. Roberts grew up in England and took his Ph.D. at Sheffield University before emigrating to the United States, a classic case of the "brain drain" that cost Britain many of its most gifted people in the postwar years. He spent twenty years at Cold Spring Harbor Laboratory and won the Nobel Prize for the discovery of split genes.

ROLLAND, ROMAIN (France, Switzerland; 1866–1944). Literature, 1915. Despite suffering from TB most of his life, Rolland became an excellent pianist, studied history at the Ecole Normale Supérieure and in Rome, and earned a doctorate in musicology at the Sorbonne, where he became a professor. His magnum opus, the ten-volume *Jean Christophe*, completed in 1919, concerned the artist as lonely genius. A socialist and pacifist, Rolland spent World War I in Switzerland but was pro-French and anti-Nazi during World War II.

ROOSEVELT, THEODORE (USA, 1858–1919). Peace, 1906. Roosevelt became governor of New York in 1898, the same year he led his regiment of Rough Riders to Cuba. In 1900, he became vice president, and with William McKinley's assassination in 1901 he became the twenty-sixth and youngest president of the United States. Although Roosevelet was honored for negotiating an end to the Russo-Japanese War in 1905, he was probably the most militaristic recipient of the Nobel Peace Prize. A champion of the vigorous life, a liberal, and a populist, Roosevelt wrote twenty-nine books and over one thousand magazine articles.

RUBBIA, CARLO (Italy, USA; born 1934). Physics, 1984. Rubbia studied physics at the universities of Pisa, Columbia, and Rome. He divided his time between Harvard and CERN (Centre Européen pour la Recherche Nucléaire) in Geneva. He shared the Nobel Prize for his contribution to the discovery of three subatomic particles.

 RUSSELL, BERTRAND (Britain, 1872–1970). Literature, 1950. Born into a liberal aristocratic family, Lord Russell became Britain's leading mathematician and philosopher. He was fired from his Cambridge fellowship and imprisoned for his opposition to World War I. He was an author of the Einstein-Russell manifesto against nuclear weapons in 1955 and was arrested in his eighties for joining antinuclear sit-ins in London. His bibliography numbers more than four thousand items; his most popular book was his 1945 *History of Western Philosophy*.

RUTHERFORD, ERNEST (New Zealand, Britain; 1871–1937). Chemistry, 1908. The father of modern nuclear physics, widely regarded as the greatest experimental physicist of the twentieth century, Rutherford studied at Cambridge and taught at Manchester and McGill. He was awarded the Nobel Prize for his studies of radioactivity. In 1913, he propounded the modern model of atomic structure. In 1919, he became director of the Cavendish Laboratory at Cambridge, where numerous atomic physicists trained.

SACHS, NELLY (Germany, Sweden; 1891–1970). Literature, 1966. Sachs was rescued from the Holocaust by the efforts of friends who persuaded the aged Selma Lagerlöf, with whom Sachs had corresponded for many years, to request from the king visas for Sachs and her mother. The Holocaust haunted Sachs for the rest of her life, and she became one of its leading poets. Her best-known book of poems is titled *O the Chimneys*.

SAKHAROV, ANDREI (Russia, 1921–1989). Peace, 1975. Chief physicist on the Soviet hydrogen bomb project, Sakharov subsequently moved into opposition to nuclear weapons and led the movement for civil rights, for which he was awarded the Nobel Prize by Norway and internal exile by Moscow. As Sakharov was refused permission to go to Oslo, the prize was accepted by his wife. He was rehabilitated by Gorbachev in 1986 and awarded the Order of Lenin.

SAMUELSON, PAUL (USA, born 1915). Economics, 1970. After taking his B.A. at the University of Chicago, Samuelson spent the rest of his career at Harvard and MIT. He was an adviser to President John F. Kennedy and wrote a column for *Newsweek*. He received the Nobel Prize for his fundamental contributions to nearly all branches of economic theory. Gifted in expressing economic theory in mathematical terms and lucid prose, he wrote an influential textbook, *Economics: An Introductory Analysis*, which sold millions of copies worldwide.

SARAMAGO, JOSÉ (Portugal, born 1922). Literature, 1998. Born to a family of poor peasants, Saramago trained and worked as an auto mechanic. Frequently persecuted in Portugal for his communist politics, he supported himself for long periods by translation. His earlier books were mainly poetry; after 1980 he wrote mostly novels, the best known of which is *Blindness*.

SARTRE, JEAN-PAUL (France, 1905–1980). Literature, 1964. During World War II, Sartre served in the Meteorological Corps, was captured, escaped, and joined the Resistance. By 1945, he had become the leading voice of existentialism. He was awarded the Nobel Prize for his huge body of work in literature, drama, and philosophy; he rejected it, saying that he did not want to become an institution. His stubborn defense of Soviet communism eventually led to his intellectual isolation.

SCHWEITZER, ALBERT (Germany, France, Gabon; 1875-1965). Peace, 1952. Born in Alsace-Lorraine, Schweitzer was a renowned organist, with doctorates in philosophy, theology, and medicine. In 1913, he left Europe to found a hospital in Lambaréné, in French Equatorial Africa. During World War I, he was interned in France as an enemy alien. He returned to Africa in 1924 and rebuilt the hospital, added a leper colony, and worked at Lambaréné until his death.

SEABORG, GLENN (USA, 1912-1999). Chemistry, 1951. Seaborg won the Nobel Prize for his discovery of nine new elements, including plutonium, which he discovered at the age of twenty-eight. He gave his acceptance speech in Stockholm in Swedish, his first language. Element 106 was named seaborgium in his honor. Seaborg was chancellor of the University of California, Berkeley, chairman of the Atomic Energy Commission, and scientific adviser to nine presidents. He held the record for the longest entry in *Who's Who in America*.

SEFERIS, GIORGOS (Greece, 1900-1971). Literature, 1963. Seferis was born in Smyrna and educated in Paris. A diplomat for thirty years, he ended his career as ambassador to London in 1957-1961. He celebrated in vivid poetry the landscape and color of Greece, and the glory and tragedy of its history, sharpened by his own sense of distance from his homeland. He died in Athens, where people wept in the streets on the news of his death.

SEN, AMARTYA (India, Britain; born 1933). Economics, 1998. Sen was born in India and educated in Calcutta and at Cambridge. He taught at Cambridge, Delhi, the London School of Economics, Oxford, and Harvard, before becoming master of Trinity College, Cambridge in 1998-2004. He was awarded the Nobel Prize for his work on welfare economics, with a particular interest in poverty and famine in developing nations.

SHAW, GEORGE BERNARD (Ireland, Britain; 1856-1950). Literature, 1925. Shaw modernized British drama. A vegetarian, self-taught musician, popular orator, critic, pro-feminist, and polemicist, he advocated the simplification of English spelling and was a leading member of the influential socialist Fabian Society. In more than fifty plays he showed himself a master of comedy, tragedy, satire, and intellectual argument. His best-known works are *Pygmalion* and *St. Joan*.

SIENKIEWICZ, HENRYK (Poland, 1846-1916). Literature, 1905. Most of Sienkiewicz's epic novels were set in Poland during the mid-seventeenth century, but the best known today is *Quo Vadis*, set in the time of Christ. In 1876-1878, he paid an extended visit to the United States, traveling across the country by train, and recording his impressions in his *Letters from America*. The utopian agricultural colony that he and a group of fellow intellectuals attempted to establish in California failed after a few years.

SIMON, HERBERT (USA, 1916-2001). Economics, 1978. Simon taught at Carnegie Mellon University for forty-four years. He received the Nobel Prize for his work on decision making in economic organizations. Multilingual, a pianist, painter, and expert chess player, Simon was often described as a Renaissance man. He made contributions in the fields of mathematics, administrative theory, psychology, political science, and artificial intelligence.

SINGER, ISAAC BASHEVIS (Poland, USA; 1904-1991). Literature, 1978. Singer spent his teenage years in Bilgoraj, a Polish shtetl virtually unchanged since the Middle Ages. He moved to the United States in 1935 to join the staff of a Jewish newspaper in Brooklyn, New York. His much-loved books for adults and children about the world of East European Jewry in the early twentieth century were written in Yiddish. His best-known works are *Enemies: A Love Story* and *Yentl*.

SMOOT, GEORGE F. (USA, born 1945). Physics, 2006. Born in Florida to scientist parents, Smoot graduated from MIT and is now a professor at the University of California, Berkeley. He was honored with John C. Mather for their work with the Cosmic Background Explorer satellite. Smoot was responsible for the instruments that determined with great precision the temperature of the black body radiation emanating from the earliest state of the universe.

SOLOW, ROBERT (USA, born 1924). Economics, 1987. Solow served three years in the U.S. Army in North Africa and Sicily. He taught at MIT for forty-five years. His research showed that the rate of technological progress is more important to economic growth than capital accumulation. His studies were influential in persuading governments to support technological research and development.

SOLZHENITSYN, ALEXANDR (Russia, born 1918). Literature, 1970. A decorated artillery captain in World War II, Solzhenitsyn served eight years in prison camps for criticizing Stalin. During a brief cultural thaw in 1962, his novel *One Day in the Life of Ivan Denisovitch*, describing conditions in a labor camp, was published. After a resumption of censorship, his books could be published only outside the USSR. He was not permitted to go to Stockholm to receive his Nobel Prize. In 1974, he was expelled from the USSR, and lived in the United States until 1994, when he returned to Russia.

SOYINKA, WOLE (Nigeria, born 1934). Literature, 1986. The first African to win a Nobel Prize in Literature, Soyinka writes poetry, plays, novels, and criticism. After his return from study in Britain, he founded a national theater company. In 1967, during the civil war between Nigeria and Biafra, he published an appeal for peace and was imprisoned for twenty-two months. Subsequently, he has been frequently exiled.

STEINBECK, JOHN (USA, 1902-1968). Literature, 1962. Steinbeck's life-long advocacy for the oppressed, expressed in such novels as *The Grapes of Wrath* and *Of Mice and Men*, earned him a large FBI file. His book *The Moon Is Down* became an inspiration to occupied Europe during World War II, when Steinbeck served as a war correspondent. He wrote the screenplay for the movie *Viva Zapata!* and speeches for President Lyndon Johnson.

STIGLER, GEORGE (USA, 1911-1991). Economics, 1982. Stigler, an economist at the University of Chicago, where he was head of the Center for the Study of the Economy and the State, was honored for his work on industry, markets, and regulatory legislation.

STIGLITZ, JOSEPH (USA, born 1943). Economics, 2001. Stiglitz studied economics at MIT under four future Nobel laureates. In 1992, he became chairman of President Bill Clinton's Council of Economic Advisors, where he developed the concept of the "third way" between the roles of government and the market. In 1997, he moved to the World Bank as chief economist. Disagreeing with the bank's practice of imposing neoliberal policies on developing countries, he resigned in 2000.

SULSTON, JOHN (Britain, born 1942). Medicine, 2002. The son of an Anglican priest, Sulston was educated at Cambridge. In his prize-winning work, he "identified the first mutation of a gene participating in the cell death process." In the 1990s, he led Britain's involvement in the Human Genome Project and successfully fought to keep the results of the research in the public domain and prevent privatization of the genome by commercial interests.

SZENT-GYÖRGYI, ALBERT (Hungary, USA; 1893–1986). Medicine, 1937. From a family of landed nobility, Szent-Györgyi served in the Austrian army during World War I. He studied at several universities and laboratories in Europe, taking his doctorate at Cambridge. Between the wars, he did pioneering research on muscle contraction. He received the Nobel Prize for his work on vitamin C. During World War II, he joined the Hungarian Resistance, and his arrest was personally ordered by Hitler. In 1945, he moved to Woods Hole, Massachusetts, where he worked on cancer research for the rest of his life.

SZYMBORSKA, WISLAWA (Poland, born 1923). Literature, 1996. The poet Szymborska has lived almost all her life in Kraków, Poland. During the German occupation, she worked with an illegal underground theater. The Nobel Committee cited her "poetry that with ironic precision allows the historical and biological context to come to light in fragments of human reality."

TAGORE, RABINDRANATH (India, 1861–1941). Literature, 1913. A nationalist and friend of Gandhi, the Bengali poet Tagore also wrote novels, plays, short stories, and essays, all of which reflected his mystical beliefs and his Indian background. He wrote the words to the national anthem of India. Tagore studied in Britain and received a knighthood in 1915, which he repudiated in 1919 in protest against the Amritsar Massacre, in which British troops killed several hundred unarmed demonstrators.

TANAKA, KOICHI (Japan, born 1959). Chemistry, 2002. Tanaka's mother died a month after his birth. He was educated at Tohoku University and then went to work for the Shimadzu Corporation, where six out of nine Japanese science laureates had been employed. He shared the Nobel Prize for his contribution to the development of "soft desorption ionisation methods for mass spectrometric analyses of biological macromolecules."

TERESA, MOTHER (Yugoslavia, India; 1910–1997). Peace, 1979. Agnes Gonxha Bojaxhiu, known as Mother Teresa, went to India in 1928 as a Catholic missionary. In 1950, she founded her own order, the Society of Missionaries of Charity, to care for the destitute, the dying, and the orphaned. The society now operates in more than twenty-five countries.

THOMSON, J. J. (Britain, 1856–1940). Physics, 1906. The son of a Manchester bookseller, Thomson went to college at fourteen and arrived in Cambridge at nineteen. He spent the rest of his life at Cambridge, rising to be master of Trinity College. While he was head of the Cavendish Laboratory, seven future Nobel laureates worked under him. He won the Nobel Prize for his work on the conduction of electricity through gases, but more important was his discovery of the electron in 1897.

TRIMBLE, DAVID (Northern Ireland, born 1944). Peace, 1998. A lecturer in law at Queen's University, Belfast, Trimble, leader of the Ulster Unionist Party, became first minister of Northern Ireland in 1999. Originally a hardline Protestant, he won the Nobel Prize with John Hume for their work for peace in Northern Ireland that resulted in the 1998 peace agreement.

TUTU, DESMOND (South Africa, born 1931). Peace, 1984. An Anglican priest, Tutu spent several years working and studying in Britain. As secretary-general of the South African Council of Churches, he became a leading spokesman against apartheid. The Nobel Committee cited his lifelong concern for "human dignity, fraternity, and democracy." Subsequent to the Nobel Prize, Tutu became archbishop of Cape Town. After the end of apartheid, he chaired the Truth and Reconciliation Commission.

WALCOTT, DEREK (St. Lucia, Trinidad; born 1930). Literature, 1992. One of two Nobels from the tiny and isolated volcanic island of St. Lucia, Walcott is of African, Dutch, and English descent. A poet and playwright, he taught school in the Caribbean for some years; he now divides his time between Trinidad and Boston, where he teaches at Boston

University. "In him," the Swedish Academy stated, "West Indian culture has found its great poet."

WALD, GEORGE (USA, 1906–1997). Medicine, 1967. Wald was born on New York's Lower East Side. A professor at Harvard for forty years, he received the Nobel for research on the role of vitamin A in forming the three color pigments in the retina. In addition to his scientific work, he was a dedicated teacher and a dogged campaigner against nuclear weapons. His opposition to the United States' involvement in Vietnam earned him a place on President Richard Nixon's "enemies list."

WALESA, LECH (Poland, born 1943). Peace, 1983. Walesa was honored for his nonviolent efforts to win the right of Polish workers to organize freely. He was leader of the union Solidarity, which originated in the Lenin Shipyard in Gdansk. When martial law was imposed in 1981, Solidarity was banned and Walesa was imprisoned for a year. With the end of martial law, Solidarity won a majority in parliamentary elections. Walesa was president of Poland in 1990–1995.

WATSON, JAMES (USA, born 1928). Medicine, 1962. Watson entered the University of Chicago at fifteen. At twenty-four, he became codiscoverer of the double helix structure of DNA. Watson's views were often provocative; his 1968 book, *The Double Helix*, became a best seller. He taught at Harvard for twenty years and then moved to the Cold Spring Harbor Laboratory in New York, which he made a world center for molecular biology. He helped direct the Human Genome Project at the National Institutes of Health from 1988 to 1992.

WEINBERG, STEVEN (USA, born 1933). Physics, 1979. A graduate of the Bronx High School of Science, Cornell, and Princeton, Weinberg taught at the University of California at Berkeley, MIT, Harvard, and the University of Texas at Austin. He shared the Nobel Prize for formulating the electroweak theory. He is well known for his 1977 book, *The First Three Minutes*, on the origin of the universe.

WHITE, PATRICK (Australia, 1912–1990). Literature, 1973. The son of a sheep rancher, White spent several years in Britain, attended Cambridge, and served during World War II in Royal Air Force Intelligence. After his return to Australia, he produced a series of novels and plays that reflected the Australian landscape and experience. The Swedish Academy praised his "epic and psychological narrative art which has introduced a new continent into literature."

WIEMAN, CARL (USA, born 1951). Physics, 2001. Wieman grew up in the forests of the Oregon coastal range. A professor at the University of Colorado since 1984, he is married to a physicist and is deeply involved in efforts to improve undergraduate physics education, to which project he dedicated the Nobel Prize money. He shared the Nobel award for the creation of Bose-Einstein condensate in 1995.

WIESCHAUS, ERIC (USA, born 1947). Medicine, 1995. Wieschaus studied at Notre Dame, Yale, and Zurich. He has been at Princeton since 1981. In high school he was interested in music and the arts; he was captivated by science at a National Science Foundation summer school. Wieschaus shared the Nobel Prize for his work on drosophila genetics, which promised greater understanding of human congenital malformation.

WIESEL, ELIE (Romania, France, USA; born 1928). Peace, 1986. Elie Wiesel said that his youth died in the cattle cars in which he was deported in 1944 from Romania to Auschwitz. He survived ten months in different concentration camps, in which he lost a sister and both parents, until he was liberated at Buchenwald. He moved to Paris in 1948, and in 1955 to the United States. He has written extensively about the Holocaust and is a champion of the oppressed everywhere.

WIESEL, TORSTEN (Sweden, USA; born 1924). Medicine, 1981. The son of a psychiatrist, Wiesel took medical degrees in Sweden and the United States. At Harvard for twenty-four years, he moved to Rockefeller University in 1983, becoming president in 1991. Wiesel shared the Nobel Prize for his work on information processing in the visual system. This research lent strong support to the view that prompt surgery is imperative in correcting certain eye defects that are detectable in newborn children.

WIGNER, EUGENE (Hungary, USA; 1902–1995). Physics, 1963. Born in Hungary, Wigner immigrated to the United States in 1930 and worked at Princeton for more than forty years. He was one of the group of physicists that persuaded the U.S. government of the need for an atomic bomb project, and he worked with Enrico Fermi at the University of Chicago in building the first atomic reactor. He received the Nobel Prize for his contributions to elementary particle physics, particularly the principles of symmetry. His five hundred papers fill eight volumes.

WILKINS, MAURICE (New Zealand, Britain; 1916–2004). Medicine, 1962. Born in New Zealand, Wilkins moved to England at the age of six, studied physics at Cambridge, and spent most of his career at the University of London. He worked on the Manhattan Project in World War II, subsequently moving to the field of biophysics. With Francis Crick and James Watson, he discovered the structure of DNA.

WILLIAMS, BETTY (Northern Ireland, USA; born 1943). Peace, 1976. Williams, an office receptionist, witnessed a tragic accident in 1976, when a car driven by a terrorist who had been shot by British soldiers crashed and killed three children. With Mairead Corrigan, aunt of the slain children, she launched the organization Peace People, for which the two women received the Nobel Prize. In 1982, Betty Williams moved to the United States.

WILLIAMS, JODY (USA; born 1950). Peace, 1997. Lifelong human rights activist Williams shared the Nobel Prize with the International Campaign to Ban Landmines, which she coordinated. Their work culminated in the 1997 treaty to ban landmines signed by 121 countries, but not including Russia, China, or the United States.

WILSON, WOODROW (USA, 1856–1924). Peace, 1919. The son and grandson of Presbyterian ministers, Wilson became professor of jurisprudence and later president of Princeton University. He was governor of New Jersey in 1911–1913, and the twenty-eighth president of the United States in 1912–1920, the only president with an earned doctorate. He was awarded the Nobel Prize for his "Fourteen Points," an effort to secure a just and lasting peace at the end of World War I.

XINGJIAN, GAO (China, France; born 1940). Literature, 2000. Xingjian took a degree in French in Beijing. During the Cultural Revolution, he was sent to a reeducation camp for six years. He produced many stories, essays, and plays between 1980 and 1986, when they began to be banned. In 1987, he left China and settled in France. He paints in ink and has held many international exhibitions of his work.

YALOW, ROSALYN (USA, born 1921). Medicine, 1977. Rosalyn Yalow earned a Ph.D. in nuclear physics in 1945. Married, with two children, she worked for three decades at Bronx Veterans Administration Medical Center. Yalow shared the Nobel Prize "for the development of radioimmunoassays of peptide hormones." After a stroke in 1995, she was rejected as a suspected indigent by a New York hospital whose parent university had conferred on her an honorary degree.

YANG, CHEN NING (China, USA; born 1922). Physics, 1957. The son of a mathematics professor, Yang was educated in China, then went to the United States in 1945 for graduate studies at the University of Chicago, where he worked with Enrico Fermi. From 1965, he taught at SUNY, Stony Brook. He shared the Nobel Prize with Tsung-Dao Lee for their investigation of the parity laws with respect to subatomic particles.

YEATS, WILLIAM BUTLER (Ireland, 1865–1939). Literature, 1923. Yeats received the Nobel Prize for his dramatic works but is remembered more for his poetry, the finest of which he wrote after the age of fifty. An Irish patriot who served six years in the Irish Senate, Yeats led an Irish literary revival through his writing and his leadership of the Abbey Theatre in Dublin.

YUNUS, MUHAMMAD (Bangladesh, born 1940). Peace, 2006. Known as "banker to the poor," Yunus earned a Ph.D. in economics from Vanderbilt University in 1969. In 1974, he gave twenty-seven dollars to a group of poor women to save them from the clutches of moneylenders. This led in 1976 to his foundation of Grameen Bank to make small loans to the poor to enable them to achieve self-sufficiency. Since then the bank has loaned $6 billion to 7 million villagers in Bangladesh, 97 percent of them women. The bank has a 99 percent repayment rate, makes a profit, and has extensive programs of housing, scholarships, and telecommunications.

NOBEL LAUREATES, 1901–2006

CHEMISTRY

1901 Jacobus H. van 't Hoff
1902 Emil Fischer
1903 Svante Arrhenius
1904 William Ramsay
1905 Adolf von Baeyer
1906 Henri Moissan
1907 Eduard Buchner
1908 Ernest Rutherford
1909 Wilhelm Ostwald
1910 Otto Wallach
1911 Marie Curie
1912 Victor Grignard, Paul Sabatier
1913 Alfred Werner
1914 Theodore W. Richards
1915 Richard Willstätter
1916 no prize awarded
1917 no prize awarded
1918 Fritz Haber
1919 no prize awarded
1920 Walther Nernst
1921 Frederick Soddy
1922 Francis W. Aston
1923 Fritz Pregl
1924 no prize awarded
1925 Richard Zsigmondy
1926 Theodor Svedberg
1927 Heinrich Wieland
1928 Adolf Windaus
1929 Hans von Euler-Chelpin, Arthur Harden

1930 Hans Fischer
1931 Friedrich Bergius, Carl Bosch
1932 Irving Langmuir
1933 no prize awarded
1934 Harold C. Urey
1935 Frédéric Joliot-Curie, Irène Joliot-Curie
1936 Peter Debye
1937 Norman Haworth, Paul Karrer
1938 Richard Kuhn
1939 Adolf Butenandt, Leopold Ružička
1940 no prize awarded
1941 no prize awarded
1942 no prize awarded
1943 George de Hevesy
1944 Otto Hahn
1945 Artturi Virtanen
1946 John H. Northrop, Wendell M. Stanley, James B. Sumner
1947 Robert Robinson
1948 Arne Tiselius
1949 William F. Giauque
1950 Kurt Alder, Otto Diels
1951 Edwin M. McMillan, Glenn Seaborg
1952 Archer Martin, Richard L. M. Synge
1953 Hermann Staudinger
1954 Linus Pauling
1955 Vincent du Vigneaud
1956 Cyril Hinshelwood, Nikolay Semenov
1957 Alexander Todd

1958	Frederick Sanger	1998	Walter Kohn, John Pople
1959	Jaroslav Heyrovsky	1999	Ahmed Zewail
1960	Willard F. Libby	2000	Alan Heeger, Alan MacDiarmid,
1961	Melvin Calvin		Hideki Shirakawa
1962	John Kendrew, Max Perutz	2001	William S. Knowles, Ryoji Noyori,
1963	Giulio Natta, Karl Ziegler		K. Barry Sharpless
1964	Dorothy Crowfoot Hodgkin	2002	John B. Fenn, Koichi Tanaka, Kurt
1965	Robert B. Woodward		Wüthrich
1966	Robert S. Mulliken	2003	Peter Agre, Roderick MacKinnon
1967	Manfred Eigen, George Porter,	2004	Aaron Ciechanover, Avram Hershko,
	Ronald G. W. Norrish		Irwin Rose
1968	Lars Onsager	2005	Yves Chauvin, Robert H. Grubbs,
1969	Odd Hassel, Derek Barton		Richard R. Schrock
1970	Luis Leloir	2006	Roger D. Kornberg
1971	Gerhard Herzberg		

1972	Christian Anfinsen, Stanford Moore, William H. Stein
1973	Ernst Otto Fischer, Geoffrey Wilkinson
1974	Paul J. Flory
1975	John Cornforth, Vladimir Prelog
1976	William Lipscomb
1977	Ilya Prigogine
1978	Peter Mitchell
1979	Georg Wittig, Herbert C. Brown
1980	Paul Berg, Walter Gilbert, Frederick Sanger
1981	Kenichi Fukui, Roald Hoffmann
1982	Aaron Klug
1983	Henry Taube
1984	Bruce Merrifield
1985	Herbert A. Hauptman, Jerome Karle
1986	John Polanyi, Dudley Herschbach, Yuan T. Lee
1987	Donald J. Cram, Charles J. Pedersen, Jean-Marie Lehn
1988	Johann Deisenhofer, Robert Huber, Hartmut Michel
1989	Sidney Altman, Thomas R. Cech
1990	Elias James Corey
1991	Richard Ernst
1992	Rudolph A. Marcus
1993	Kary Mullis, Michael Smith
1994	George A. Olah
1995	Paul Crutzen, Mario J. Molina, F. Sherwood Rowland
1996	Robert F. Curl, Harold Kroto, Richard E. Smalley
1997	Paul Boyer, John E. Walker, Jens C. Skou

ECONOMICS — (THE BANK OF SWEDEN PRIZE IN ECONOMIC SCIENCES IN MEMORY OF ALFRED NOBEL WAS ESTABLISHED IN 1969.)

1969	Ragnar Frisch, Jan Tinbergen
1970	Paul Samuelson
1971	Simon Kuznets
1972	John R. Hicks, Kenneth J. Arrow
1973	Wassily Leontief
1974	Gunnar Myrdal, Friederich von Hayek
1975	Leonid Vitaliyevich Kantorovich, Tjalling C. Koopmans
1976	Milton Friedman
1977	Bertil Ohlin, James E. Meade
1978	Herbert Simon
1979	Theodore Schultz, Arthur Lewis
1980	Lawrence R. Klein
1981	James Tobin
1982	George Stigler
1983	Gerard Debreu
1984	Richard Stone
1985	Franco Modigliani
1986	James M. Buchanan
1987	Robert Solow
1988	Maurice Allais
1989	Trygve Haavelmo
1990	Harry M. Markowitz, Merton H. Miller, William F. Sharpe
1991	Ronald H. Coase
1992	Gary S. Becker
1993	Robert W. Fogel, Douglass C. North
1994	John C. Harsanyi, John F. Nash, Reinhard Selten

1995	Robert E. Lucas, Jr.
1996	James A. Mirrlees, William Vickrey
1997	Robert C. Merton, Myron S. Scholes
1998	Amartya Sen
1999	Robert A. Mundell
2000	James Heckman, Daniel McFadden
2001	George A. Akerlof, A. Michael Spence, Joseph Stiglitz
2002	Daniel Kahneman, Vernon L. Smith
2003	Robert F. Engle III, Clive W. J. Granger
2004	Finn E. Kydland, Edward C. Prescott
2005	Robert Aumann, Thomas C. Schelling
2006	Edmund Phelps

LITERATURE

1901	Sully Prudhomme
1902	Theodor Mommsen
1903	Bjørnstjerne Bjørnson
1904	Frédéric Mistral, José Echegaray
1905	Henryk Sienkiewicz
1906	Giosuè Carducci
1907	Rudyard Kipling
1908	Rudolf Eucken
1909	Selma Lagerlöf
1910	Paul Heyse
1911	Maurice Maeterlinck
1912	Gerhart Hauptmann
1913	Rabindranath Tagore
1914	no prize awarded
1915	Romain Rolland
1916	Verner von Heidenstam
1917	Karl Gjellerup, Henrik Pontoppidan
1918	no prize awarded
1919	Carl Spitteler
1920	Knut Hamsun
1921	Anatole France
1922	Jacinto Benavente
1923	William Butler Yeats
1924	Wladyslaw Reymont
1925	George Bernard Shaw
1926	Grazia Deledda
1927	Henri Bergson
1928	Sigrid Undset
1929	Thomas Mann
1930	Sinclair Lewis
1931	Erik Axel Karlfeldt
1932	John Galsworthy

1933	Ivan Bunin
1934	Luigi Pirandello
1936	Eugene O'Neill
1937	Roger Martin du Gard
1938	Pearl S. Buck
1939	Frans Eemil Sillanpää
1940	no prize awarded
1941	no prize awarded
1942	no prize awarded
1943	no prize awarded
1944	Johannes V. Jensen
1945	Gabriela Mistral
1946	Hermann Hesse
1947	André Gide
1948	T. S. Eliot
1949	William Faulkner
1950	Bertrand Russell
1951	Pär Lagerkvist
1952	François Mauriac
1953	Winston Churchill
1954	Ernest Hemingway
1955	Halldór Laxness
1956	Juan Ramón Jiménez
1957	Albert Camus
1958	Boris Pasternak
1959	Salvatore Quasimodo
1960	Saint-John Perse
1961	Ivo Andrić
1962	John Steinbeck
1963	Giorgos Seferis
1964	Jean-Paul Sartre
1965	Mikhail Sholokhov
1966	Shmuel Agnon, Nelly Sachs
1967	Miguel Ángel Asturias
1968	Yasunari Kawabata
1969	Samuel Beckett
1970	Alexandr Solzhenitsyn
1971	Pablo Neruda
1972	Heinrich Böll
1973	Patrick White
1974	Eyvind Johnson, Harry Martinson
1975	Eugenio Montale
1976	Saul Bellow
1977	Vicente Aleixandre
1978	Isaac Bashevis Singer
1979	Odysseus Elytis
1980	Czeslaw Milosz
1981	Elias Canetti
1982	Gabriel García Márquez
1983	William Golding

1984	Jaroslav Seifert	1926	Johannes Fibiger
1985	Claude Simon	1927	Julius Wagner-Jauregg
1986	Wole Soyinka	1928	Charles Nicolle
1987	Joseph Brodsky	1929	Christiaan Eijkman, Frederick
1988	Naguib Mahfouz		Hopkins
1989	Camilo José Cela	1930	Karl Landsteiner
1990	Octavio Paz	1931	Otto Warburg
1991	Nadine Gordimer	1932	Charles Sherrington, Edgar Adrian
1992	Derek Walcott	1933	Thomas Morgan
1993	Toni Morrison	1934	George H. Whipple, George R.
1994	Kenzaburo Oe		Minot, William P. Murphy
1995	Seamus Heaney	1935	Hans Spemann
1996	Wislawa Szymborska	1936	Henry Dale, Otto Loewi
1997	Dario Fo	1937	Albert Szent-Györgyi
1998	José Saramago	1938	Corneille Heymans
1999	Günter Grass	1939	Gerhard Domagk
2000	Gao Xingjian	1943	Henrik Dam, Edward A. Doisy
2001	V. S. Naipaul	1944	Joseph Erlanger, Herbert S. Gasser
2002	Imre Kertész	1945	Alexander Fleming, Ernst Chain,
2003	J. M. Coetzee		Howard Florey
2004	Elfriede Jelinek	1946	Hermann J. Muller
2005	Harold Pinter	1947	Carl Cori, Gerty Cori, Bernardo
2006	Orhan Pamuk		Houssay
		1948	Paul Müller

MEDICINE

		1949	Walter Hess, Egas Moniz
1901	Emil von Behring	1950	Edward C. Kendall, Tadeus
1902	Ronald Ross		Reichstein, Philip S. Hench
1903	Niels Ryberg Finsen	1951	Max Theiler
1904	Ivan Pavlov	1952	Selman A. Waksman
1905	Robert Koch	1953	Hans Krebs, Fritz Lipmann
1906	Camillo Golgi, Santiago Ramón y	1954	John F. Enders, Thomas H. Weller,
	Cajal		Frederick C. Robbins
1907	Alphonse Laveran	1955	Hugo Theorell
1908	Ilya Mechnikov, Paul Ehrlich	1956	André F. Cournand, Werner
1909	Theodor Kocher		Forssmann, Dickinson W. Richards
1910	Albrecht Kossel	1957	Daniel Bovet
1911	Allvar Gullstrand	1958	George Beadle, Edward Tatum,
1912	Alexis Carrel		Joshua Lederberg
1913	Charles Richet	1959	Severo Ochoa, Arthur Kornberg
1914	Robert Bárány	1960	Frank Macfarlane Burnet, Peter
1915	no prize awarded		Medawar
1916	no prize awarded	1961	Georg von Békésy
1917	no prize awarded	1962	Francis Crick, James Watson,
1918	no prize awarded		Maurice Wilkins
1919	Jules Bordet	1963	John Eccles, Alan L. Hodgkin,
1920	August Krogh		Andrew F. Huxley
1922	Archibald Hill, Otto Meyerhof	1964	Konrad Bloch, Feodor Lynen
1923	Frederick Banting, John Macleod	1965	François Jacob, André Lwoff,
1924	Willem Einthoven		Jacques Monod
1925	no prize awarded	1966	Peyton Rous, Charles B. Huggins

1967	Ragnar Granit, Haldan K. Hartline, George Wald	1998	Robert F. Furchgott, Louis J. Ignarro, Ferid Murad
1968	Robert W. Holley, H. Gobind Khorana, Marshall W. Nirenberg	1999	Günter Blobel
		2000	Arvid Carlsson, Paul Greengard, Eric R. Kandel
1969	Max Delbrück, Alfred D. Hershey, Salvador Luria	2001	Leland H. Hartwell, Tim Hunt, Paul Nurse
1970	Bernard Katz, Ulf von Euler, Julius Axelrod		
1971	Earl W. Sutherland Jr.	2002	Sydney Brenner, H. Robert Horvitz, John Sulston
1972	Gerald Edelman, Rodney R. Porter	2003	Paul Lauterbur, Peter Mansfield
1973	Karl von Frisch, Konrad Lorenz, Nikolaas Tinbergen	2004	Richard Axel, Linda Buck
		2005	Barry Marshall, J. Robin Warren
1974	Albert Claude, Christian de Duve, George E. Palade	2006	Andrew Z. Fire, Craig C. Mello

PEACE

1975	David Baltimore, Renato Dulbecco, Howard M. Temin	1901	Henri Dunant, Frédéric Passy
1976	Baruch S. Blumberg, Carleton Gajdusek	1902	Élie Ducommun, Albert Gobat
		1903	Randal Cremer
1977	Roger Guillemin, Andrew V. Schally, Rosalyn Yalow	1904	Institut de Droit International
		1905	Bertha von Suttner
1978	Werner Arber, Daniel Nathans, Hamilton O. Smith	1906	Theodore Roosevelt
		1907	Ernesto Teodoro Moneta, Louis Renault
1979	Allan M. Cormack, Godfrey N. Hounsfield	1908	Klas Arnoldson, Fredrik Bajer
1980	Baruj Benacerraf, Jean Dausset, George D. Snell	1909	Auguste Beernaert, Paul Henri d'Estournelles de Constant
1981	Roger W. Sperry, David H. Hubel, Torsten N. Wiesel	1910	Bureau International Permanent de la Paix
1982	Sune K. Bergström, Bengt I. Samuelsson, John R. Vane	1911	Tobias Asser, Alfred Fried
		1912	Elihu Root
1983	Barbara McClintock	1913	Henri La Fontaine
1984	Niels K. Jerne, Georges J. F. Köhler, César Milstein	1914	no prize awarded
		1915	no prize awarded
1985	Michael S. Brown, Joseph L. Goldstein	1916	no prize awarded
		1917	International Committee of the Red Cross
1986	Stanley Cohen, Rita Levi-Montalcini		
1987	Susumu Tonegawa	1918	no prize awarded
1988	James W. Black, Gertrude Elion, George Hitchings	1919	Woodrow Wilson
		1920	Léon Bourgeois
1989	J. Michael Bishop, Harold E. Varmus	1921	Hjalmar Branting, Christian Lange
1990	Joseph Murray, E. Donnall Thomas	1922	Fridtjof Nansen
1991	Erwin Neher, Bert Sakmann	1923	no prize awarded
1992	Edmond H. Fischer, Edwin G. Krebs	1924	no prize awarded
1993	Richard Roberts, Phillip A. Sharp	1925	Austen Chamberlain, Charles G. Dawes
1994	Alfred Gilman, Martin Rodbell		
1995	Edward B. Lewis, Christiane Nüsslein-Volhard, Eric Wieschaus	1926	Aristide Briand, Gustav Stresemann
		1927	Ferdinand Buisson, Ludwig Quidde
1996	Peter C. Doherty, Rolf M. Zinkernagel	1928	no prize awarded
		1929	Frank B. Kellogg
1997	Stanley B. Prusiner	1930	Nathan Söderblom

1931	Jane Addams, Nicholas Murray Butler	1972	no prize awarded
1932	no prize awarded	1973	Henry Kissinger, Le Duc Tho
1933	Norman Angell	1974	Seán MacBride, Eisaku Sato
1934	Arthur Henderson	1975	Andrei Sakharov
1935	Carl von Ossietzky	1976	Betty Williams, Mairead Corrigan
1936	Carlos Saavedra Lamas	1977	Amnesty International
1937	Robert Cecil	1978	Anwar al-Sadat, Menachem Begin
1938	Nansen International Office for Refugees	1979	Mother Teresa
1939	no prize awarded	1980	Adolfo Pérez Esquivel
1940	no prize awarded	1981	Office of the United Nations High Commissioner for Refugees
1941	no prize awarded	1982	Alva Myrdal, Alfonso García Robles
1942	no prize awarded	1983	Lech Walesa
1943	no prize awarded	1984	Desmond Tutu
1944	International Committee of the Red Cross	1985	International Physicians for the Prevention of Nuclear War
1945	Cordell Hull	1986	Elie Wiesel
1946	Emily Balch, John R. Mott	1987	Oscar Arias Sánchez
1947	Friends Service Council (UK), American Friends Service Committee (USA), on behalf of the Religious Society of Friends, better known as the Quakers	1988	United Nations Peacekeeping Forces
		1989	the Fourteenth Dalai Lama
		1990	Mikhail Gorbachev
		1991	Aung San Suu Kyi
		1992	Rigoberta Menchú Tum
		1993	Nelson Mandela, F. W. de Klerk
1948	no prize awarded	1994	Yasser Arafat, Shimon Peres, Yitzhak Rabin
1949	John Boyd Orr		
1950	Ralph Bunche	1995	Joseph Rotblat, Pugwash Conferences on Science and World Affairs
1951	Léon Jouhaux		
1952	Albert Schweitzer		
1953	George C. Marshall	1996	Carlos Belo, José Ramos-Horta
1954	Office of the United Nations High Commissioner for Refugees	1997	International Campaign to Ban Landmines, Jody Williams
1955	no prize awarded	1998	John Hume, David Trimble
1956	no prize awarded	1999	Médecins Sans Frontières
1957	Lester Pearson	2000	Kim Dae-jung
1958	Georges Pire	2001	United Nations, Kofi Annan
1959	Philip Noel-Baker	2002	Jimmy Carter
1960	Albert Lutuli	2003	Shirin Ebadi
1961	Dag Hammarskjöld	2004	Wangari Maathai
1962	Linus Pauling	2005	Mohamed ElBaradei, International Atomic Energy Agency
1963	International Committee of the Red Cross, League of Red Cross Societies	2006	Muhammad Yunus
1964	Martin Luther King		
1965	United Nation's Children's Fund	**PHYSICS**	
1966	no prize awarded	1901	Wilhelm Conrad Röntgen
1967	no prize awarded	1902	Hendrik A. Lorentz, Pieter Zeeman
1968	René Cassin	1903	Henri Becquerel, Pierre Curie, Marie Curie
1969	International Labour Organization		
1970	Norman Borlaug	1904	Lord Rayleigh
1971	Willy Brandt	1905	Philipp Lenard

1906	J. J. Thomson	1952	Felix Bloch, E. M. Purcell
1907	Albert A. Michelson	1953	Frits Zernike
1908	Gabriel Lippmann	1954	Max Born, Walther Bothe
1909	Guglielmo Marconi, Ferdinand Braun	1955	Willis E. Lamb, Polykarp Kusch
		1956	William B. Shockley, John Bardeen, Walter H. Brattain
1910	Johannes Diderik van der Waals		
1911	Wilhelm Wien	1957	Chen Ning Yang, Tsung-Dao Lee
1912	Gustaf Dalén	1958	Pavel A. Cherenkov, Il'ja M. Frank, Igor Y. Tamm
1913	Heike Kamerlingh Onnes		
1914	Max von Laue	1959	Emilio Segrè, Owen Chamberlain
1915	William Henry Bragg, Lawrence Bragg	1960	Donald A. Glaser
		1961	Robert Hofstadter, Rudolf Mössbauer
1916	no prize awarded		
1917	Charles Glover Barkla	1962	Lev Landau
1918	Max Planck	1963	Eugene Wigner, Maria Goeppert-Mayer, J. Hans D. Jensen
1919	Johannes Stark		
1920	Charles Edouard Guillaume	1964	Charles H. Townes, Nicolay G. Basov, Aleksandr M. Prokhorov
1921	Albert Einstein		
1922	Niels Bohr	1965	Sin-Itiro Tomonaga, Julian Schwinger, Richard Feynman
1923	Robert A. Millikan		
1924	Manne Siegbahn	1966	Alfred Kastler
1925	James Franck, Gustav Hertz	1967	Hans Bethe
1926	Jean-Baptiste Perrin	1968	Luis Alvarez
1927	Arthur Compton, Charles T. R. Wilson	1969	Murray Gell-Mann
		1970	Hannes Alfvén, Louis Néel
1928	Owen Willans Richardson	1971	Dennis Gabor
1929	Louis de Broglie	1972	John Bardeen, Leon N. Cooper, Robert Schrieffer
1930	Venkata Raman		
1931	no prize awarded	1973	Leo Esaki, Ivar Giaever, Brian D. Josephson
1932	Werner Heisenberg		
1933	Erwin Schrödinger, Paul Dirac	1974	Martin Ryle, Antony Hewish
1934	no prize awarded	1975	Aage N. Bohr, Ben R. Mottelson, James Rainwater
1935	James Chadwick		
1936	Victor F. Hess, Carl D. Anderson	1976	Burton Richter, Samuel C. C. Ting
1937	Clinton Davisson, George Paget Thomson	1977	Philip Anderson, Nevill F. Mott, John H. Van Vleck
1938	Enrico Fermi	1978	Pyotr Kapitsa, Arno Penzias, Robert Woodrow Wilson
1939	Ernest Lawrence		
1940	no prize awarded	1979	Sheldon Glashow, Abdus Salam, Steven Weinberg
1941	no prize awarded		
1942	no prize awarded	1980	James Cronin, Val Fitch
1943	Otto Stern	1981	Nicolaas Bloembergen, Arthur L. Schawlow, Kai M. Siegbahn
1944	Isidor Isaac Rabi		
1945	Wolfgang Pauli	1982	Kenneth G. Wilson
1946	Percy Bridgman	1983	Subrahmanyan Chandrasekhar, William A. Fowler
1947	Edward Appleton		
1948	Patrick Blackett	1984	Carlo Rubbia, Simon van der Meer
1949	Hideki Yukawa	1985	Klaus von Klitzing
1950	Cecil Powell	1986	Ernst Ruska, Gerd Binnig, Heinrich Rohrer
1951	John Cockcroft, Ernest T. S. Walton		

1987 J. Georg Bednorz, K. Alex Müller
1988 Leon Lederman, Melvin Schwartz,
Jack Steinberger
1989 Norman F. Ramsey, Hans G.
Dehmelt, Wolfang Paul
1990 Jerome I. Friedman, Henry Kendall,
Richard E. Taylor
1991 Pierre-Gilles De Gennes
1992 Georges Charpak
1993 Russell A. Hulse, Joseph H. Taylor
1994 Bertram N. Brockhouse, Clifford G.
Shull
1995 Martin Perl, Frederick Reines
1996 David M. Lee, Douglas D. Osheroff,
Robert C. Richardson
1997 Steven Chu, Claude Cohen-
Tannoudji, William Phillips

1998 Robert Laughlin, Horst L. Störmer,
Daniel C. Tsui
1999 Gerardus 't Hooft, Martinus J. G.
Veltman
2000 Zhores I. Alferov, Herbert Kroemer,
Jack S. Kilby
2001 Eric Cornell, Wolfgang Ketterle,
Carl Wieman
2002 Raymond Davis Jr., Masatoshi
Koshiba, Riccardo Giacconi
2003 Alexei A. Abrikosov, Vitaly L.
Ginzburg, Anthony J. Leggett
2004 David J. Gross, H. David Politzer,
Frank Wilczek
2005 Roy J. Glauber, John L. Hall,
Theodor W. Hänsch
2006 John C. Mather, George F. Smoot

INDEX TO NOBEL
LAUREATES QUOTED

A NOTE ON THE AUTHOR

A lifelong collector of quotations, David Pratt was born in England and studied at Oxford, Harvard, and the University of Toronto. He is a Professor Emeritus at Queen's University in Canada, where he taught from 1969 to 1997. He is the author of numerous academic books and papers, and his poetry and short stories have appeared in more than one hundred literary journals in the United States, Canada, Britain, and Australia.